KIPLINGER'S

Home•ology

How to Be Sure the House You Buy Is the Home You *Really* Want

By Carolyn Janik

Kiplinger Books, Washington, D.C.

**KIPLINGER
BOOKS**

Published by
The Kiplinger Washington Editors, Inc.
1729 H Street, N.W.
Washington, D.C. 20006

Library of Congress Cataloging-in-Publication Data

Janik, Carolyn.
     Kiplinger's home-ology : how to be sure the house you buy is the
home you really want / Carolyn Janik.
               p.   cm.
     Includes index.
     ISBN 0-938721-52-6 (paperback)
     1. House buying--United States. I. Title.
HD255.J34 1998
643'.12--dc21
                                                          98-12429
                                                          CIP

This publication is intended to provide guidance in regard to the subject matter covered. It is sold with the understanding that the author and publisher are not herein engaged in rendering legal, accounting, tax or other professional services. If such services are required, professional assistance should be sought.

9 8 7 6 5 4 3 2 1

First edition. Printed in the United States of America.

Book designed by S. Laird Jenkins Corp.

Table of Contents

PART 1: Choosing Your Gateway to Comfort and Financial Security

What's Beyond This Gateway: Fixer-Uppers, Renovation, Rehabilitation, Restoration • Why Enter This Gateway? • Self-Test Before You Enter This Gateway • Tips and Trouble Spots • One Gateway to Another

What's Beyond this Gateway: Unusual Purchase Opportunities: Foreclosures, REOs, Government-Owned Houses, Public Auctions, Private Auctions, Tax Sales • Unconventional Homes: Conversions • Controversial Neighborhoods: Turn-Around Neighborhoods • Why Enter This Gateway? • Self-Test Before You Enter This Gateway • Tips and Trouble Spots • One Gateway to Another

What's Beyond this Gateway: Far-Out Locations; Far-Out Farms; Lost Lots; Doing Business in the Neighborhood: Above the store, Telecommuting, In-Home Offices, Add-on Options, Bed & Breakfasts, In-Home Child Care • Why Enter This Gateway? • Self-Test Before You Enter This Gateway • Tips and Trouble Spots • One Gateway to Another

PART II: Getting the Best Possible Deal

Why I Wrote This Book

I began my education in the real estate marketplace as an observer, a curious toddler who peered out from behind her father's legs as he collected monthly rents and listened to tenants. With such a career start, it's no surprise that I should see home as more than a mere building.

Home touches every part of our lives. We even use the word "home" to connote "love" or "happiness" just about as often as we use it to refer to a specific house or apartment. Until now, however, home-buying books have focused on helping consumers buy a specific piece of property. Home was the "emotional" element in the purchase, not to be taken too seriously. Despite the good advice, people still sometimes made inappropriate purchases because their personalities, lifestyles and long-term goals weren't considered in the home-buying decision.

I saw a need and I had an idea.

Why not write a book that would consider what makes a home right for a particular home buyer? Why not do a book that would teach the reader how to evaluate property not only for its resale value but also for its appropriateness to the "self" of each person who would live in it? And why not extend the book's scope to help each purchaser use home-buying as a step toward achieving his or her long-term goal of financial independence?

Why not indeed? People responded:

"Big order!"

"Kind of complex."

"Not exactly easy."

"Not very appealing to publishing houses marching to the beat of the biggest drummer."

So I want to thank David Harrison, publisher of Kiplinger Books, for taking a chance on something a little different. His high standards, focused vision and unwavering support have helped to create *Home·ology*. (He also gets the credit for coming up with a great title!)

My equally sincere and heartfelt thanks go to Pat Mertz Esswein, my editor. She took the role of the educated consumer and asked *why? how? where?* and *what for?* She never hesitated to say, "We need more explanation here" or "more information there," even when I objected that we were far over the proposed word count. To her, the quality of the project was the only standard of judgement. Thank you, Pat, for your patience and perseverance. And your kindness.

Like a Broadway show, book production is a group effort. For careful and extensive fact checking, I sincerely thank Jennifer Cliff O'Donnell. For accurate, light-handed and fair-minded copyediting, I take my hat off to Rosemary Neff. For word-for-word proofreading, my thanks to Dianne Olsufka. And kudos to Dan Kohan for cover design and to S. Laird Jenkins Corp. for interior book design.

Closer to home, many dear friends listened to my venting or made me tea as I struggled through the ups and downs of trying to do something that had never been done before and to meet Kiplinger's high standards. Love and thanks to Kathy Kainer, Linda Lech, Julie Leiter, CeeCee Martin, Ruth Rejnis, Suzy Roberti, Sandy Weber and Ruth Zimmerman. Special thanks to my agent Jeanne Fredericks, for putting the deal together and standing by me along its entire route.

And what can I say but, "Thanks, honey," to my husband, Joe, who grew accustomed to the bedroom lights going on at 2 or 3 A.M. as I scribbled some idea on the night-table scratch pad. Thanks for the love and patience, and the faith that I could do it.

I wrote this book to help home buyers everywhere, but at its very heart is all the advice I have wanted to give to my favorite home buyers, my children: David Janik and his wife, Jeanne, who are on their third home, buying, selling and building in New Hampshire; Laura Janik Cronin and her husband, Chris, now in their first home in New Jersey; and Bill Janik, an ensign in the Navy Nurse Corps who looks forward to building his own home someday.

To my readers and my children, I wish you "Good luck!" in the marketplace. To help make that good luck happen, ask yourself, "Does it feel right?" Then ask yourself, "Why?" That's where the thinking comes in.

Carolyn Janik

Home-Buying for a Better Life

Everyone talks about real estate. You can overhear the conversations on commuter trains, in the cloakroom at the day-care center, and in the locker room at the gym. Home buying is probably one of the top ten cocktail-party conversation topics. Perhaps you've heard stories about people like these.

After looking at 23 houses in two days, Dick and Jane were totally confused. "4 Bdrs 2.5 Ba" seemed to describe everything...and nothing. Then the real estate agent called with a new listing, perfect for them! They saw it, fell in love with it and bought it. It was months before they realized that they had bought the most expensive house in the neighborhood. Years later, they discovered that they couldn't sell their big house for much more than their neighbors could sell their small house.

John decided to buy *something* on April 15, 1985, shoving his tax return—with a hefty check—into the mailbox and vowing, "Never again!" "But you're *single,*" said his friends and relatives, "what do you need a *house* for?" So John bought a brand-spanking-new condo. Three years later the bottom had fallen out of the condo market and John was about to be married. He sold the condo for a little more than half of what he had paid. Because the loss wiped out his equity, the only purchase he could afford was a 3% down multifamily dwelling where collecting the rent would help pay his mortgage. Then he learned to be a handyman and landlord.

Penny for Your Thoughts

Haste in every business brings failures.

Herodotus
(5th century BC),
Greek historian known as
"the father of history"

Alice and Tom thought they wanted comfort more than convenience. So they passed over all the modest, middle-aged houses in the usual commuter towns and chose a big, new house beyond the far suburbs. Travel to and from work ate up time and money. Child care on those days when both parents had to work late was difficult to get, and even when they didn't work late, Tom and Alice rarely got home in time to participate in their children's after-school activities. Exasperated, Alice wanted to leave work and give her full attention to family matters, but they needed both incomes to meet the mortgage payment. A company transfer saved Tom and Alice.

———

Put in different names and change a detail here or there and you can probably tell your own versions of these stories. Perhaps you've even thought, "Hard luck! They bought the wrong house. They should have been more careful. They should have known better." But have you ever stopped to think why stories of people buying the wrong house are so common?

Home buying is a major and complex life event. Yet many Americans spend more time and effort deciding which car to buy or trying to get tickets to the Super Bowl than preparing to buy a house. That's true despite media bombardment with the reminder that buying a home is the biggest financial commitment most people ever make.

In fact, buying a home is *more* than the biggest financial commitment in most people's lives. It is also the purchase requiring the most complex process and procedures. If you put marriage, children and divorce aside, buying a home is the most legally entangled and life-changing decision that most of us make. Yet most of us do it without consideration of its demands as well as its pleasures. We do it without a plan for the future. Without much knowledge of the real estate marketplace. Without good counseling. And often with haste and impatience.

Consider some of the consequences:

- **Overwhelmed by the sheer number of potential pitfalls in buying,** first-time buyers rely heavily on their real estate agents or their relatives. Rather than making their own choice, they allow themselves to be persuaded. Sometimes the purchase fulfills the dreams of others, not the buyers.

- **Some buyers proceed where even angels fear to tread** because they don't know the risks that are hidden in the type of home or purchase strategy they choose. Sometimes they win; more often they lose.

- **Some buyers are pretty good at choosing a house that is right for their needs, but they pay too much for it.** Later, they can't sell without taking a loss.

- **Some buyers choose the wrong location,** one that is not right for their personal needs or not appropriate to their goal of potential profit. And they can't fix that error because, while almost anything else in real estate can be altered, location can't be.

- **Some buyers don't consider their future lifestyle changes and needs for space,** and are forced to move much sooner than they would like. Sometimes before they've unpacked all the boxes, these buyers find themselves incurring all the costs of buying and selling—again.

- **Some buyers are tempted by bargains in properties with limited appeal** that have been on the market for long periods of time. Later, when they want to sell the property, they find it difficult to find a buyer or realize a profit.

- **Some buyers get a good deal on a fixer-upper** but realize too late that the last thing they want to do is spend every weekend working on the house. If they decide to pay professionals to do the work, their purchase becomes much less of a bargain.

- **Less than a year after purchase, some owners find themselves applying for second mortgages** to fix the roof or other major problems.

- **Conversations at the dinner table end with: "I hate it here.** And we can't afford to move. Why did we ever buy this place anyway!"

Mistakes in home buying can be so expensive that they wipe out both your past savings and the potential for future investment. They can be so legally devastating that they paralyze mobility, keeping you where you don't want to be. They can be so time-consuming that they make some homeowners not only house-poor but also house-indentured.

How This Book Will Help

Will reading this book prevent you from making all these mistakes? Is it the silver bullet or a magic pill that will guarantee home-buying success? Hardly. Mistakes are always possible. Even experts make them. But *Home•ology* will help you improve the odds—tremendously!

Using the tools in these pages will help you to get the best possible house for the best possible price. Now, that's a big promise but it's not the pot of gold at the end of the rainbow. *Best possible* anchors us to realities imposed by time, money and market conditions.

In the quest for the best possible house, a home buyer should keep three goals in mind every time he or she enters the real estate marketplace. Look for the house that is:

- **Most appropriate to your current needs** and, insofar as you can anticipate them, your future needs for shelter and comfort;

- **Most likely to be a positive step** in achieving a future housing goal; and

- **Most likely to contribute** to your achieving financial independence.

"Nice goals, on paper," you say. "But does anyone *really* go out into the real estate marketplace with *goals*? I mean, does anyone think beyond the happily-ever-after notion of a dream house?"

Most people don't. *You* can.

If you do, it can make a real difference in your life. What you're about to read in the next 366 pages will help you to set your goals and work toward achieving them. This book is about *planning* before you buy a house. It's about how to buy that house. *And,* it's about how to make each buying experience contribute positively to your lifetime efforts for financial independence, physical comfort and emotional contentment.

Home·ology will help you understand real estate concepts and theories, not just follow the steps. If you understand *why* you must do this or *what will happen* if you do that, you will be able to make good decisions when the unexpected or unusual pops up. (It always does.) Beyond theory, this book will help you get things done in the most practical and efficient way possible. And finally, it will help you to make choices that are right for you and your family.

Let's take a minute for an overview of what's ahead:

Part I, Choosing Your Gateway to Comfort and Financial Security

Part I focuses on matching *you,* the individual, unique home buyer to the right home-buying opportunities. It will help you to define your vision of "home," set your goals, identify and define your temperament, ownership skills, coping abilities and financial resources, and recognize and evaluate appropriate buying and owning choices. Those many choices are organized into the seven gateways to home-buying and home-owning success, discussed in Chapters 3 through 9. The name of each gateway reflects the nature of the opportunities—or homeownership style—that lie within.

In the gateway chapters, you will get help with these very important questions:

- **Why should I consider this type of house?**

- **Is this purchase right for me**—my homeowning temperament, abilities and goals?

Your answers to those two questions will help you to choose from among the housing opportunities available to you at any given stage of your life. They will help you to decide when to get into or out of a particular homeownership style. You can use them to test the appropriateness of a purchase before you sign a contract. Finally, they will help

Penny for Your Thoughts

First ponder, then dare.

Count Helmuth von Moltke
(1800-1891),
Prussian soldier

you to maximize equity growth with each purchase, contributing to your achievement of future housing goals and, in the longer term, your financial independence.

The gateway chapters therefore are your key to choosing the right house for your current needs, planning your home-buying goals, and being able to revise those goals if necessary. They are essential to your successful plan.

Part II, Getting the Best Possible Deal

While Part I offers special tips, strategies and caveats to help you make the most of each gateway's opportunities, Part II will help you successfully navigate in any area of the real estate marketplace. It will help you get the best possible deal, no matter which gateway you choose. It will show you how to judge value, weigh options and consider alternatives. It will take you from noticing that first ad that sounds good in the real estate section of the newspaper, through the hunt and the negotiating, and right to the settlement table where you will collect the key to your new home.

Making It Happen:
The Essentials of Home Financing

The "tabbed" pages in the middle of the book are about how to get the money for your new home. Mortgage financing today is a huge and very competitive industry. There are entire books written on the subject that would put you to sleep despite three cups of "real" coffee. This special insert cuts to the heart of the matter, telling you what you need to know in order to ask the right questions, the questions that will lead to successful results.

Some extra features

Throughout *Home•ology*, you'll find examples, quizzes and checklists to help you hone general theories down to your particular questions, needs and decisions. Graphs and other illustrations will give you quick and comparative overviews. You'll also find five different kinds of bonus material regularly highlighted in boxes. Look for them under these headings:

- **Words to the Wise.** To function effectively, accurately and safely in the real estate marketplace, you must understand its language. You'll find technical terms and words that have unusual marketplace usage defined in boxes located on the page near the topic being discussed. Whenever appropriate, there's an example of how to use the word correctly in everyday speech. (That's so you won't *sound* like a neophyte, even if you are!)

- **Don't Assume.** This is the warnings box. It will alert you about things to watch for and things to watch out for. Sometimes it will tell you that there's more work for you to do just when you thought you could leave it all to someone else.

- **It's the Law.** This box will explain how a real estate law might affect some aspect of your purchase. Sometimes it will warn you of what you can't do. Sometimes it will tell you what you should or must do to protect your interests.

- **More, More, More.** Look here for sources of additional information. Often these boxes will tell you where to go when you don't know where to go. Sometimes they'll direct you to sources of in-depth information on specialized topics.

- **Penny for Your Thoughts.** For your amusement or bemusement, these quotations come to you from minds great and not-so-great. They might add inspiration, a new perspective, or just a smile.

Equity Growth Works For You

The best plans are only dreams unless you have the means and know-how to get from one step to the next. Say that in ten years you want to own a four-bedroom, 2½-bath colonial-style home and you are currently living in a one-bedroom condominium apartment. How will you get from here to there? You may be scratching your head in puzzlement. No realistic estimate of increased income over the next ten years produces a number that will make mortgage payments on that colonial affordable.

But what if you could make a larger down payment on each house that you bought? Remember: It's usually not the bigger *house* you can't afford, it's the bigger mortgage payment. Both homeowners and prospective home buyers sometimes get discouraged because they look ahead with limited information. They estimate the monthly payment on the larger house of their dreams based on the financial resources they currently have. It doesn't cross their minds to consider a different perspective.

A Lifetime of Tax Angles

Uncle Sam believes in homeownership! Your favorite uncle will actually put money in your pocket because you've become a homeowner with a mortgage. The property taxes that you pay on your home and all of the interest you pay on your mortgage loan are deductible items on your federal income-tax return. (The exceptions? Your mortgage interest may not be fully deductible if your mortgage debt exceeds $1 million or if your adjusted gross income exceeds $124,500 in 1998.) Whether you're trading in nondeductible rent for mortgage payments or moving up to a more expensive home, those deductions will most certainly cut your tax bill and reduce your true, *after-tax* cost of owning a home. If, for example, you're in the 28% tax bracket, every $1,000 of deductible interest and taxes translates to a $280 subsidy from Uncle Sam.

And there's more! With the 1997 changes in the tax law, almost all home sellers can avoid paying capital-gains tax on their profits. (Unlike the old law, the new one doesn't require you to buy a more expensive house as your next purchase.) As long as the profit from the sale of a principal residence is less than $500,000 for a married couple filing jointly, or less than $250,000 for a single taxpayer, head of household, or married person filing separately, it can be excluded from taxation.

Still more bonuses from your ever-more-dear Uncle Sam: There's no age requirement for this break and unlike the once-in-a-lifetime restriction on the old $125,000 break, you can use this one over and over again, as long as you don't use it more than once in any two-year period.

There are, however, some limiting factors. For instance, you must have owned and lived in the house for two of the five years leading up to the sale.

And even then there are exceptions. If medical reasons or a job transfer force you to sell and move in less than two years, a portion of the $500,000 profit allowance (calculated by the amount of time you have lived in the house) will be tax-free. For example, if you have lived in the house for one year and then get transferred, your prorated allowance is half of the two-year allowance, or $250,000. That will usually mean a free ticket since very few home sales realize a $250,000 *profit* in one year!

For better understanding of how this new tax law might affect your home-buying decisions, consult with your accountant or books such as *Kiplinger's Cut Your Taxes.*

Instead of struggling to break out of that odious box labeled *Financial Constraints*, step away from it and look at "home" as both a source of comfort and an investment in financial independence. No matter what the size of its mortgage, a home is the major wealth-building vehicle for the majority of Americans.

In the foreseeable future, house prices are unlikely to get the rocket boosts that they got in the '70s and early '80s (more about that in a moment). But home buying is still a fine method of securing and growing your money. It is a rather reliable hedge against the devaluation of our currency that we call inflation, and it provides shelter from the hungry hand of the IRS. Most important to this discussion, however, it gives us the opportunity to increase equity by paying off the mortgage loan and by choosing properties that can increase in value.

> ## *Words to the Wise*
> •
>
> **Equity** is the cash value an owner has in a property after the mortgage debts have been deducted from its fair market value. It increases both with appreciation and with time as you gradually pay off the mortgage debt. It's correct to say, "We have $60,000 equity in this house."

Homeowners who create a significant increase in equity with each ownership period can progressively sell and buy into a more expensive home without an unmanageable increase in monthly payment. Besides winning the lottery or earning colossal salary increases, growing *equity* is the major financial key to achieving your housing goals.

For Those Just Getting Started

If you're reading this in a rented loft in lower Manhattan or in a "cozy corner" of the studio apartment your spouse's parents have created out of their basement family room "to help out the young couple," you may be ready to close the book and give up. "Growing equity! That's just great," you say. "How am I going to grow equity when I can't save enough to make the down payment?"

Don't close the book! There are ways to get started with a minimal down payment, and we'll go through them together. Once you get into the marketplace and work out

So often we rob tomorrow's memories by today's economics.

John Mason Brown (1900-1969), American literary critic [from *The Arts of Living,* Simon & Schuster, 1954]

a home-buying plan for achieving your goals, you'll be working on growing equity.

If you're like most people, you'll find that there will be times in your homeowning life when you'll be growing equity by maintaining and improving the property you have while paying down your mortgage. At other times, you'll be growing equity by buying and selling houses profitably every few years. (Chapter 2, "You and Your Plan," will introduce you to these two "styles" of profitable homeownership.)

Home-Buying Challenges

A lot of people who bought homes in the '60s and '70s are now sitting on sizable "nest" eggs that will support comfortable retirements. Those were the golden years of home buying. House prices were going up far faster than the rate of inflation. No one worried about making a bad deal because virtually every piece of real estate on the market sold for a profit. And of course, no one bothered to make a plan for homeownership. Strategies were superfluous when the weather was fine, the wind steady and the ship sound.

But the storm struck in the mid '80s, and a decade later the home-buying waters are still sometimes a little rough. Today, many economists are saying that we are approaching zero inflation, and in some areas of the nation, homeowners are complaining about *zero appreciation.* What most of those dejected would-be home *sellers* really mean is that the rate of rising house prices is running neck and neck with the rate of inflation and, as a result, they're not feeling any oomph in their equity growth.

Conditioned by the huge profits in home selling during the inflationary decades, these would-be sellers often cry over a "flat" market. In reality, they should save their tears. Many homeowners haven't yet realized, or simply refuse to recognize, that a small increase in home value in a low-inflation economy can be worth more in real dollars than a seemingly large increase in an inflationary economy. To give you a simplified example: If the rate of inflation in the overall economy is 7% (slightly less than the average rate during the 1970s) and a house bought for $100,000 sells for $107,500 after one year, the approximate inflation-adjusted value is $107,000 and the approximate real gain is $500. If the overall rate of inflation is 3% and a house bought for $100,000 sells for $105,000 after one year, the approximate inflation-adjusted value is $103,000 and the approximate real gain is $2,000.

The change from rapid inflation and a high demand for housing to low and steady inflation and a moderate demand for housing means that some properties will increase in value, some won't change, and some even may decrease. For home buyers, these conditions mean that they must make purchases more carefully, consider house prices with more attention to the marketplace, and factor the cost of buying and selling (including real estate commissions and the cost of improvements) into the cost of homeownership.

In other parts of the nation, you may find yourself in a market where house prices are rising at a strident and sometimes even staggering rate. A hot home-buying market may seem like a boom to home sellers, but it poses new problems. Sellers must be extra careful to price their home accurately or they may find themselves short the cash they'll need to buy a similar house in a fast market. All buyers must take care not to get caught up in the tempo of a fast market and jump at a desirable property, usually paying too much.

In a word, home buying at the turn of the millennium is more *challenging!* And the challenges are different depending upon *where* in the nation you are house hunting. But if you work at it well, you can still use each purchase and sale to improve your life and your wealth.

Words to the Wise
• •

The term **appreciation** has commonly been used to mean a rapid increase in house value due to inflation. More correctly, it means an increase in value due to an improvement in the area (such as an urban-renewal project or the building of much higher-priced houses very close by); to an improvement in the property itself (such as regrading and landscaping, or a new kitchen and bathrooms); or to economic conditions that increase the demand in an area (such as the housing needs of employees transferred to the new location of a corporate headquarters or manufacturing plant).

Rising to the Challenge

Some of the numbers that both buyers and sellers must deal with when negotiating for a home will result from economic factors beyond their control, and others will result from the choices they make. When dollar values change less rapidly and less drastically and profits are measured in smaller numbers, mistakes are likely to be costly. Most will be difficult to remedy. When dollar values are increasing rapidly, mistakes are easy to make. You'll feel most of them as a lower return on your home-buying investment.

So what should you do? Some people will choose to rent and watch the market. Some will choose to stay put in the houses that they already own. Others will choose to meet the new challenges of home buying head-on and enter the marketplace with the goal of using homeownership to improve the quality of their lives.

If you belong to this last group, you must:

- **Learn as much as possible** about the real estate marketplace,

- **Look inward,** both at your needs and wants and at your skills and character traits that will help you meet the demands of homeownership,

- **Choose a housing style** or a particular means of purchase that fits your needs and skills,

- **Make a long-term plan** that you can work to achieve, and

- **Get started.**

Since you've read this far, you've already started on the learning journey that will continue as long as you buy and sell property. The next chapter will help you to look at your home-buyer personality and begin to tailor an appropriate plan.

You and Your Plan

Obsession: it's not just a fragrance. Some house-hunters start out as really nice people and somewhere along the way become unreasonable, driven, incorrigible and paranoid. Even though (they think) everyone is against them, by golly, they're out to get what they want, when they want it! Most of them make bad deals.

Usually these are people who have "fallen in love" with a house and believe they must have it or be heartbroken. They generally have difficulty making rational evaluations because they have become tightly focused on, even obsessed with, getting a particular property. They have allowed their emotions to take over and won't even let their minds get an evaluating (or restraining) thought in for consideration. They are determined to buy a certain house, and they either have no concept of a home-buying plan or have conveniently forgotten the one they did have.

Don't allow obsession with a particular piece of property or an immediate housing goal to restrict your options and opportunities. If you want to achieve your future housing goal—not just "someday," but sooner rather than later—you should never become so focused on a particular deal that you lose sight of the big picture. Each time you purchase a house, you should evaluate every aspect of the purchase against your homeowning "personality" as well as your current needs and desires, your long-term goals and an appropriate strategy to achieve them. This chapter will help you begin to pin down all those elements—to create *your* plan.

Making a plan is more important than reading every ad in the Homes for Sale section of the newspaper. More important than drive-bys. More important than open houses. More important than seeing every single house for sale

Penny for Your Thoughts

A house is a home when it shelters the body and comforts the soul.

Phillip Moffitt, writing in
Esquire, April 1986

in your price range. More important than haggling, worrying, and fighting over a small difference in price!

If you'll stop to do a plan or reevaluate it before you go house-hunting, and stop again to check it point by point before you sign a purchase contract, you can save yourself some colossal headaches, not to mention some significant money and the possibility of an unwanted move.

Bear in mind always that there is neither a perfect mate nor a perfect house in all the world.

Your Type: Movable or Rooted?

Recognition of your home-buyer personality profile is an essential element in building and implementing a plan for home buying. Like your overall personality, your home-buyer personality develops in response to both external and internal factors. It is, therefore, both multifaceted and complex, and it is subject to change. In alphabetical order, here are some aspects of everyday life that influence home-buying styles: age, ambition, anxiety, children, employment, family connections, financial security, income, marital status, need for community, rootedness, social status (both your awareness of it and your perception of its importance), and tolerance for risk. Almost everything, right? Well, where we live affects almost everything, too.

As you read the following descriptions of the two major types of home buyers, remember that in these profiles there is no right or wrong, no better or worse. People simply tend to be one type or the other. And circumstances can influence people to change from one to the other and back again.

Unknown future demands that can and will affect your needs are part of the challenge of home buying. So hang loose while you gather the facts and try to draw your own profile.

Perennially On the Move

Like perennial plants, movable people thrive with frequent uprooting and transplanting. They usually buy and

14

sell many houses over a lifetime, rarely spending more than five years in one place.

Profit potential is one of the most important purchase factors to movable buyers because they are using appreciation and equity growth to enhance their wealth and comfort. In choosing a house, they carefully consider future resale value—a measure of the property's desirability to a large potential buying public that results in a combination of potential profit and the likelihood of a quick and easy sale.

Buyers often choose location with emphasis on easy commuting to areas of major employment and for the highest possible desirability to the largest possible number of people. They often count the value of a home not only in its convenience and comfort but also (and usually more important) in its potential for increasing wealth and comfort in the near future.

Don't Assume

Don't assume that home buying offers the best housing deal you can get. Yes, there are tax benefits, security benefits, control benefits, and the probability of growing equity and reaping a profit. But there are costs and commitments in ownership, and real estate is an illiquid investment (one that can't be converted to cash or sold in a short time at a price that is close to its true value; stock is considered a liquid investment). Under some circumstances, renting is the preferred choice.

Deeply Rooted

Like trees, rooted people put down strong, deep roots. Some buy only one house in a lifetime, while others change houses only after a stay of many years. Comfort and the suitability of style and floor plan are among the most important purchase factors for rooted buyers because their personal needs and wants motivate them without a lot of consideration for profitable resale in the near future. They often choose location with particular consideration for the size and beauty of the lot, the proximity to extended family, the quality of local schools, the continuation of long-established friendships, and the opportunity for participation in community activities. Rooted buyers often count the value of a home in its contribution to the richness of life, not in how much monetary profit it will bring when sold.

Changing Identity

Some people start out with a typical movable or root-ed profile and never change throughout their lives. Others seem to shift back and forth with each life-changing event or new decade.

Usually, movable-type home buyers are people who work for major corporations that frequently transfer their employees, people who change jobs frequently, and peo-ple in the military. Once in executive positions or upon re-tirement from the military, many of them choose to set down roots and take on related characteristics. Others however, go right on having adventures in the real estate marketplace.

Some young home buyers function as movable types until they reach a level of income that will support the home "of their dreams," then settle down and grow roots like an oak tree for 20 or more years. On the other hand, a rooted person might become divorced or widowed and suddenly become an aggressive movable type. Or a natural-ly gypsy-like movable type might be forced to settle into a rooted role because of the special needs of children or be-cause of employment constraints (such as a dentist with an office in her home).

What Does It Matter, Anyway?

Why bother with all this? Because you should consid-er your home-buying profile if you want to make the most appropriate housing decisions. In one way or another, your type *will* affect both the profitability of your purchase and your satisfaction with your home. To demonstrate all this theory, let's look at some specific situations and how they have influenced home-buying decisions to the good.

Linda and John:
Probable corporate transferees (movable)

These folks are both setting out on their careers with IBM. They want to have children in a few years, but not yet. They know their future may include job transfers, but they also know the company will support their home selling. They choose a three-bedroom, ranch-style home in a well-established neighborhood.

Although a two-bedroom home would have been large enough and less costly, they know that two-bedroom houses don't appeal to most home buyers and that the condo market, the only other two-bedroom alternative in their area, is slow. They didn't choose a house in a new development because they didn't want to put out-of-pocket money into landscaping, and they knew their resale house would have to compete with houses still being built in the neighborhood.

> # *Words to the Wise*
> •
>
> **Flag lot** is the term commonly used to mean a lot that has no road frontage of its own. (The term probably reflects the similarity of the property's outline to the "flag" on the rural mailbox that is raised to indicate mail to be picked up.) The access to a flag lot is either by an easement over the land of a neighbor who does have road frontage (often the extension of a shared driveway) or by ownership of a strip of land wide enough for a car to pass. Houses on flag lots are generally more difficult to sell, but they do provide maximum privacy for those willing to maintain a long driveway.

Ruth and Tom:
Not going anywhere soon (Rooted)

This couple has sold their split-level house, which became too small after the birth of their third child. They own a Dairy Queen franchise, two of their children are already in school, and they have no intention of moving to another town. They choose a new, four-bedroom contemporary on a *flag lot.*

Although two-story, colonial-style houses sell best in their area, Ruth and Tom wanted the extra space the contemporary offered. They planned to use both the basement and the storage lofts under the roof for living space.

They knew that a flag lot can be a difficult form of property to resell. But this particular lot appealed to them because access wasn't provided by an easement over someone else's property. Instead, the lot included a narrow strip that connected the bulk of their land to the road. (This connecting piece of land is called a "stem" in the marketplace, as in the stem of a flower or a flag.) And that lot was huge—more than five acres—big enough to allow Tom to build the barn he wants for his antique cars and the children's pony. Chances are, resale value won't be a factor for Ruth and Tom until retirement.

Janice and Jack:
Get in, fix it up, get out (Movable)

Janice and Jack are both teachers who have the summer off. They also both enjoy home remodeling and are good at it. They choose a 22-year-old, four-bedroom, two-story home that was once the builder's model in its neighborhood but has been uncared for during most of its life.

Planning to *leverage* their investment, they make a minimum down payment. They plan to refurbish the house while living in it and sell for a profit within three years. They don't need four bedrooms, but they know that buyers most often ask for that size house in their town.

Andrea: Too soon to commit (Movable)

AT&T has just promoted this young up-and-comer into an excellent management position, and she sees many opportunities ahead. She has a big enough down payment

Words to the Wise

Leverage was a term heard frequently in every corner of the real estate marketplace during the '70s. It is defined as the use of borrowed money to purchase an asset that is likely to appreciate, but it was taken to mean using a big mortgage to allow a small amount of cash to purchase property.

When house values were going up rapidly and interest rates on borrowed money were relatively low, the prevailing theory was: the smaller the down payment, the greater the percentage of potential increase on the investment. A person who bought a $100,000 house with a $5,000 (5%) down payment and sold two years later for $130,000 might say, "I leveraged five grand into 30 grand in two years!" In other words, a spectacular, 600% return on the original

investment of $5,000 Which is true in gross numbers, but he or she isn't taking into account the effects of inflation (see the discussion beginning on page 7 of Chapter 1), the interest paid on the mortgage (although they recouped some of that via tax savings from the mortgage-interest tax deduction), and the cost of selling. Still, there probably was a sizable profit in real dollars.

Leveraging (putting the minimum down with the expectation of maximum profit) is dangerous in times of high interest rates, or low inflation and stable house prices, because the cost of carrying the mortgage and selling the property may easily exceed the gross profit. Such a loss is called negative leveraging.

to buy a small house or a large condo, and friends and relatives urge her to grab the tax benefits of homeownership. Instead, Andrea chooses to rent an apartment.

AT&T offers excellent transfer benefits, so Andrea should have little fear that a transfer would result in a financial loss if she were to buy and then be forced by transfer to sell her home.

So why did Andrea rent? Because she's good at her work and ambitious. During the next three years, she may choose to stay with AT&T, go to one of its competitors or open her own consulting firm. She does not want to be tied to property and the attendant responsibilities anywhere, anyhow. In addition, she has done some research and come up with figures to indicate that expected appreciation in her area during the next three years would not cover the cost of selling if she had to do so without company support.

> # *Words to the Wise*
> ●
>
> **Sweat equity** is an expression commonly used to mean the value added to a home through work and improvements done by the owner.

Paul: Settling in (once Movable, now Rooted)

After taking an early retirement from the Navy at age 43, Paul found a position as a head nurse on a cardiac floor in a large and well-established hospital. He chooses a run-down lakefront cottage that he plans to rebuild as needed, remodel to his satisfaction and winterize.

He is aware that there is little community around his home in the off-season, but he has many links to friends through his employment and hobbies. He sees his new home as an excellent place to entertain his children when they visit and as a potential retirement haven when he really retires 20 years in the future. The fact that his home's resale value as a year-round property will be less than the value of comparable properties within the city limits has no impact on him since (1) his cash investment is small, (2) much of the property value will be *"sweat equity,"* and (3) even if his life changes and he decides to move back into the city, he has enough income to keep the property as a vacation home.

A Plan That Fits You

To draw up a home-buying plan that will help you achieve your long-term housing goals (which include comfort and wealth), you must come up with a home-buyer profile of yourself now and as you see yourself in the future. Start by assessing the status of certain life factors that affect home buying. Use the worksheet on page 21 to help you organize and focus your particular concerns.

- **If you are just starting out as a home buyer,** ask yourself what your goals and plans are. Which type are you now? What, if anything, could make you shift your profile?

- **If you have already bought and sold at least one** home, you will already have functioned as one home-buyer type. Are you about to change the profile? Do you think you could change? What would make you change?

    If you'll share the purchase with a partner, copy the sheet so each of you can do the work separately. Then get together and compare your notes just to be sure you are both looking at life through the same lens. If you don't think this is important, picture two horses harnessed to the same cart. If they pull at opposite diagonals, the cart will have a slow and bumpy ride at best, go nowhere, or, at worst, go backward. Review your charts after you have read the gateway chapters to be sure you are still looking at housing opportunities in the same way.

Strategies to Achieve Your Goals

Once you know where you want to go, the next question is how to get there. Different strategies will work for each type of buyer.

    You can expect this section to give you an overview of the issues you need to consider in developing your strategy. This book offers specific tips for both types of home buyer in each of the gateway chapters. Part Two covers many of them in much greater detail. You'll find cross-references to those chapters where it's appropriate.

Continued on page 24

What Type of Home Buyer Are You?

Think about how each of these life factors will affect your buyer profile now and in the future. Which factors will incline you to rootedness, and which to movability and profit motive? Indicate on paper your current buyer profile and probable profiles for the future. Make a copy of this worksheet for your spouse or buying partner so you can compare your expectations and identify any potential conflicts.

Life factors	Movable or Rooted?			
	Now	In 10 years	In 20 years	In retirement
Ages of home buyers	_____	_____	_____	_____
Children (number and ages)				
	_____	_____	_____	_____
Employment (consider possible transfers, advancement or career changes?				
	_____	_____	_____	_____
	_____	_____	_____	_____
Income (anticipated increases or decreases?)				
	_____	_____	_____	_____
Financial security (anticipated increases or decreases in your accumulated wealth?)				
	_____	_____	_____	_____
	_____	_____	_____	_____
Community involvement	_____	_____	_____	_____
	_____	_____	_____	_____
Commitments to extended family				
	_____	_____	_____	_____
	_____	_____	_____	_____
Ability to take risks	_____	_____	_____	_____
	_____	_____	_____	_____
Importance of how others perceive you				
	_____	_____	_____	_____
	_____	_____	_____	_____
Other concerns	_____	_____	_____	_____

Considering all the factors, are you or will you be mostly a movable or rooted type?
Your buyer profile _____ _____ _____ _____

Set Your Goals and Go for It!

Once you understand how you will be approaching the home-buying role, you should set your housing goals for the current purchase and for each decade mark in the future. Don't include fantasies for a castle in the sky; they will only distort the plan. Do try to come up with realistic and achievable goals.

This worksheet will help you organize and focus your goals. Again, if there is more than one home buyer, each one should do this exercise separately. Differences of opinion expressed on paper before going house shopping are much easier to resolve than differences discovered in the process of choosing, in the heat of negotiating or,

heaven forbid, after you've committed yourselves and bought the property.

As you work, bear in mind that this is only a plan and subject to revision. Financial planners say that it's a good idea to review and revise all your financial plans at five-year intervals. Likewise, it's a good idea to revisit your homeowning goals every several years.

But it's likely you'll want to revisit this worksheet even sooner. Your goals may well change as you read this book, identify appropriate opportunities for homeownership and refine your ideas of what comfort means to you (see Chapter 10).

Location Where? (state, town, neighborhood, gated community)

Your goal now _____

In 10 years _____

In 20 years _____

In retirement _____

Land How much? Terrain?

Your goal now _____

In 10 years _____

In 20 years _____

In retirement _____

Size of house Total number of rooms? Bedrooms? Bathrooms? Special-use rooms such as for music, sewing, home office? Garages?

Your goal now _____

In 10 years _____

In 20 years _____

In retirement _____

Square footage Proportion of private space to public (eg., entertaining)

Your goal now _____

In 10 years _____

In 20 years _____

In retirement _____

_____

Style of house Formal or informal? Traditional or contemporary? Single- or multistory?

Your goal now _____

In 10 years _____

In 20 years _____

In retirement _____

_____

Special features Pool? Fireplace? Luxury bath? Privacy? View?

Your goal now _____

In 10 years _____

In 20 years _____

In retirement _____

Other factors _____

Your goal now _____

In 10 years _____

In 20 years _____

In retirement _____

Penny for Your Thoughts

Every man is the smith of his own fortune.

Appius Claudius Caecus (3rd century B.C.), Roman politician and dictator famed for reforms giving more privileges to the common people.

To Make a Profit and Move On (Movable)

Location

Look for towns with the criteria most buyers set: low tax rates and a reputation for good schools. Choose a neighborhood of houses similar to each other in style, size, age and price, and then choose a house priced in the midrange of the neighborhood. If possible choose a lot that is regular in shape and level. Try to avoid corner properties and through streets that are main arteries of the town.

The newer the house, the better. But don't buy in a development still under construction; the out-of-pocket costs for landscaping, decorating and finishing touches will be high, and you won't get that extra money back because you'll be competing with the price tags on the new construction. (The exception: If home prices have been going up *rapidly* over the past two years in the town, you might buy one of the first houses in a development and grab some rapid appreciation as the builder increases the asking prices of similar houses. But don't put too much heart into landscaping and decorating!) On the other hand, buying one of the *last* few houses to be built in the development is also usually a good way to get maximum appreciation since there won't be any new construction to compete with your house. (See also Chapter 9, "New Construction," and Chapter 11, "Your Piece of the Earth.")

Style and floor plan

Choose from among the house styles that are currently popular in the area. Avoid anything with an unusual facade. Choose a conventional floor plan that is likely to appeal to the largest possible number of people. Especially avoid houses with additions, with rooms that you can access only by walking through another room, and with in-law apartments. The number, size and convenience of the bathrooms is important (the more the better). Eat-in kitchens are a major plus. Porches and decks increase salability. It's preferable to have all bedrooms on one level. (See also Chapter 10, "The Comforts of Home.")

Condition

If you enjoy doing home decorating and repairs, you can indeed make a profit by doing some cosmetic house surgery. Just be sure your professional inspection report shows the house to be structurally sound and with all systems in good working order. (See also Chapter 14.)

If you are not a putter-around-the-house type, choose a property in the best possible condition. If you're lucky you can live in it for three years or so and sell before it needs redecorating or refurbishing.

The idea is to try to avoid large out-of-pocket expenditures, which will cut deeply into your supply of cash for day-to-day living and limit your ability to save for a bigger down payment on your next house.

Price

Study the market carefully and negotiate hard. Do not pay more than the home's estimated fair market value. Remember, the further below market value you get the price, the more profit you're likely to enjoy when you sell.

But beware the bargain property that has been on the market "forever." Ask the real estate agent, the seller and yourself, "Why has this property not sold?" The answers you get now as a buyer may be the same you would get as a seller three years down the road. Try to find highly motivated sellers—those dealing, for example, with foreclosure, divorce, transfer, more than one mortgage, or an expected sale that has fallen through. (See also Chapter 12, "The Price and Value Question.")

To Put Down Deep Roots (Rooted)

Location

Choose the area of the country, town and neighborhood, and even the piece of land, that meet your needs and make you comfortable. If you think you may want to put on an addition at some time, be sure the lot is large enough and zoning ordinances will permit expansion. (See also Chapter 11, "Your Piece of the Earth.")

Style and floor plan

Choose what works for you now and consider how it will work for you in the future. Consider your special room needs and traffic-pattern preferences. Give some weight to accommodating your hobbies and leisure activities. Carefully consider the possibilities for expanding or remodeling in the event your needs and preferences should change over the years. (See also Chapter 10, "The Comforts of Home.")

Condition

Structural soundness is essential to a cash-effective purchase. But obsolescence (too few bathrooms, for example), the visible effects of ordinary wear and tear, the need for cosmetic refurbishing, and just plain decorating in poor taste are not always detriments to a long-term purchase. If you feel comfortable with the location and the style of the house, you can make many changes over time to suit your preferences. (See also Chapter 14, "Good Working Order.")

Price

Get the best deal you can, of course. But if you must pay a *little* more than you think quite fair in order to buy the property that will be your place for many years to come, do it. The extra thousands of dollars will be spread out over time. If you expect to live in the house more than ten years, the sum that looks so painful when it's written into the purchase contract may turn out to be just a few extra dollars per month. Also, buying the right property can save deep-rooted people thousands of dollars and considerable stress because they won't outgrow the house and have to move.

Pick Your Gateway

Next, let's look at the seven home-buying gateways that can lead to equity growth. At each one, you'll be introduced to the types of purchases available through that gateway and to the buying and selling strategies specific to that part of the marketplace.

To help you evaluate whether a gateway is right for

you, each chapter includes a self-test of your ability to meet the gateway's specific demands, based on ten important homeowner characteristics (discussed below); a brief explanation of why those characteristics are important to success; and a graph showing the relative demands made on homeowners.

Each of these seven gateways is open to both movable and rooted home buyers, but some of the options are more suited to one or the other. Whenever appropriate, it's been noted who does best with a given type of housing.

It's unlikely that anyone will be interested in all seven gateways at once. It's very likely, however, that many people will enter into several of them during a lifetime of home buying, exploring new parts of the marketplace as their needs and goals change with each stage of life.

But it is also possible that a single gateway could provide for a lifetime of homeownership. You could pursue each of its options in turn to the end of your homeowning career, maximizing your comfort and equity as you go. Some gateways lend themselves to this better than others. For example, Chapter 8, "Model Neighborhoods: The American Image Gateway," outlines a course of ownership from starter home to step-up home to status home.

Don't Assume

• •

Don't assume that you should just skip over the chapters covering home buying options that currently seem unlikely to meet your needs and preferences. You can transfer many tips and insights elsewhere.

Remember: A lifetime home-buying plan is never carved in stone. Don't look for one "right" gateway. There may be several. Keep an open mind. Weigh all the possibilities. Future purchases may pose entirely different challenges and satisfy entirely different needs.

The Seven Gateways to Homeowning Success

The Craft and Creativity Gateway

If there could be a statue at this gateway, it would be of Benjamin Franklin. He was one of the most innovative, creative and multitalented of America's founding fathers. If something didn't work, he fixed it or found a new way.

That's the image to remember for those home buyers who are willing to take on the three R's of real estate: rehabilitation, renovation and remodeling.

The Risk-Taking Gateway

Maybe Indiana Jones should be the caretaker of this gateway. That movie hero certainly got himself into and out of some dangerous situations. His image could well serve as a marker for home buyers willing to venture into some of real estate's less common and sometimes high-risk situations, such as tax sales, foreclosures, inner-city renewals and conversions.

The Independent Spirit Gateway

Should we choose frontiersman Davy Crockett or poet Gertrude Stein to welcome you at this gateway? Both were unafraid to take on the untamed and unfamiliar. This is a gateway for home buyers who choose to live on the various "frontiers" of home buying as the 21st century approaches.

The Shared-Space Gateway

Donald Trump could surely tell you a bit about shared-space buildings and managing investment property, probably more than you ever wanted to know. We'll invite him to hang out around this gateway for home buyers who choose to manage real estate as well as live in it, and for those who choose to live in a shared space with shared responsibility for the real estate and the community—albeit on a much smaller scale than Donald will ever know.

The Additions and Division Gateway

No, you won't have to take Albert Einstein along if you decide to enter this gateway, although there is certainly a bit of mathematics required. "Additions" are for home buyers who choose to buy a house that has already been added to, or to which they will add on themselves. "Division" is for home buyers who hope to buy a small home on a large piece of land and then subdivide the land into buildable lots for resale.

The American Image Gateway

Who personifies America to the rest of the world? Maybe George Washington and Barbara Bush could stand beside this gateway, and we could invite Bill Gates and Tiger Woods for the younger crowd. Most people will think quintessential "American" when they see hear those names, just as most people would look at pictures of builders' developments and think "American houses." The American Image Gateway is for home buyers who choose to begin with a tract house and then continue to buy within builders' developments, ever increasing the comfort, value, and beauty of each "estate" they buy.

The New-Construction Gateway

America's most famous architect, Frank Lloyd Wright, would certainly be an appropriate figure to associate with homes to be built from the ground up. But he'd need a lot of company. In your mind gather around this gateway a general contractor, a plumber, a roofer, a carpenter, a mason, a drywall specialist, a painter, a heating contractor, an electrician, a building inspector, and a bunch of your relatives to give advice. This part of the marketplace is for home buyers who choose to buy raw land and build a house on it.

10 Important Characteristics

Each of these seven gateways has a chapter of its own. But right now, let's get back to those homeowner characteristics that will play such a large part in your success no matter which gateway you decide to enter. You'll have to consider each of them against your lifestyle, resources and personality.

As you read along, however, don't worry if you can't rate yourself most highly in all these categories. No one could! And none of the gateways requires you to do that, anyway. The idea is to find the strengths in yourself and your buying partner(s), and match them to those parts of the marketplace where they will be most effective. Remember: Your goals in each home purchase are both comfortable living in the present and financial security in the future through growth of your equity.

These characteristics are presented in order as they come into play, from the moment a property catches your eye—and your imagination—to the point of negotiating the best possible deal for its purchase.

Creative Vision

More often than not, success in real estate is rooted in one's ability to imagine what *could be* there when others can see only what *is* there. Home buyers with creative vision can transform the ugly into the beautiful or create something appealing where once there was nothing.

Time and Skills for Maintenance

The home buyer who can fix the leaking faucet, wallpaper the kitchen, clear the autumn leaves from the roof gutters and replace the sump pump in the basement is going to save on repair and decorating costs. Even large projects such as an addition or an attic expansion can often be brought within budget when the homeowner does some of the work. Since most housing requires some time, knowledge and money, almost every homeowner must allow for some demands. For those home-buying gateways that require improvements, however, this characteristic is especially important.

Self-Confidence

Just about everyone, even your Uncle Harold, can tell you about people who got better deals in real estate than the one you're considering at the moment. Most relatives are especially good at telling you what's *wrong* with a piece of property. The only catch is: *They are not buying.* You can boost your confidence by doing a careful inspection and evaluation of a property. And you'll need every ounce of it. Demands on your self-confidence can increase exponentially when all your relatives are crying "No! No! No!" Self-confidence can also increase your perseverance and give you the willpower to continue a project despite obstacles and setbacks. Some people call it stubbornness.

Flexibility and Adaptability

Can you see yourself transforming a bedroom into a dining room? Or vice versa? Can you live without a basement? A garage? Would it bother you if your house were different from all of your neighbors'? Some home-buying opportunities call for the ability to bend one's lifestyle around the hard corners of standing buildings. Others call for skills in dealing with other people, including family members, neighbors, tenants and local government officials. Still others call for the ability to live in dust and disarray while changes are in progress.

Willingness to Take Risks

There's no way around it—some parts of the marketplace are riskier than others. Your willingness and ability to take risks may depend on your financial situation, your age, your family obligations, your personality, or any combination of these. And money isn't the only thing that can be at risk. Sometimes you might be risking time, financial liquidity, comfort, convenience or even security.

Perseverance

Some home-buying gateways require more commitment than others. Consider your willingness to see a project through to completion or a problem through to resolution. Sometimes perseverance means chasing down a local official to get answers to zoning questions. Sometimes it means fitting dentil moldings against the living room ceiling until you're seeing teeth-like projections in your sleep. Sometimes it means continuing to negotiate even when you've already heard, "That's my final offer!" three times. Perseverance is more than stick-to-itiveness; it's an assertive force that keeps you moving forward, sometimes against great odds. Often, it's tied to self-confidence, especially when the odds are against you or the opinions expressed by those not involved in the deal are negative.

Attention to Detail

In the early 18th century, the Comte de Buffon, a mathematician and natural scientist, said, "Genius is patience." In 20th century America, Richard Soloway, pianist and composer, teaches his students that, "Genius is attention to detail." Of course neither man is entirely right, but attention to detail does require great patience, and it does usually result in a finer product. If that makes you a genius, so be it. Just about everyone agrees that attention to detail is a necessary component of success in all the home-buying opportunities that require hammer-and-nail work. But you may not realize that it's also a necessary component of every opportunity that involves legal restrictions. And that is *every single real estate deal!* If attention to detail isn't your strong suit, hire someone who *will* attend to the details, and reserve your energy for judging the quality of the work when it is done.

Planning and Evaluation Skills

The premise of this book is that you can increase your comfort and wealth by buying the right home. Think of that idea as a beautiful frame house. Now where are you going to put it? Unless it stands on a strong foundation, the house will decay and crumble. Planning and evaluation skills are the foundation on which the growing-equity theory is built. To achieve success in home buying, you must be willing to make many plans, both long-term and short-term, both conceptual and specific, and to evaluate them along the way. Some home-buying gateways require both more planning and more evaluation than others.

Tact and Communication Skills

Almost all people live in communities of some sort, but some people live closer to their neighbors than others.

Continued on page 34

Your Personal Home Buyer Profile: Check Your First Impressions

Now it's time for you to stop and think a bit. The idea is for you to rate yourself on each of the ten homeownership characteristics just described. The rating scale is 1 to 5. A 1 means, "Not my area of strength, I'll avoid making these demands of myself if I can." A 5 means, "I feel secure here and enjoy calling on these characteristics." Use the worksheet provided below to fill in your self-ratings. If you have a spouse or home-buying partner, ask him or her to do the same.

You'll have the opportunity to further refine your profile in response to specific questions and situations likely to arise with each of the seven gateways. If you compare your ratings from those self-tests with this initial one, you'll probably find differences—that is, you'll find that you've rated yourself higher or lower than you might first have expected, depending on the situation presented to you. This makes the point that home-buying is a fluid experience. Just as no two home buyers will respond alike to an opportunity, you may respond differently to—and enjoy varying degrees of success with—different home-buying opportunities.

Depending on the degree of difference between your ratings and the recommended ratings of characteristics for the gateway, you may want to think twice before you cross the threshold. However, if you have a buying partner, remember that you can compensate for each other's weaknesses and build on each other's strengths. The person who is stronger in each category will usually take primary responsibility in that area.

One word of caution: If you are buying a home again in the future, do another evaluation. Just as our home-buying needs and goals change over the years, so do some of our home-buyer character traits.

Characteristic	Your self-rating	Partner's self-rating
Creative vision	_____	_____
Times and skills available for maintenance	_____	_____
Self-confidence	_____	_____
Flexibility and adaptability	_____	_____
Willingness to take risks	_____	_____
Perseverance	_____	_____
Attention to detail	_____	_____
Planning and evaluation skills	_____	_____
Tact and communication skills	_____	_____
Negotiating skills	_____	_____

Different styles of housing require varying degrees of interpersonal skills. If maximum privacy is essential to your comfort, for example, you may not do well in a shared-space condominium lifestyle. On the other hand, if interacting with your neighbors is important to you and your children, you may want to avoid buying on large tracts of land. Some home-buying gateways also make demands on your ability to speak up for your rights or to present your position in writing.

Negotiating Skills

Some 3-year-olds successfully negotiate the postponement of their bedtimes several times a week. Is this something inborn? Many experts think so. But there are just about as many who say negotiating skills can be learned. The important point here is that you rate your current level of negotiating ability. Some home-buying gateways require more negotiating skills than others because the negotiations don't stop with the signing of the purchase contract. It can involve local officials, contractors and subcontractors, and even tenants and neighbors. Knowing your negotiating ability and not overextending it, however, can help to get you through even the stickiest of situations.

With Hammer & Paintbrush:
The Craft and Creativity Gateway

Artists, home decorators, craftspeople, musicians, writers...These are the people who often hear the accolade, "Oh, you're so *creative.*" Almost no one thinks of the home renovator when that magical word comes up. But creativity is the key element to this gateway.

This part of the marketplace is reserved for home buyers who intend to increase both comfort and equity by improving the buildings they buy. All of the home-buying opportunities beyond this gateway require that substantial changes and improvements be made in the property to be purchased. Some purchases are suitable only to rooted people, who look forward to living in the home for quite some time, and others appeal to turnover-oriented, movable people.

If this is the home-buying route you choose, you'll need the creative vision to look at a home in disrepair and see what it might become. For the maximum growth of equity and optimum return on your investment of fix-up dollars, you'll want to participate in the work of refurbishing or rebuilding. Your labor—called sweat equity—saves you from paying someone else to do the improvements that will increase the value of your property and thus your equity. That's the do-it-yourself part and, yes, it does demand a fair degree of home-maintenance skill and craftsmanship in addition to creativity.

Creativity, however, is not just the ability to make

Penny for Your Thoughts

Time is money.

Ben Franklin
(1706-1790)

things beautiful or make beautiful things. It includes the ability to see new and different ways of solving problems, thus saving time, saving money or simply making life more comfortable.

What's Beyond This Gateway?

There's an American fantasy that surfaces in every age group from the early twenties to the late sixties. It goes: *We can make money by buying an old house and fixing it up.* And some people do, but it's not a sure thing. There are variables hidden in the words *old house* and *fixing* that can affect the success or failure of your particular purchase. This chapter will reveal and explore them.

Let's start with a closer look at the four key terms often confused by newcomers to this marketplace area: fixer-upper, renovation, rehabilitation and restoration.

Fixer-Upper

One of the most common opening lines spoken by in-experienced home buyers in a Realtor's office is, "We'd like something that needs some work so we can buy it cheap and fix it up the way we want." With so many people starting out with this goal, you would think run-down properties would be among the fastest movers in the marketplace. But even at bargain prices, they are among the slowest.

Why the discrepancy? Because most people think they want a fixer-upper until they actually *see* the three D's that characterize just about every fixer-upper: dirt, damage and disarray.

For example, try to imagine looking at a house with dirt-encrusted cabinet hardware, handprints on the walls, cracked window panes, pet-scratched doors, chipped trim, black mold between the tiles in the shower, and an unused dining room cluttered with a standing ironing board, piles of laundry, stacks of unopened junk mail, and weeks' worth of buy-one-get-one-free grocery specials that won't fit into the already packed pantry. And that's just a starter list of factors that can push a property into the fixer-upper category.

Even novice homeowners can remedy most of these faults. Yet most house hunters have difficulty "seeing" beyond what they actually see. Their unconscious vision of themselves living in the house *as it is* clouds their conscious effort to imagine what the house *could be* with all evidence of the current owners removed. Because of their distaste for the lifestyle of the current owners, many house hunters turn away from potential purchases that could significantly increase their equity. The dirty, damaged, cluttered and poorly decorated property purchased at 15% or more below fair market value (see Chapter 12, "The Price and Value Question"), can be a genuine bargain if dirt, surface damage and disarray are its only flaws. *If* and *only* are the operative words here.

Don't Assume

Don't assume that the dirty, banged-up and messy house is also structurally unsound with poor working systems. Appearances aren't everything. Imagine a filthy, stray dog or cat that you find asleep in your garage. A good grooming could make him a competitor for the next Lassie or Morris. A house that is an eyesore could be your ticket into profitable homeownership.

On the other hand, don't assume that the faults you can see and think you can fix are the only ones in the property. Get professional inspections and estimates! The house with an array of hidden flaws might prove to be a pit into which you pour money.

Is it your type?

When purchased carefully (you'll need to read all of Part II to understand "carefully"), a fixer-upper can be a good housing investment for both movable and rooted people. A person who plans to fix up and sell can make a quick profit and use the extra money to go on to better housing. A person who plans to stay can make the property especially comfortable and suitable to his or her particular needs.

Just plain fixing up—and *really* fixing up

Be aware that real estate advertising uses the words "fixer" and "fixer-upper" rather indiscriminately. When you answer a fixer ad, you never know whether you'll merely want to keep your hands in your pockets while looking at the black, gummy stuff creeping out around the edges of the kitchen sink or whether you'll feel as though you should be wearing a hard-hat while inspecting the basement.

Learning to differentiate the "fixer" from the "rehab" (defined later in this chapter) is among the very first requirements for a successful purchase through this gateway. The fixer-upper is the property in need of cosmetic repair, most of which the homeowner can do.

The following items are typical of the work required on a fixer-upper:

- scrubbing and cleaning everything

- spackling holes or cracks in wallboard or plaster

- painting, interior and/or exterior

- replacing missing or broken exterior shingles

- removing wallpaper and repapering

- replacing broken windows

- replacing gouged, scratched and dented moldings

- sanding or replacing scratched or broken doors

- sanding wood flooring, replacing carpets, and redoing kitchen and bathroom floors

- replacing doorknobs, hinges and all cabinet hardware

- cleaning up and landscaping the yard

Renovation

You can start a renovation by purchasing either a fixer-upper, as defined above, or a well-maintained older house. But instead of just fixing, you *improve*. (The word actually means *make new again*.) You not only "make new" the appearance of the house, but you also improve and update the working systems. (*Working systems* means virtually everything added to the structural elements to make the house habitable and comfortable, from the attic fan to the waste-disposal pipes.)

You can limit the goal of a renovation to achieving minimum comfort and acceptable appearance levels (of course, you can set the standard for minimum, and acceptable). Or you can transform an old, tired property into a new-girl-in-town (although not a debutante) that can compete with new construction.

Renovation requires all the work of the fixer-upper plus additional money, skills and usually professional help to make the upgrades. The return on this investment is more comfort and pride while you're living in the property and usually a higher price when you sell it.

What's a Renovation Worth?

How much of your renovation investment will you get back in a higher price for your house if you sell within three to five years of completing the job? (That's how long the market usually considers a renovation new rather than used and worn.) Because every property and every project is unique, there are no sure-fire answers. But in the table below, you'll find some ballpark estimates gathered over the years from the opinions of professional appraisers and real estate agents.

If you multiply out these estimates of return on your time and money, you'll see that $500 invested in paint (that you apply yourself to the exterior of your house) is likely to increase the selling price by $5,000.

A $5,000 professional basement conversion, however, is likely to increase the selling price by only $1,500.

Keep in mind that these are estimates. Use them as a starting point for your thinking, then get or do estimates for the cost of the work on the house you are considering. Enlist a real estate agent to help you find renovated houses similar to yours on the computer or in the listing files. What were the renovations, and how much value did they add to the house? If any of these comparable properties are currently on the market, make an appointment to inspect them, even if the price is out of your range. That inspection will help you to estimate the potential increase in value.

| | Percentage of cost you can expect to recoup | |
Project	With professional work	If you do-it-yourself
Interior face lift	90%	150%
Bathroom renovation	77	200
Kitchen renovation	90–94	150
Deck/Porch expansion or repair	72	200
Exterior painting	60	1,000
New, high-quality exterior siding	70	90–110
Attic conversion	84	150
Basement conversion	30	65

Be aware, however, that you can overimprove a house for the price range of its neighborhood. If you should do that, you might *not* get the financial return you had hoped for (see the box on the previous page).

The line between fix-up and renovation is often hazy. Renovation will add some or all of the following projects to the work required on a fixer-upper:

- **Kitchen remodeling,** including new cabinets, appliances, countertops, floor covering, paint and wallpaper, lighting

- **Bathroom remodeling,** including new fixtures (toilet, sink, tub and/or shower), vanity, medicine cabinet, lighting and flooring

- **New windows,** including skylights, picture windows and sliding-glass doors

- **Porch or deck repair or expansion,** including roof, screens, enclosure with sliding windows, and skylights

Who's right for renovation?

This set of opportunities is appropriate for rooted people who will live in the home long enough to complete the work and enjoy the lifestyle improvements that the renovation brings. It is less appropriate for moveable people because they may not recoup the high cost of some renovation projects with a short ownership span.

Rehabilitation

Among the Webster's Collegiate Dictionary definitions for *rehabilitate* are (1) *to restore to a former capacity* and (2) *to restore to a former state (as of efficiency, good management or solvency)*. Rehabilitating a house means bringing it back to usefulness, making it livable. That very definition implies a state of considerable deterioration.

A rehab is a much bigger challenge and usually a greater risk than a fixer-upper or a renovation. It often includes rebuilding structural elements such as the foundation, the cross timbers beneath the floors, the studs or the roof. The price of this kind of structural repair costs you in today's dollars, yet when it's complete, the marketplace still regards the house as an "old" one with some repair work done. There is always the very real risk that a future buyer will not give proper credit for the cost and quality of the rehabilitation.

To estimate how much value your rehab work will add, you must also consider the surrounding houses. If other houses in the neighborhood need rehabbing and they don't get it, the location will hold down the value of your property. (Be sure to read Chapter 11, "Your Piece of the Earth," and the section on inner city houses in Chapter 4, "For the Few and the Brave: The Risk-Taking Gateway.")

On the other hand, if you rehab the one really run-down house in an otherwise well-maintained neighborhood, your rehabbing may be even more profitable than, say, a fixer-upper because the purchase price of a rehab house should be far less than that of a fixer-upper. When complete, the work you have done on it can return many times its cost because the value of your house will be competitive with its neighbors.

When there are no neighbors (farms and mountain cabins, for example), the marketplace judges value by location, size and condition. Your rehab work can make an "uninhabitable" property desirable. With desirability comes price increase.

Up to code

Potential rehabs are also called *slums, shacks, shanties, huts, wrecks, haunted*—you get the idea. Rarely can they be made livable again without hiring several professionals (people like plumbers, roofers, heating contractors and electricians). And don't forget that a rehab virtually never

---

Don't Assume

Don't assume, with any of the options in this chapter, that you have plenty of time and money to complete all the improvement projects you plan and then start doing them all at once. Choose one project, complete it, and then go on to the next. This protective strategy will serve you well if you should suddenly need to sell. Prospective buyers will see a home with some improvements completed rather than a home completely "in process." Most buyers won't want to complete the work you've begun. They usually have their own ideas.

takes place without application for building permits and the required inspections by the local building inspector.

Most communities require these permits and inspections whenever an owner changes the structural elements or working systems of a house. Getting them can cause delays and sometimes entanglements in red tape. A homeowner must have good communication skills because an offended or angered inspector can sometimes find many additional things that just *have* to be fixed before he will grant approval.

It's the Law

• •

Municipal building codes: Once you decide to rehab a run-down structure, local ordinances almost always require that you make all structural elements and systems conform with local building codes. Systems requiring particular attention are the plumbing, waste disposal, heating and electrical wiring. Inspectors could also insist that smoke detectors be installed, however, or that the attic venting be improved, or even that railings be added to front steps.

Whenever you consider a rehab purchase, you should get professional help with interpretation of the building codes and with cost estimates for compliance. You might call two or three local independent home contractors and have each give you an estimate of the work needed to comply and the probable cost to do the work. Be sure to compare the reports and estimates. Show them to the building inspector and ask if he thinks the estimates will bring the building into compliance.

In some of the nation's largest cities where rehabbing is ever-ongoing in one part of town or another, full-time, professional building-code consultants are available. You can hire them as you would an architect—that is, they may be responsible for all of the work, all aspects of some specific portion of the work, or a single task or assignment. For example, they can make a plan for meeting the code requirements and write an estimate of its costs, or they can supervise the entire project from start to finish. Code consultants can be paid by the hour, by a negotiated flat fee, or by a percentage of the project's cost.

If you find it difficult to locate professional building-code consultants, ask your city or county buildings inspection department for names and numbers of consultants. Since many code consultants are also engineers or architects, you can also contact local or state chapters of the American Institute of Architects for leads (see page 187).

Do home inspectors fit somewhere in this process? Not usually. Because the buildings obviously need so much work, few rehab buyers hire home inspectors. It really is easier and more reliable to go right to the contractors who will be responsible for the work because most rehab work is beyond the scope of even well-trained home inspectors.

What about do-it-yourself rehabbing?

If you have the skills, do-it-yourself saves megabucks. When you own and live in the house that is being refurbished, or intend to live in it as soon as the work is finished, most local laws allow you to do the rehab work yourself. Check with your local building inspector for the law in your town. If you don't live in the house or don't intend to (if you are planning to rent it, for example), licensed professionals must do this work.

Should you take on the big project?

Rehab is not usually recommended for movable-type people unless professionals will do the work (the most ex-

---

It's the Law

Living below code: "Whoa!" you say. "What if I don't want to take on all this 'rehab' and 'up to code' stuff? What if I just want to buy an old, run-down house (one that's still livable) for a very cheap price and just live in it, repairing things only when they break?"

You can do that, and legally, too. When the structural elements and working systems of an old house were installed before the current building codes came into effect, they are said to be **grandfathered.** Those elements can continue in use, exempt from compliance with current building codes even though they may be far below code, or

"sub-code." As an owner, you can make repairs as needed.

You will most likely have to bring all systems up to code, however, if you apply for a building permit to do such things as put on an addition, change the window placement in the outside walls, raise the roof for another story, convert the building from a single-family to a multifamily dwelling, or do a historic restoration. If the building has been foreclosed on a tax lien and has been vacant, the town may require that it be brought up to code before anyone can inhabit it again.

pensive way to go) immediately after purchase. When the owner does the work, the time commitment often runs over several years. A homeowner who is subject to a corporate or military transfer, therefore, might not complete the rehab before the need to move comes around. That homeowner could even *lose* equity because unfinished projects usually sell slowly and poorly, forcing the owner to accept a lower price than otherwise.

For rooted people, however, a rehab might present an opportunity to create a "new" and customized dwelling, especially in an already developed area where land would otherwise be impossible to get. Sometimes city locations of several blocks undergo rehab by owners of individual properties, who have purchased and refurbished the properties with government-supported mortgage loans (more about these loans on page 58). The harbor area in Baltimore is perhaps the best-known example, though the Hoboken, New Jersey, waterfront, Denver's Larimer Square and

More, More, More

Books & magazines

If you want some help with the specifics of refurbishing, check your library or bookstore for the following:

- *The Complete Home Restoration Manual*, by Albert Jackson and David Day (Simon & Schuster, 1992; out of print, look for it at your public library). A step-by-step guide with color photos for restoring authentic period detail, from exterior siding and brickwork to fan lights, moldings, plumbing fixtures, windows, and roof.

- *Find It, Buy It, Fix It*, by Robert Irwin (Real Estate Education Co, 1996). A step-by-step guide to fixer-uppers.

- *The Home Remodeling Organizer,* by Robert Irwin (Real Estate Education Co., 1995).

Helps the novice homeowner to estimate the cost, time requirements, and degree of difficulty of the most common fix-up and renovation projects.

- *Old House Journal* (P.O. Box 50214, Boulder, CO 80323–0214; 800–234–3797; www.old-housejournal.com) This magazine is written exclusively for people interested in houses built before 1940. Advertisements include many catalogs for renovators' supplies. A subscription costs $27 a year (6 issues).

- *Interior Renovation and Restoration of Private Dwellings*, by Byron W. Maguire (Prentice Hall, 1994). A technical manual written for professionals in the field but easily used by the experienced do-it-yourselfer.

LoDo (for Lower Downtown), and St. Louis's Benton Place (currently in development) have garnered attention, too.

In addition to the projects mentioned under fixer-upper and renovation, rehabilitation often includes the following work:

- Bracing, buttressing or rebuilding the foundation

- Waterproofing the foundation and/or regrading adjacent land to slope away from the house

- Hanging new exterior siding

- Replacing the roof

- Replacing windows

- Upgrading plumbing, electricity, heating, insulation and wastewater removal

- Eradicating termites and repairing any damage

Organizations

- **The National Trust for Historic Preservation** (1785 Massachusetts Ave., N.W., Washington, DC 20036; 202–588–6000; www.nationaltrust.org) The trust offers the booklet *Buyer's Guide to Older and Historic Houses* and provides information on building codes, appraisals of older homes and insurance programs. The trust also has several regional offices where you can visit and browse among its books and pamphlets. Some of the offices have extensive public libraries. Call for more information on hours and availability.

- **The Victorian Society in America** (219 South 6th St., Philadelphia, PA 19106; 215–627–4252; www.libertynet.org/~vicsoc) Although Queen Victoria reigned from 1837 to 1901, the Victorian Society in America concerns itself with homes and cultural life in the United States from 1790 to the end of World War I. Membership is $40 a year for an individual, $50 for a household. The society publishes periodicals and advises its members on local craftspeople, officials and materials suppliers. (It will also advise on serving a proper Victorian tea, if you so desire.)

Your state historic preservation officer

Every state has one. He or she will help you find your way through the historic-designation process. For the name, address and phone number of your "SHPO" call or write to the: National Register of Historic Places (National Park Service, P.O. Box 37127, Washington, DC 20013–7127; www.cr.nps.gov/nr/nrhome.html; 202–343–9536).

- Repairing the chimney and fireplace

- Repairing the driveway

Restoration

Restoration is for practicing or would-be artists and historians. It's usually most successful when undertaken by home buyers with some previous experience in fix-up and renovation and more than a passing interest in the world of the past. The word restoration is generally applied to houses more than 50 years old and has come to mean bringing a home back to its original appearance—with some modifications, of course. Central heating and air conditioning, for example, are valuable nods to the present.

Some restorations are simply old houses redone with an effort to capture and preserve the charm of their youth. Other houses with national historic or architectural significance can be designated historic and named to the National Register of Historic Places, administered by the National Park Service. Owners of such houses must apply for this designation, and once it's granted, they may have to comply with the National Register's rules for restoration and maintenance. Other houses might be designated historic by state or local groups. The rules for historic houses and the effects of those rules differ from one area to another; they're typically more strict at the state and local levels. And some houses will be historic because *you* have researched the former owners, found the hidden panel behind the fireplace and made the effort to preserve a bit of history.

An antique restoration could include all of the work in the above categories plus the extensive hunt for authentic materials, colors, fabrics and so on. If you take on restoration of a designated historic house or a house that's part of a historic district, government officials could supervise your decisions and your work for compliance with established standards for the district or the housing style.

What do you know about wainscoting?

Restoration is very rarely appropriate for movable people because it takes even more time than renovation. Selling profitably also requires finding the exceptional buyer who will appreciate—and pay for—the authenticity of the restoration.

Some rooted people, however, find that restoration is just their cup of tea. Doing the essential research and finding appropriate materials and competent crafters takes time that is rarely—and then, probably not entirely—compensated for with money. Though you might eventually sell the home, say at retirement or when the kids leave the nest, the primary reward is in the ongoing joy of living in an artistic creation, your own piece of history. Rooted people who undertake restorations often make their homes their primary hobby.

Why Enter This Gateway?

Why would anyone want to buy a home spelled *w-o-r-k?* If you've read this far, you may already have an answer or two. But let's run through some of the most common reasons that home buyers choose the Craft and Creativity Gateway. (Weigh these motives carefully. If this gateway seems like a good fit with your homeowner personality, confirm your hunch with the self-test that follows.)

To make money and move on

Cash-poor first-home buyers often seek out a property they can buy *cheap* and sell *dear* as a means of increasing down-payment money for their next home purchase. Of all the options in this chapter, the fixer-upper is the recommended starting point. Renovation may be too expensive, requiring substantial cash outlay for the labor and materials, but is a possibility if the owner can do much of the work. Rehab is more risky and more demanding but a potential purchase for the careful buyer with adequate skills.

Less commonly, some buyers use a home purchase as a means of increasing spendable wealth. Some experienced home buyers come to a stage in their lives where converting some portion of their home equity to income is important. They keep a constant equity amount from home to home and use the *profit* from each sale for college tuition, a yacht, a vacation home, a year off with travel, or some other major purchase.

Continued on page 52

Self-Test Before You Choose This Gateway

The following, three-part self-assessment will help you evaluate whether you have what it takes to successfully pursue the homeowning options outlined in this chapter. It focuses on the ten important home-buyer personality characteristics introduced in Chapter 2.

PART I, RATE YOURSELF

In Part I, below, read each of the self-descriptive statements for each characteristic and decide how well it describes you. Grade your responses on a scale from 1, "Not me at all!" to 5, "That's me all the way!" Encourage your spouse or home-buying partner(s) to do the same.

Certain statements pertain to only one or two home-buying opportunities. If those don't interest you, just skip those statements.

If your ratings vary within a category, average them.

Turn to the following page and Parts II and III to see how you've fared.

Creative vision

____ I can look at a room full of dirt and debris and see it as I would like it to be.

____ I am aware of the cabinets, fixtures, floor coverings, and appliances available for home improvement and can visualize the effects they would have upon a room.

____ **Category average**

Time and skills for work and maintenance

____ Not only am I good at painting and wallpapering, I feel pride when the job is done.

____ I know I can fix leaky faucets, broken windowpanes, and nailholes in the walls. I also know whether a hired contractor has done a good job—or not.

____ I can see myself working the better part of most weekends on my house.

____ **Category average**

Self-confidence

____ I look at most projects and say, "I think I can."

____ I know my own limitations and know when to call in the pros.

____ I can tell a contractor that I don't think the job has been properly done and I can insist that the faults be corrected.

____ **Category average**

Flexibility and adaptability

____ I could use the dining room as a bedroom while refurbishing.

____ I don't mind a little sawdust on my toast—once in a while.

____ If we're without water for several days, we'll eat off paper plates and take showers at my in-laws.

____ **Category average**

Willingness to take risks

____ If I feel there's a good opportunity for profit, I'm willing to go ahead even when my mother-in-law and my favorite uncle are both saying, "You'll never get your money back on this one!"

____ I'm not afraid to make a mistake because I can usually correct it or pick myself up and start the project over again.

____ **Category average**

Perseverance

___ I finish what I start.

___ When the going gets tough, I try to find ways to make the job easier.

___ **Category average**

Attention to detail

___ When I do a job, I do it right.

___ If I notice something that has been overlooked, I'll go back to fix it.

___ I strive to ensure that all elements in a room work well together. That usually keeps me from doing things like hanging our "incredible" antique chandelier in my new contemporary dining room.

___ **Category average**

Planning and evaluation skills

___ I can put aside emotions about loving or not loving a house to evaluate cost of purchase and repairs, and future value.

___ I schedule projects and set goals for myself.

___ I can change a p. r a rational evaluation indicates that another approach might be better.

___ **Category average**

Tact and communication skills

___ When working with contractors, I can clearly state my goals and anticipated results, and give explicit directions.

___ I can maintain an attitude of friendly courtesy and respect when working with building inspectors and other local officials.

___ **Category average**

Negotiating skills

___ Since I want to buy the property in need of refurbishing at well below the going price for similar properties in good shape, I know I will need to feel confident in my ability to estimate fair market value. (And I've read Chapter 12 of this book.)

___ I have the patience and perseverance to start low and yield with higher offers gradually while adding as many extras and concessions to the deal as possible.

___ **Category average**

PART II, WHAT'S IMPORTANT AND WHY

Now let's turn the tables and look at the home-buyer personality characteristics from the point of view of demand—that is, how vital the characteristic is to success through this gateway, and why. Each characteristic is rated from 1 to 5 (1 being low demand, 3 being variable demand that might be higher in some instances and lower in others, and 5 being high demand).

Creative vision: 5

As we said at the beginning of this chapter, creativity is the key element for success.

Time and skills for work and maintenance: 4

Profits are generally greater if you have the time and skills to do much of the work. Some work can be hired out, however, especially if the pros will do a better job.

Self-confidence: 3

Too much or too little confidence can be a problem. Being too tentative towards new projects and hiring contractors unnecessarily can cut deeply into profits. On the other hand, it can be costly to repair the mistakes that can be made when homeowners dive into projects beyond their abilities.

Flexibility and adaptability: 4

Living in a house that is undergoing repair, renovation or restoration is never "ordinary living." Just how much "I-can-put-up-

Self-Test, Cont'd.

with-this" outlook you'll need will depend on the project, the time it takes and how it might stress your family life.

Willingness to take risks: 3

The level of risk depends on many factors, such as the amount and cost of repair work, the location and housing style of the property, the state of the local marketplace, the local and national economy, and the financial position of you, the buyers. For example, inaccurate estimates of cost could put you at risk for financial difficulties in the future; doing a rehab in a neighborhood that doesn't follow suit could be a moneyloser; buying for a quick fix-up and resale could backfire if the economy turned down. Read all of Part II before you evaluate risk for any property you will purchase.

Perseverance: 5

Unfinished projects will hurt the sale of property. Don't enter this gateway unless you are committed to finishing up the work.

Attention to detail: 4

Quality work is the result of care at each step. The homeowner with a "make-it-look-good-and-let's-get-on-with-it" attitude will rarely succeed at creating a comfortable and desirable home.

Planning and evaluation skills: 5

The head must control the heart when pursuing this gateway's options. Careful estimates of costs and well-thought-out plans for the completion of projects can make the difference between success and failure.

Tact and communication skills: 3

Although you must articulate exactly what you want done, choosing just the right words and worrying about hurt feelings aren't necessarily factors, contractors are businesspeople. Still, most homeowners take a little more care with building inspectors.

Negotiating skills: 4

It's important to get the best possible price for the needs-work property that you purchase and for the work you contract to have done. But knowledge of the marketplace is more important than haggling ability; you must know where your purchase fits in the price-range of the community in order to estimate its value after completion.

PART III, THE CRITICAL COMPARISON

Now you can compare your self-ratings with the importance ratings for each characteristic to see how likely you are to measure up to the demands of this gateway. In the graph's left column, the characteristics are presented in descending order from highest to lowest demand for this gateway. The grey bars show each characteristic's importance rating. Use the space allowed to draw in your and your buying partner's results.

- If you rated yourself *most* highly on this gateway's *most* important characteristics (at least 4 on characteristics rated 5, and at least 3 on those rated 4), this gateway may be the one for you.

- If you *also* rated yourself highly on the gateway's *least* important characteristics (4s or 5s on characteristics rated 3 or less), other gateways might provide additional options suited to your strengths.

- If you rated yourself highly *only* on the gateway's *least* important characteristics (those rated 3 or less), look to another gateway for your best home-buying opportunities.

- Be sure to look at your partner's strengths and weaknesses. Is your partner strong where you're weak? Is it realistic to expect your partner to pick up the slack?

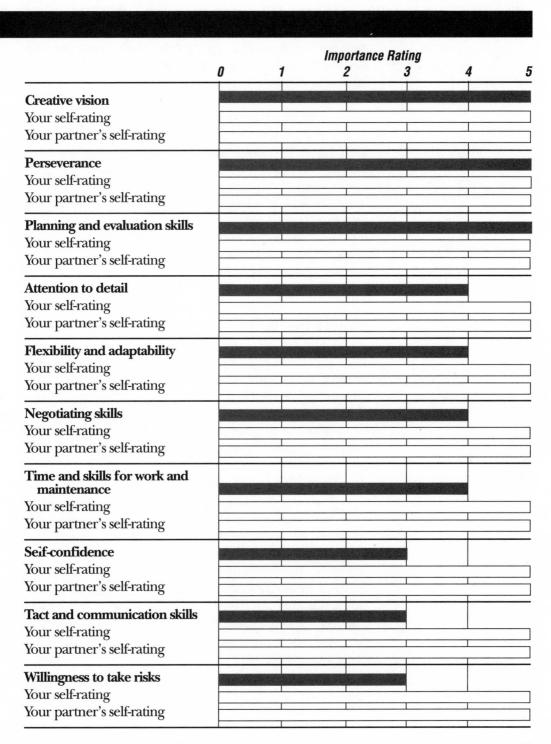

Importance Rating

	0	1	2	3	4	5

Creative vision
Your self-rating
Your partner's self-rating

Perseverance
Your self-rating
Your partner's self-rating

Planning and evaluation skills
Your self-rating
Your partner's self-rating

Attention to detail
Your self-rating
Your partner's self-rating

Flexibility and adaptability
Your self-rating
Your partner's self-rating

Negotiating skills
Your self-rating
Your partner's self-rating

Time and skills for work and maintenance
Your self-rating
Your partner's self-rating

Self-confidence
Your self-rating
Your partner's self-rating

Tact and communication skills
Your self-rating
Your partner's self-rating

Willingness to take risks
Your self-rating
Your partner's self-rating

Tax law changes enacted in 1997 enhance this opportunity to a "dreams-come-true" status for most movable-type home sellers. The new law allows a home seller who has owned and lived in a home for two or more years to take up to $500,000 in profit, *tax-free.*

Unlike the old law which required the home seller to buy a more expensive house to avoid paying taxes on profit or to be over age 55 for a one-time-only exemption, the 1997 law has no age requirement to qualify for this fabulous tax break and it has no limit on the number of times it can be used. Even very movable types who must sell in less than two years because of a job change or for health reasons can qualify for a prorated exemption.

Like all tax laws, there are some "ifs" and "whens" and "except fors" in this one, not to mention forms to be filled out. So be sure to consult with your accountant or tax advisor before you decide to claim its benefits.

To get a bigger house

Getting more space for the available dollar can motivate both movable and rooted home buyers, but the time factor gives the advantage to the latter. Remember: The larger the house, the more time required for repair and improvement. The rooted home buyer can spread the work over many years without risk; the frequent mover risks having to sell before the necessary work is completed.

To afford the otherwise unaffordable

The run-down house priced below its neighbors in an otherwise desirable neighborhood is often one of the plums of the marketplace. Both movable and rooted buyers could move into a house in a neighborhood where they couldn't afford to buy any other house, do the fix-up, and—presto!—they are not only living in the neighborhood, but they can afford it. Because location is the most important factor in determining home value, this motivator usually guarantees success. (Be sure to read Chapter 11, "Your Piece of the Earth.")

For the creativity of it all

Some people enjoy the process and the challenge of home improvement. You know the type: He or she finishes a project and then feels a sense of emptiness. Almost before the paint is dry on the last bedroom wall, these home buyers are out looking for something else. Profit is a secondary motivator to pride in achievement.

Tips and Trouble Spots

If you decide to give this gateway a try, you'll want to choose your property with a primary focus on *potential profit* if you are currently a movable person or on *maximum comfort* if you are currently a rooted person. To do that you'll need to know all the basic principles of home-buying (Part II), plus some very important specifics for working this chapter's options. Let's look at some tips for finding and getting good buys in properties that need improvement.

How to Find "Needs Work" Properties

Most home buyers think they should look in older areas of the city or in suburban developments built in the late 1940s and early '50s to find properties in need of improvement. But there are also eligible properties in small towns, far suburbs and rural areas. Even houses as young as ten years that are located in very upscale neighborhoods can qualify if their owners have neglected maintenance work.

Look for "For Rent" signs

Some house hunters begin their work by driving around areas where they would like to live. This is a good tactic for developing familiarity with the local real estate market. Watch for "For Rent" signs in addition to "For Sale" signs. Many landlords are open to offers, especially when a property is in need of refurbishing.

Look for "Needs Work" listings

Besides your driving about, you should make contact with a reliable real estate agent in each town or geographic area that you are considering. Ask the agent to go into the computer and pull all the properties that have been on the market for more than six months. There's always a reason why they haven't sold, and "needs work" is a common one. Then look for older properties and those that have "needs work" noted on the listing.

Active, full-time real estate agents who *really* know their marketplace are also a good source of information on properties that need repair, often with owners anxious to sell. The data provided on the computer listings doesn't always note these factors. Agents learn about "need-for-improvement" properties and anxious, stressed-out owners when they show houses to other customers through office-sponsored, visit-the-new-listings caravans, through "brokers-only" open houses or through word of mouth in the real estate community.

Don't Assume

• •

Don't assume that you'll look foolish if you ask for *several* appointments to see the house, each accompanied by a different home-repair contractor. The Craft and Creativity Gateway is a part of the marketplace where the smart money is cautious. Go through the property as many times as needed for you to get as accurate an estimate as possible of necessary repairs and their costs. Negotiate the price *only after* you have the facts and the numbers in hand.

The rented-condo option

If you have minimal funds and minimal time for maintenance activities, you can sometimes find a good buy in a previously rented condominium apartment that is advertised for rent again. Many of these apartments have been roughly treated by their tenants. Some owners would rather sell at a loss than refurbish and rent again. You'll have to decide whether you can or want to live there during the refurbishing.

But condos are accessed through another gateway and make some very different demands upon their owners. If refurbishing that is limited to indoors-only work sounds appealing to you, read Chapter 6.

Real estate–owned properties (REOs)

Another source of needs-work properties are the *REOs* of local lenders. If you are looking for a possible purchase in this ballpark, you should read more about bank-owned properties in Chapter 4, on the Risk-Taking Gateway. Some lenders list these properties with local real estate agents. Others, however, market them themselves.

To find these properties, you can simply call every mortgage lender listed in the local Yellow Pages. Ask for the real estate–owned department. When you get to a person with some knowledge in that department, ask whether there are any bank-owned properties for sale. Most lenders will send you printed sheets with the addresses, features and prices of their REOs. To inspect a property, make an appointment through the bank representative, or through a Realtor if the property is listed.

> ## *Words to the Wise*
> ●
>
> **REO** stands for real estate owned. These are properties now owned by lenders because of foreclosure or because the threat of foreclosure prompted owners to deed their properties over to the mortgage holder. Another term commonly used for such properties is nonperforming assets.

Estimating Fix-Up Costs

Once you find a property that you might consider purchasing, don't begin negotiating until you carefully estimate the cost of the refurbishing. Even if you intend to do some or all of the work yourself, estimating fix-up costs on your own will increase your risk of getting into financial trouble.

You don't need to pay for a professional home inspection, nor do you need a contract to purchase in order to get fix-up estimates. To find contractors, you can get referrals from friends who have had similar experiences or from real estate professionals. Or you can consult your phone book. Get *at least* two professional estimates for any work you think you want done, whether general contracting (see the definition on page 183) or specific tasks such as painting, plastering and so on. When your real estate agent arranges "showings" for each of the contractors, be there! Ask questions and watch what the contractor inspects. You should give the contractor a list of what *you* think needs to be done or what you *want* done, then ask if there is anything else that *should* be done.

Ask the contractors to break down their estimates into two categories: materials and labor. This will get you at least ballpark estimates for the cost of materials if you decide to do the work yourself. On the other hand, you will also have fallback figures should you try to do the work and then decide that you want it finished by a pro.

Be aware that these estimates don't replace a home-inspection contingency in the contract (more in Chapters 14 and 15). Except for rehabs, which are usually sold "as is," the professional inspection is a safeguard that will give you an unbiased opinion, one that's not based on contractors' bids for a job. Compare the data from the contractors with that from the home inspector. A good contract will let you get out of the deal if you don't like what you find. (Be sure to read Chapter 15, "Protection Under the Law.")

You Might Offer to Pay More

There is a creative way to negotiate savings on the cost of repairs when buying a needs-work property, but it is somewhat risky and not all sellers are receptive to the idea. Once you have negotiated the as-is price down as far as you think the seller will go, you can offer to pay more for the property if certain repair work is completed—to your satisfaction—before the closing. Be aware that you can't include all the work necessary for refurbishing in such an agreement. Some of the most common repairs negotiated this way are a new roof, exterior painting or new siding, new windows, deck or porch repairs, basement waterproofing, and regrading of the land around the house.

"But why should I offer to pay more?" you ask. "And how much more?"

If you do the repairs after you close on the house, you must either pay cash or finance the cost. Financing usually means a second mortgage (also called a second trust) or a home-equity loan (which is akin to a second mortgage), both of which usually have higher interest rates than a typical home mortgage. If the repairs have been completed before you close on the house, however, you can include their cost in the purchase price and thus finance it over the entire term of the loan.

Long-term financing means that the cost of the repairs will make only a small monthly demand on your paycheck. If you are a movable person, you'll probably pay off only a tiny portion of the money borrowed to pay for the repairs before you sell the property while reaping all the rewards of improving it.

You can offer to pay the seller the entire estimated cost of the repairs by adding that cost to the as-is purchase price you agree on. Or you can use the repairs as a negotiating tool, agreeing to split the cost with the seller, and then adding your portion to the purchase price.

If this is such a great money saver, why isn't everyone doing it? Because there are some problems that require negotiating talent, perseverance and attention to detail, not to mention faith. A risk for both the seller and the buyer is that the repairs won't meet with the buyer's approval. But close and careful supervision of the project and good communication between buyer and seller can usually decrease that risk significantly.

Another very real risk is that the repairs will end up costing more than their estimated price. Both parties can agree, however, to split the additional cost in the same proportions as the estimate or for the buyer to pick up any additional cost above the estimate.

Who will pay the contractors isn't so much a risk factor as it is a difficult problem to solve. It's a common reason that many sellers are reluctant to agree to such a proposal. Since the seller technically owns the house until closing, it follows that he should pay for the repairs and let the buyer reimburse him at the closing. But sellers worry, "What if the buyer backs out? We'll be stuck!" Some buyers and sellers solve this problem by arranging to pay contractors out of the proceeds of the sale, using mechanics' liens as a safety measure. Not all contractors, however, will agree to this.

In an alternative method, the buyers put enough money into their earnest-money escrow deposit (see page 352) to cover the cost of the repairs. When all contingencies in the contract are met and the repairs are completed to the buyer's satisfaction, the escrow money is released to the sellers to pay the contractors. This release of escrow money is perfectly legal as long as all parties agree to it—in writing. Some buyers choose to have the fiduciary agent who is holding the escrow money (usually a lawyer, the closing agent, or the real estate broker who made the sale) pay the contractors.

If everyone is honest and does what he or she promises, this all works fine. But as in every real estate deal everywhere, the more complicated it is and the more people involved, the more likely that problems will arise. Consider whether this technique is worth the effort and the hassle before you suggest it.

Financing for Fixer-Uppers and Rehabs

There are a number of mortgages specifically available to help with financing for houses in need of improvement. (For more on home financing generally, see the special section beginning on page 209.) Some mortgage loans are even supported by federal and state government programs and are written at below-market interest rates. There's a catch, however. You'll need extraordinary perseverance to find them and make your way both *through* the red tape and *beyond* the usual initial response, "That's not possible."

The 203(k) program

Through the Federal Housing Administration (FHA), the Department of Housing and Urban Development (HUD) sponsors a program called 203(k) that enables the buyer of a one- to four-family house to borrow more than the sale price of a property that is in need of repairs and improvements. The loan amount is based on the property's estimated value after improvement.

The maximum loan amount is still subject to the FHA's lending guidelines for the area of purchase, which effectively limits the price of the house (there are no income caps, however). The maximum loan-to-value ratio is about 95% for an owner-occupant, which means the lender will finance up to 95% of the estimated value after refurbishing is complete.

Here's how it works:

- **You make a list of all repairs** and improvements that you intend to do.

- **If your plan includes additions,** you go to an architect or home designer and have drawings made.

- **You get professional estimates for completed work** on all the improvements. This figure can include repairs outside the structure itself, such as those to landscaping, patios, terraces or garages.

- **Then you present everything to a 203(k) lender** who will give your plans and estimates to a professional appraiser for a written projection of the property's value when all the repairs and improvements are completed.

- **You can borrow up to 95% of the appraiser's estimate** of value after refurbishing, and you can use the borrowed money to pay loan-procurement fees and closing costs.

Homeowners do *not* have to make payments on the mortgage loan while repairs are under way if they can't occupy the property, for up to six months. (They may have to make property tax and homeowners insurance payments, however.)

FHA-insured 203(k) loans are available through conventional lenders across the nation. You just have to seek out lenders who are participating in the program. Your nearest FHA office (check your phone book's blue pages) can put you on the trail. Some responsible mortgage brokers will also help you to find these loans (though some brokers don't think they're worth the effort).

State and local help

If you want to find other financial help for home buying, you must do some digging yourself in your state or local government's banking and insurance offices (listed in the blue pages) and sometimes in the regional offices of Realtor boards. It's also a good idea to watch your local newspapers because such programs, if they exist, will be announced there, usually in the real estate or financial sections. For information on state-sponsored programs, both advertised and unadvertised, you can call your state housing finance agency (also listed in the blue pages).

More, More, More •

For the price of a first-class stamp, HUD will send you a list of mortgage lenders in your area who are participating in the 203(k) program. Send your request, with a self-addressed, stamped envelope (the long, business type), to: **HUD 203(k) Program** (Room 9270, 451 7th St., S.W., Washington, DC 20410) or visit the Web site (www.HUD.gov/FHA/203kmenu.html).

If you are having trouble locating your state housing finance agency, or if you would like information about the 180 public agencies that provide financial assistance to home buyers, you can contact the **National Council of State Housing Agencies** (444 North Capitol St., N.W., Suite 438, Washington, DC 20001; 202–624–7710; www.ncsha.org).

Life After the Closing

You come away from the closing ecstatic. You just bought a house for $47,000 less than its identical neighbor next door! You're a homeowner! An entrepreneur! You're heading straight for Easy Street!

Think again.

Improving a house while living in it is anything but an easy road. No matter how carefully you inspected and estimated, you're probably going to discover a few more objectionable features after you move in—and a few more hidden costs. What should have been a simple repair will turn out to be more complicated and time-consuming once you get into it. When you're feeling frustrated, angry or discouraged, it's important to remember that you've embarked on a long-term project. There are bound to be squalls along the way. Stick to your goals…and don't forget to take some time off.

And if you have children, be careful! Living with work in progress is especially dangerous for preschoolers. Toddlers can easily pop screws into their mouths and swallow them. Wet paint especially invites touching and tasting. Exposed electrical wires just seem meant to be explored. Keep children and repair projects separate as much as possible. To limit the danger zone in your home, complete one project before taking on another.

One Gateway to Another

Many home buyers who start out with a small fixer-upper never make it to a renovation or rehab. Some make enough profit on that first house to move on to housing that requires less time, work and commitment. Others realize that home improvement is not their forte, sell before a project is complete and seek a more comfortable lifestyle.

Movable-type people who stay in the Craft and Creativity marketplace area often progress to finer and finer—and bigger and bigger—housing in need of fixing up or improvement. Rooted people often choose antique restoration or upscale renovation of a home where they can enjoy the fruits of their intensive labors for years.

Certain members of both groups will branch out into vacation-home purchases, usually "cottages" in need of improvement. Some people even go through the Craft and Creativity gateway to get to unfinished new construction, a riskier option (see Chapter 9).

Many creative people who have significantly increased their wealth over time by doing home improvements choose retirement housing that requires absolutely minimal maintenance work and lifestyle disruption. You can think of their luxury retirement condo as a kind of pot-of-gold at the end of the rainbow. But for some of them the joy of swinging a hammer is a strong lure that leads them full circle. For these homeowners, the fixer-upper is often the investment vehicle of choice during retirement. A lifetime of experience contributes significantly to success in buying, fixing up and selling small houses. This is a particularly good investment because starter homes are in great demand, and they're not being built fast enough to meet that demand.

Home buyers who leave this marketplace area usually find that their experiences in Craft and Creativity contribute to success in every other type of home-buying venture. The maintenance and repair skills they learned will save money and ensure good work from future contractors. For a home buyer whose personality and goals match the demands of this style, it is among the best of the first-home opportunities.

Penny for
Your Thoughts

After ecstasy, the laundry.

saying from
Zen Buddhism

- **Unusual Purchase Opportunities**

- **Unconventional Homes**

- **Controversial Neighborhoods**

For the Few and the Brave:

The Risk-Taking

Gateway

Foreclosures, tax sales, conversions, turnaround neighborhoods: This chapter gathers together an unusual mix of offbeat purchase methods, unconventional housing styles and controversial locations. It's a gateway that might be nicknamed *opportunity*. And just like opportunity in the workplace, it usually comes with a demand for extra work.

Besides opportunity, the common element in this marketplace area is risk. The return in equity growth and lifestyle comfort from your investment of time and money can be tremendous. Or horrendous. You can buy a wonderful house with little or nothing down, and you can buy a house at half its fair market value. Or you can buy a house into which you'll pour thousands of dollars and hundreds of hours of labor and which will later be difficult, perhaps very difficult, to sell.

It takes a committed and persevering person to house-hunt in this marketplace area successfully. It also requires strong motivation, even determination. If you choose to enter this gateway, you might, from time to time, pause in your house-hunting to make "possibilities" lists. On one side of the page write down what would happen if everything went well (your rewards). On the other side of the page, write down what could happen if things were to go wrong (your risks).

What's Beyond This Gateway?

Bankers hold weeklong seminars on foreclosures. Lawyers study tax certificates and tax deeds in specialized classes. Whole books have been written about converting barns and carriage houses, never mind lighthouses, churches, schools and chicken coops (well, maybe not chicken coops). And in national magazines and the feature pages of local newspapers, you'll regularly find stories of buyers who successfully chose houses in neighborhoods that were turned around from "the part of town you that drive around rather than through" to "the part of town where everybody wants to live."

So what can we accomplish in one short chapter? An introduction of sorts, an overview.

Housing purchases made through the Risk-Taking Gateway are complex because they often include unusual purchase constraints and red tape, legal issues, and structural changes. If any of the home-buying opportunities in this marketplace area seems to fit your needs and interests, you'll have to do a bit more research and perhaps get some professional advice from some of the sources described later in this chapter. But let's get you started.

Unusual Purchase Opportunities

Understanding Foreclosure

A mortgage is a voluntary lien on real estate (more about liens in Chapter 15, "Protection Under the Law"). That means the borrower voluntarily gives the lender the right to take the property if the borrower fails to repay the loan. But it's not that simple. Each state has its own laws as to how the assets (the property) are to be liquidated (turned into cash) in order to satisfy the debt. The process is called *foreclosure,* and there are three types:

- **Judicial foreclosure.** The lender's attorney files suit to foreclose the lien. The facts are presented in court and

Penny for Your Thoughts

In every enterprise consider where you would come out.

Publilius Syrus (1st century BC), Latin writer and actor

the court orders a public sale. The property is sold to the highest bidder.

- **Nonjudicial foreclosure.** No court action is required if the loan instrument contains a *power-of-sale* clause, usually present in states that use *trust deeds* rather than mortgages. (Read the discussion of promissory notes and trust deeds beginning on page 209 in "The Nuts and Bolts of Home Financing.") A *notice of default* is recorded at the county records office, a public sale is advertised in local newspapers, and the property is sold to the highest bidder.

- **Strict foreclosure.** In some states, the lender can acquire the property rather than wait for the proceeds from a sale. The lender must give appropriate notice to the borrower in default, and the court sets deadlines for repayment. If the borrower does not repay the loan in full by the deadline, the court awards full legal title to the lender. There is no public sale.

> ## *Words to the Wise*
> •
>
> **Deed in lieu of foreclosure** is an alternative that some borrowers choose to avoid the stigma of public foreclosure. It is sometimes called friendly foreclosure, an oxymoron if there ever was one! When foreclosure looms, the borrower and the lender mutually agree to settle the debt by the lender's accepting title to the property. (The borrower signs a deed transferring ownership to the lender.) There's a catch, however: A second mortgage and all other liens (also known as junior liens) on the property remain in effect. These are clouds on the title (see Chapter 15) and could present some problems to the person who later buys that property from the lender.

If you are going to explore opportunities in foreclosed properties, it's essential that you understand the foreclosure procedure in your state. Call your state attorney general's office or talk with your own real estate attorney. Ask which of the above three methods of foreclosure is used. Also ask about the statutory redemption period and possession during redemption (more about these two factors in just a bit).

REOs (Real Estate Owned by the Lender)

Lenders end up owning houses because they accepted *deeds in lieu of foreclosure,* as described above, or because the lender placed the highest (or only) bid at the public sale of the foreclosed property. Houses owned by the lender usually sell at below-market prices, even though the asking price may be pretty close to that of similar properties. This is a case where bankers are often giving the very best deals, the lowest prices in the neighborhood.

"Why would they do that?" you ask. "They're in business to make money. How could they sell properties for less than their real value?"

Because, regardless of the acquisition method, there's a cushion. When a house is deeded to the lender, the original owners/borrowers forfeit their down payment. That plus any accumulated equity is now in the hands of the lender. When lenders bid at public auction, they offer an amount equal to the outstanding debt plus their expenses and thus usually acquire the property at below-market value. These acquisition methods make the lower price feasible. Interested in recouping the outstanding balance on the loan and not in managing property, the lender then wants to sell the property as quickly and efficiently as possible. The usual result is that properties are sold for a reduced or negotiated-down price in order to get them off the books.

REOs have already been introduced in Chapter 3 as a source of properties likely to need repair, renovation or rehabilitation (see page 55). Their poor condition invariably lowers the price, but it also adds a particular risk factor to buying lender-owned houses. It's important to remember, however, that not all REOs are run-down properties. Buying foreclosed property is a purchase method whose ap-

Don't Assume

Don't assume that the "mint condition" REO you inspect is just as good as new. Some lender-owners refurbish foreclosed properties in order to facilitate the sale and increase their return. Sometimes the repairs are more cosmetic than substantive.

Some REO listings specify that the property is to be sold in "as is" condition. That stipulation does not mean, however, that you should not hire a home inspector (you should). It does mean that you will not be able to renegotiate the price because of faults the inspector finds. You can still make your contract contingent on an inspection that is satisfactory to you. You can, after all, be satisfied with less than perfect, for the right price! (Be sure to read Chapter 14, "Good Working Order.")

peal isn't necessarily restricted to people interested in handyman work.

But this *is* a risky gateway. Why is there more risk than normal in foreclosed properties? Because many properties under looming foreclosure have tax liens, mechanic's liens or other clouds on the title. And because of financial strain, some owners stop maintaining their properties, allowing working systems and structural elements to deteriorate.

Prospective buyers need to pay special attention to getting clear title, even if that means hiring a real estate lawyer. They should also hire a professional home inspector and examine the report carefully. If the inspector raises any questions, it's advisable to hire specialized contractors (such as plumbers, heating engineers, roofers, and so on) for a more detailed report. (Be sure to read Chapter 14.)

More, More, More

● ●

Fannie Mae (Consumer Resource Center, 3900 Wisconsin Ave., N.W., Washington, DC 20016; 800–732–6643; http://www.FannieMae.com), is the largest player in the secondary mortgage market and therefore the largest mortgage holder in the nation. Fannie Mae (formerly The Federal National Mortgage Corporation) sells the houses it has acquired through foreclosure or deed in lieu of foreclosure by means of direct sale and agent listings. For a list of properties in your area, you can call the real estate agent of your choice, write or call Fannie Mae at the address and number above, or visit Fannie Mae's Web site.

Unfinished builders' tracts

Another group of REOs is unfinished houses in developments abandoned by failed builders. Lenders usually look for another developer to buy the unfinished portion of the project for the amount of the outstanding debt (or some portion of it), but sometimes they will sell some of the lots or partially built houses individually.

There are bargains in failed builders' tracts, but don't expect a free lunch. You can evaluate how much of a bargain you're being offered by getting professional estimates for the cost of completion, then comparing the offering price plus the cost of completion with the price of a similar, finished new house. Don't forget to add in some money to compensate you for the stress, your time and the uncertainties of buying an incomplete house.

After closing on the property, the buyer must either hire another builder to complete construction or do some of the work and act as his or her own general contractor for those jobs needing heavy equipment or professional skills. (If you buy an unfinished house, you'll encounter many of the challenges found beyond the Craft and Creativity Gateway and the New-Construction Gateway. See Chapters 3 and 9.)

Do you need to worry about any future financial or legal entanglements with your new home because of the original builder's failure? No, not if you've received clear title to the property. And who assumes responsibility for any unfinished infrastructure in the development, such as roads? The lender who foreclosed will include that responsibility with the sale of the remainder of the tract to another builder. The town, meanwhile, has usually required that road bonds be posted when subdivision approval was granted. That money is forfeited, and the town can use it to pay for putting in the roads, curbing and storm sewers or require the subsequent builder to complete the work. So, although you may not get all the infrastructure right away, you will get it.

Individual properties in lender-owned unfinished developments aren't usually advertised. A good real estate agent will know about such projects in the local area. Or you can call local lenders and ask to speak to someone about nonperforming assets.

Government-Owned Houses

Besides lenders, the federal government also owns and sells properties acquired because of default on mortgage loans. Purchase of these houses carries all the same risk factors as purchase of other REOs.

In the late 1980s, the federal government became the owner of thousands of properties when it embarked on the bailout of hundreds of failed thrifts (savings banks and savings and loan institutions). Most of these properties were sold at huge auctions run by the Resolution Trust Corporation (RTC). People got to thinking of the RTC as the agent for government REOs. In fact, the federal government owned and sold foreclosed properties long before the bailout, and still does even though the bailout is long over.

The U.S. Department of Housing and Urban Development (HUD) acquires properties through foreclosures on FHA and insured loans. Properties are sold through agents in the real estate marketplace and sometimes through sealed-bid auctions.

Depending on the specific program, HUD may pay some of the closing costs and even help with repair costs. There are some incentive programs requiring a downpayment of only $1,000 or less. In these programs, all closing costs and the mortgage insurance premium can be financed with an FHA-insured mortgage.

Don't Assume

● ●

Don't assume that you can take possession and move into a house that you just bought at a foreclosure auction. Many states, but not all, have a **statutory redemption period** during which the previous owner can pay off all debt and redeem the property. The length of time varies by state and ranges from 75 days to two years. Most states that have a statutory redemption period also allow the defaulting borrower to remain in possession (and occupancy) of the property during the allowed redemption time. This possession can and often does result in a maintenance disaster for the new owner.

If you are pursuing a bargain in foreclosed property, call your state attorney general's office and ask whether the state has a statutory redemption period for foreclosed mortgages, how long that period is, and whether the purchaser or the mortgagor (defaulting borrower) has possession during the statutory redemption period.

Interested? Contact your local or regional HUD office (check the blue pages of your telephone book to locate the office nearest you) or call HUD at 202–708–1422, or visit HUD's Web site (http://www.hud.gov) for links to state offices and lists of HUD houses for sale.

The Department of Veterans Affairs (VA), like HUD, handles the sale of some foreclosed properties. You can get lists of available properties in your area from your regional VA office; to locate the one nearest you, check the blue pages of your phone book or the VA's Website (http://www.va.gov).

Public Auctions

Properties sold under judicial or nonjudicial foreclosure are sold at public auction. Notice of the date, time, and properties involved (and usually the amount of the outstanding debt) is posted in county records offices and generally advertised in local newspapers. A government official (usually the sheriff) conducts the auction.

The successful bidder at the auction receives a deed to the property executed by the sheriff or other official. The property is sold free of the foreclosing mortgage and all other junior liens. So you'll get clear title, right?

Not guaranteed! The sheriff's deed conveys whatever title the borrower had. The deed contains no warranties. You get title without any debt attached, but not necessarily without any claims attached. This situation can make for difficulty in financing and title insurance. Don't get involved without adequate legal counsel.

More, More, More
● ●

If you want to get on the mailing lists of professional auctioneers, contact the **National Auctioneers Association** (8880 Balentine, Overland Park, KS 66214; 913–541–8084, fax 913–894–5281; www.auctioneers.org). The national trade organization will send you a free copy of its membership directory for $5.

Private Auctions

The conventional wisdom holds that you can get a bargain at an auction. This is sometimes, but not always, true in the real estate marketplace.

Be aware that some private auctions have nothing to do with foreclosure and that some are dealing with properties in default where foreclosure is imminent but not yet a reality. Private auctions are advertised in local newspapers without any notice given in county records offices or courthouses.

Usually the sellers of the properties set minimums for the bids (called floor bids.) And usually these starting prices are not blazing bargains set at fire-sale figures.

"Why not?" you ask. "Don't those owners want to sell?" Yes, they do, but because the proceeds from the auction must pay off outstanding debt plus auction costs, the price creeps up pretty fast. When lenders set floor bids, the minimum selling price usually covers the outstanding debt plus foreclosure expenses and any other liens on the property, such as back taxes.

When you buy property at private auction, you risk paying too much and not really knowing what you're getting. Some buyers get caught up in auction fever, bid higher because others are bidding, and if they fail to get the property they wanted, bid on others they have not researched. While some buyers do get bargains, you might pick up just as good a deal in the regular marketplace with some careful hunting and hard negotiating.

Tax Sales

Properties with tax and other government liens are sold to the highest bidder at a tax sale, which is generally an auction. Usually very few bidders show up. So why can't you go, bid the $20,000 in outstanding taxes and walk away with a nice $200,000 house? Because the lenders who

Don't Assume

Don't assume that every municipal tax auction leads to the ownership of the property being auctioned. Some states sell **tax certificates,** not the houses. In certificate states, you pay the outstanding taxes and get a lien on the property. The owners and other parties with an interest in the property (such as heirs, an ex-spouse or even a contractor who improved the plumbing and then put a mechanic's lien on the property because he was never paid) have a given period of time in which to redeem their ownership rights by paying you the tax balance plus a high rate of interest (say, 18%). The redemption period varies from state to state—two years is common.

If the tax certificate isn't redeemed by the owner or another party with an interest in the property, you will have to initiate foreclosure proceedings and additional legal action may be required to make the title marketable. Although they are often attractive to investors, tax certificates are not a recommended route to homeownership.

More than half of the states are tax-certificate states. To find out if yours is one of them, call your state attorney general's office.

hold mortgage liens on the properties being auctioned will be there to protect their interests. Rather than allow a property on which they hold a mortgage to be sold for taxes, they will acquire it by making sure to be the highest bidder. (Later the lender will put it on the market to recoup the outstanding amount of the mortgage loan, the taxes that were paid and all the expenses involved.) In fact, many houses never go to tax auction because nonpayment of taxes is a valid reason for foreclosure and the lenders foreclose the mortgage before the property qualifies for tax auction.

> # Words to the Wise
>
> Legal proceedings to **quiet title** are available in every state. In a **quiet title action,** all parties with a potential interest in the property are notified that a lawsuit has been filed to determine the validity of the title. The court then hears the case and rules on the matter. If you win, the title should be both marketable and insurable.

Some properties that are owned free and clear of any mortgages are sold at tax auctions, however. Are there bargains available? Absolutely! But not without some serious problems attached. Ask yourself why an owner who didn't owe anything to a mortgage holder didn't (or couldn't) pay the municipal taxes.

The primary risk in buying foreclosed property at tax auction is the validity of the title. Often title insurance companies will not insure properties purchased at tax sales until the title has been cleared from any claims by means of a legal procedure called *quiet title action.* This procedure can be both expensive and time consuming over a long period, sometimes years.

Tax-sale purchases are feasible only for rooted people, and then only if they have plenty of time to settle title questions and are willing to live with the risk of ultimately losing the property.

Unconventional Homes: Conversions

In the real estate marketplace, a conversion is a building that was intended for one purpose but has been changed so that it will function for another. Some typical conversions might be an old school building that is turned into a multifamily house, a gas station that becomes a restaurant, a warehouse that becomes office condos. The most common residential conversions are multifamily houses to single family, or visa versa (discussed in Chapter 6, on the Shared-Space Gateway), and the rebuilding and redesign of barns, carriage houses and churches.

Conversions have the elements of the Craft and Creativity Gateway (Chapter 3) and the New-Construction Gateway (Chapter 9). They demand time, handyman skills, creative vision, planning, attention to detail and commitment. The design of an interior suitable and safe for living usually requires the help of an architect. The actual conversion and construction will require working with a fairly large number of construction professionals. When completed, however, conversions are neither a renovation nor a new house but a class of real estate unto themselves.

Conversions are a high-risk home purchase because:

- **the cost of the conversion is often difficult to estimate** with all the redesign and building involved and the extras to be added;

- **estimates often prove inaccurate;**

- **some buildings never really convert well** to living space; and

- **converted buildings are usually difficult to resell.**

Not Meant for Humans

Barns are the conversion that most people fantasize about. Perhaps you've seen a magazine article with photos of those beautiful beams, the weathered wood, the high ceilings, the patterns of light from high windows.

In fact, barns are difficult to make livable. Like all other outbuildings not originally meant for human habitation—carriage houses and garages, for example—conversion is complicated by the need to add basic working systems such as heat, water, electricity, and waste disposal to an already standing building. Hook-up to utilities in the nearest road is often expensive. A well must often be dug, and driveways can be long and difficult to maintain.

Beyond the need to make an outbuilding habitable, you'll have to make it comfortable, overcoming such deficiencies as inconvenient floor plan and the lack of bathroom and closet space. If the building already has a concrete slab as a foundation or first floor, you may have to locate the kitchen and bathrooms on the second floor to avoid breaking up the concrete for installation of the plumbing and waste-water disposal systems. Sometimes exterior stairs are used to bring the entranceway to the second-story level of the house, using the first level for bedrooms, recreation area, storage or garage space.

It's the Law!

If you decide to convert a barn or other outbuilding, you will need a building permit. Your project will be subject to inspections by your town's building inspector, and you will have to meet all the current building codes.

Built for Other Human Uses

Buildings originally meant for human uses other than dwelling space are somewhat easier to convert to homes. Among the most common are old schoolhouses, small churches, lighthouses, restaurants, mills, stores and other commercial buildings. Lofts, usually the top story of a warehouse or factory, are common in large cities. They are usually a condominium conversion entailing legal work in addition to the construction work.

Since the basic working systems in these buildings generally have already been installed, conversion usually means upgrading and adapting them for living space. For example, plumbing is usually limited and not located where you want it to be, electrical outlets are too few and wiring is inadequate, and heating is inappropriate. Modification of interior space demands considerable skill, knowledge and attention in order to comfortably accommodate the typical use and movement patterns of human inhabitants. (Before you decide on a conversion, be sure to read

Chapter 10, "The Comforts of Home.")

Besides the possibility of an inconvenient floor plan, there's always a resale risk when you purchase or do a conversion. Conversions are often difficult to sell because the building usually retains a hint of its old character and always looks a little different from an ordinary house. Zoning—seldom the usual residential designation that most home-buyers expect—may add another stumbling block to profitable sale. Generally, conversions are not recommended for turnover-oriented "movable" people who may want or need to sell quickly.

Controversial Locations: Turnaround Neighborhoods

The exodus from American cities has been well documented by the census bureau and many other data-collection groups. Since the post–World War II building boom, the desire for suburban housing has grown continually, and since about 1970 virtually all new construction of single-family, detached homes has been in the suburbs, especially the outer suburbs. So where does that leave houses in the city and older suburbs? Old, often rented, dilapidated and sometimes abandoned.

But there's something going on. The Community Reinvestment Act of 1977 required lenders to meet the needs for home financing of low- and moderate-income neighborhoods. It effectively put a legal stop to the policy of *redlining*. More recently, municipalities, Fannie Mae and other secondary mortgage-market players have added their support to neighborhood revitalization.

Renters are being encouraged to learn about the advantages and possibilities of homeownership through community- and corporate-sponsored counseling, education, and training programs that are being offered not only in English but also in Spanish and other languages. And the programs have become a step to getting financing.

Fannie Mae now operates 28 Partnership Offices around the nation where low- and moderate-income lending programs are being tailored to fit the needs of the local community. The corporation is accepting loans with very low down payments with the precondition that the home buyer complete a counseling program. With this backing from the secondary mortgage market, lenders are now financing purchases with very little money down. Community organizations are often providing help with closing costs and legal services.

The financial marketplace's developing focus and positive attitude toward revitalizing older neighborhoods will help make homeownership available to low-income families, single-parent families, single people, and, perhaps most important, immigrant families.

Words to the Wise
• •

Redlining is the marketplace term for the practice of drawing a line on the street map around certain neighborhoods where new mortgage loans are to be avoided for fear of default and property devaluation. It is illegal. If you suspect that you are being denied home financing because the property you have chosen is in a turnaround area, contact your state banking commission.

As a result of the Immigration Act of 1990, the last decade of this century will see a level of immigration unequaled since the first decade. For these new immigrants, homeownership is as much a part of the American Dream as it was for the great-grandparents of most of today's young native-born Americans. Most authorities believe that their strong family values and drive to succeed will bring new life and character to our cities. The picture is positive.

But what about the older-neighborhood house *you* might choose to buy? What if the neighborhood *doesn't* turn around but continues to decay? What if yours is the only rehabilitated house on the block? Will you be able to sell for a profit? Will you be able to live there comfortably? This is an opportunity that makes many demands on the homeowner similar to those of the Craft and Creativity and Shared-Space gateways. So be sure to read Chapters 3 and 6 carefully. Chapter 11, "Your Piece of the Earth," offers additional tips for researching a neighborhood you're interested in. Realize and evaluate your risks, and then weigh them against the opportunity each property presents.

But that still doesn't tell you where to get clues that a neighborhood is experiencing a turnaround. Investors use the following points when considering a purchase:

- **The ratio of resident owners to absentee landlords.** Resident owners generally take better care of their real estate than absentee landlords and tenants. To learn this ratio, you may have to do some sleuthing. Go to the town tax maps and write down the names of the owners of each building in the neighborhood. Then go to a street directory (available in real estate offices) and compare the names of the owners with the names of the occupants of each building.

Penny for Your Thoughts
• •

"Distressed neighborhoods and inner cities will be stabilized as homeownership gives people a greater stake in their community; this can and will mean higher property values, a lower crime rate, better schools, and improved infrastructures, from streets to parks to shopping areas."

James A. Johnson, at the time Chairman and CEO of Fannie Mae, in his book *Showing America a New Way Home, Expanding Opportunities for Home Ownership* (Jossey-Bass Publishers, 1996)

- **The vacancy rate.** An area where virtually all the housing units are occupied is usually an area that is considered desirable. For clues to vacancy, look in the windows. Are there curtains? Can you see furniture or other evidence of residency? Professional management companies, real estate agents and the National Association of Realtors, and HUD all have access to vacancy-rate information. You may have to do some time-consuming investigative work, but you can get this information.

- **Conversion of nearby apartment buildings to condominiums or co-ops.** If apartments are being sold, people are finding the area desirable enough to buy into it.

- **Renovation or rehab in other houses nearby.** Houses that are well maintained (paint as needed on siding and trim, brickwork, doorways, shutters, windows, gutters and drainpipes and walkways) indicate a positive focus on the value of good housing.

- **Gardens, window boxes and well-swept stairs.** Look for small, extra lifestyle touches that indicate concern with good living space. By contrast, you won't want to see: litter, trash, brooms and buckets near the doorways, signs of overcrowding and illegal use (too many mailboxes for the size of the house), and broken glass, bottles or drug paraphernalia.

- **Neighborhood groups or associations.** People gathering together to improve life in the neighborhood is a positive sign that often leads to property and neighborhood improvement.

Why Enter This Gateway?

If higher risk is the common element of the home-buying opportunities reached through this gateway, why bother with it? There is certainly opportunity elsewhere. Why struggle with homebuying fraught with more than the usual *ifs* and *maybes*? The answers may surprise you. (Weigh the following motives carefully. If this gateway seems like a good fit with your homeowner personality, confirm your hunch with the self-test beginning on the following page.)

To break into the real estate marketplace

You can often buy property with little or no money down. FHA, VA and state-supported financing is available. If you buy a multifamily house, you may collect rents that can help you make the mortgage payments and support maintenance costs. (Be sure to read Chapter 6.)

To buy at a bargain price

Foreclosures rarely sell at the fair market value of nearby comparable properties. Most lenders want ownership turnaround to be as fast as possible, so they set an asking price to attract buyers and are very willing to negotiate. Don't be afraid to make a low offer.

For privacy and autonomy in housing

The spirit of individualism is strong in America, and most of us prefer housing with some private space around

Continued on page 82

Self-Test Before You Choose This Gateway

The following, three-part self-assessment will help you evaluate whether you have what it takes to successfully pursue the homeowning options outlined in this chapter. It focuses on the ten important home-buyer personality characteristics introduced in Chapter 2.

PART I: RATE YOURSELF

In Part I, below, read each of the self-descriptive statements for each characteristic and decide how well it describes you. Grade your responses on a scale from 1, "Not me at all!" to 5, "That's me all the way!" Encourage your spouse or home-buying partner(s) to do the same.

Certain statements pertain to only one or two home-buying opportunities. If those don't interest you, skip those statements.

If your ratings vary within a category, average them.

Turn to the following page and Parts II and III to see how you've fared.

Creative vision

___ A house's exterior doesn't define for me the use or comfort of interior space.

___ If the foundation is solid and the structure sound, I can make any building a livable space.

Time and skills for work and maintenance

___ I enjoy taking the time to work with groups of people to improve the neighborhood and the community.

___ I have the tools and the knowledge to do most home-repair jobs.

Self-confidence

___ I don't need a popular or high-status neighborhood to bolster my sense of self worth.

___ I often choose the road less traveled.

Flexibility and adaptability

___ I enjoy the rich experience of being with people of different ethnic and social backgrounds.

___ I don't mind an unusual and slightly inconvenient floor plan if I have enough space and like my home's location.

___ If a good house in a great location lacked a garage or off-street parking, I would arrange for a garage elsewhere.

Willingness to take risks

___ I'm a firm believer that you should consider all the risks, all the worst-case scenarios, and if you can live with them, go ahead.

___ Like the old saying "Nothing ventured, nothing gained," I say, "If you want it and it can be done, take a chance."

Perseverance

___ I don't quit because I'm a little scared.

___ I've removed wallpaper five layers deep and ended up with nine or ten colors under my fingernails.

Attention to detail

___ When I drive or walk through a neighborhood, I notice curtains and plants in the windows, clean stairs and walkways, mailboxes with names attached, children playing, neighbors talking, and other details that show pride in ownership and community responsibility.

____ I would buy title insurance even if it was not required.

Planning and evaluation skills

____ Before I make a purchase offer, I'll get at least two estimates of repair, conversion or completion costs.

____ Before I buy, I'll research the community. I'll know the trends for property values, crime, services, recreation programs and business opportunities.

Tact and communication skills

____ I have learned to communicate with workers and neighbors who speak a foreign language.

____ If I'm the "different" person in a neighborhood, I can wait to be accepted gradually, and I don't expect other people to think that my way is the right way or the only way to do things.

____ I'm good at dealing with red tape and bureaucrats.

Negotiating skills

____ I can hold out for a better deal whether I'm dealing with a banker or a carpenter because I base my negotiating on facts, not persuasion or power plays.

____ I won't let my heart rule my head because I know that if I don't get the deal I want on one house, I can find another just as good, maybe better.

PART II: WHAT'S IMPORTANT AND WHY

Now let's turn the tables and look at the home-buyer personality characteristics from the point of view of demand—that is, how vital the characteristic is to success through this gateway, and why. Each characteristic is rated from 1 to 5 (1 being low demand, 3 being variable demand that might be higher in some instances and lower in others, and 5 being high demand).

Creative vision: 5

These home-buying opportunities ask the prospective buyer to see beyond what is there and see what is not yet there. Creativity helps to visualize what a property could be and what a neighborhood could be.

Time and skills for work and maintenance: 5

Virtually all purchases demand owner contribution to fix-up and maintenance for success. But that's not all. Virtually all properties beyond this gateway also demand time for legal questions, planning, design, and hiring and supervising home-improvement specialists, including architects, designers and contractors. Time spent in community work also contributes to housing success when you choose a property that is unusual in the neighborhood or in a neighborhood that will be changing.

Self-confidence: 4

With risk, work and time demands high, buyers in this marketplace area need confidence that they can indeed pull off the purchase and make it successful. Confidence depends on knowledge, however, so do some extra digging for information, read, and ask questions of everyone.

Flexibility and adaptability: 5

Birch trees survive the storms, ice and blustery winds of northern New England because they can bend. Some of the demands of buying foreclosed property, doing a conversion, or choosing a house in an inner-city neighborhood may seem as harsh and isolating as a blizzard. Sometimes you'll have

Self-Test, Cont'd.

to bend and adapt like the birch. But remember: Birches straighten up beautifully after the storm.

Willingness to take risks: 5

Risk distinguishes this marketplace area. Always weigh the risk you will take against the goals you hope to achieve and the likelihood of achieving them.

Perseverance: 4

The Risk-Taking Gateway often requires that you juggle several projects simultaneously. And some of them have long timelines! Sometimes you will want to give up. Don't. Strive to complete each project.

Attention to detail: 5

Don't give in to delays and the inefficiency or incompetence of others. Maintain your high standards and insist that those who work for you meet them. There are many kinds of detail, from legal issues to structural problems, in this marketplace area, and they all demand careful attention.

Planning and evaluation skills: 5

Careful planning and accurate evaluation of the success and cost of each step is vitally important to successful risk-taking.

Tact and communication skills: 4

Purchases are often complex, and most complex projects require the cooperation of many minds. You will need the capacity to encourage minds (and personalities) to cooperate.

Negotiating skills: 5

Because these properties are all unusual in some way and comparables may be hard to find, determining fair market value is often difficult. Negotiate hard for the best possible price and terms. Don't be afraid to ask for what you want. Give ground if you must, but hold fast for points that are important to you. Don't exceed the top dollar figure you calculated you can pay. Remember: There are and will be other houses on the market.

PART III: THE CRITICAL COMPARISON

Now you can compare your self-ratings with the importance ratings for each characteristic to see how likely you are to measure up to the demands of this gateway. In the left column of the graph, the characteristics are presented in descending order from highest to lowest demand. The black bars show each characteristic's importance rating. Use the space allowed to draw in your and your buying partner's results.

- **If you rated yourself *most* highly on this gateway's *most* important characteristics** (at least 4 on characteristics rated 5, and at least 3 on those rated 4), this gateway may be the one for you.

- **If you *also* rated yourself highly on the gateway's *least* important characteristics** (4s or 5s on characteristics rated 3 or less), other gateways might provide additional options suited to your strengths.

- **If you rated yourself highly *only* on the gateway's *least* important characteristics** (those rated 3 or less), look to another gateway for your best home-buying opportunities.

- **Be sure to look at your partner's strengths and weaknesses.** Is your partner strong where you're weak? Is it realistic to expect your partner to pick up the slack?

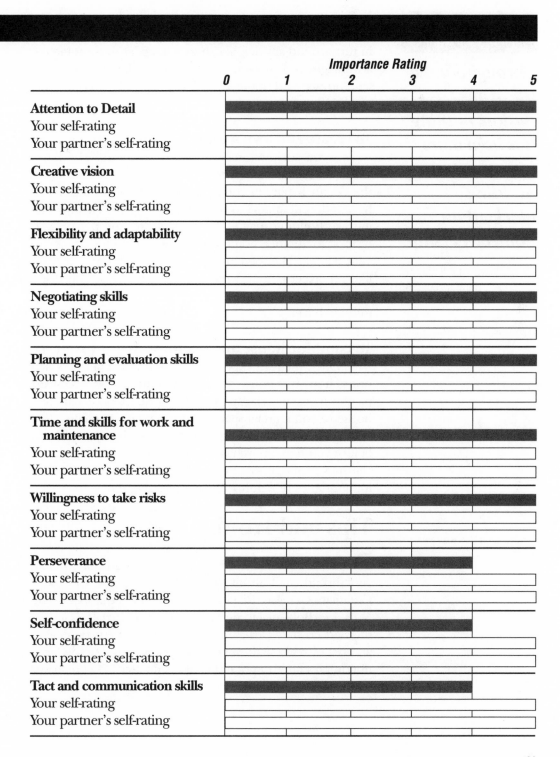

Throughout the life of our nation, nothing has been more important as a building block...than homeownership.

President Bill Clinton,
January 30, 1995

it. Some city-loving people who have lived in apartments (both renters and condo or co-op owners) choose houses in turnaround city neighborhoods in order to combine the advantages and conveniences of city dwelling with the control, privacy, and opportunity for independence of the detached house.

To create and own a unique home

Some conversions are purely aesthetic. The lighthouse looks like "home" to some buyers because a view of the ocean is part of their life's dream. Some purchases have different appeal to different buyers. For example, an in-town building may look run-down to one person and historic to another. Some properties cry out for change to another use. The foreclosed, ten-room Victorian may look like a perfect bed and breakfast inn that would provide both housing and some income to the creative, conversion-minded buyer.

To combine house and business in one property

Often the least expensive way to house a business is to house it in your house. Some savvy entrepreneurs convert part of a commercial space to living quarters or part of a house to commercial space. If this is your plan, check the zoning ordinances to be certain that the change is allowed before you sign a purchase contract. If it isn't allowed, you can make your contract contingent on a successful appeal for a variance or a nonconforming-use permit.

Tips and Trouble Spots

Before you set out to find a house through this gateway, you should read about the challenges in the Craft and Creativity Gateway (Chapter 3), the corner-tabbed "The Nuts and Bolts of Home Financing" and Part II, "Getting the Best Possible Deal." And don't skim! When you deal in an area of real estate where risk is prevalent, knowledge is not only a source of power but also a financial life preserver.

Meanwhile, here are some important tips for success.

Finding Property

We've already mentioned REOs and auctions—and, of course, you know about Realtors' MLS (multiple listing service) books. But have you thought about town tax records? Here's how a little initiative can pay off.

Lists of people who are behind on their tax payments are public record—they're even generally published in local newspapers. Go to the tax collector's office for the area you're interested in and ask for the current list, then drive by the properties. If you see something you like, consider writing a letter to the owner saying that you are looking to buy a home and ask if he or she is interested in selling.

If you don't want the owner to know you got the address from the delinquent tax list, you can send the same letter to every house on the block. (You can get the name of every owner on the street from the town tax record.) Here's a possible sample:

Dear *[the name of the homeowner],*

We are a couple looking to buy a home on *[the name of the street].* We have down-payment money and are qualified to carry the necessary mortgage. We'd like to buy and move in before school starts in September *[or any other date or time you wish to specify],* but of course we are somewhat flexible on that date. If you would consider selling your home, please call us at *[your phone number].*

Sincerely, *[your name(s), printed below for clarity]*

Often homeowners in financial trouble welcome the opportunity to sell their home without paying real estate commissions or facing tax liens and the possibility of foreclosure. Their taxes will be paid from the proceeds of the sale, and you may get a bargain. Be certain, however, that you know fair market value in the neighborhood before you send out a letter like this (read Chapter 12). If you don't, you may find yourself responding to an asking price that is out of line and ending up so frustrated that you give up your creative hunt.

Tax records are also a good place to find the owners of properties that appeal to you as conversions, whether an abandoned commercial building or a turn-of-the-19th-century house that is now being used for rental units. The current owner's name and address will appear on the tax records. Even if the property is not listed for sale and is not tax delinquent, you can approach the owners and ask if they will consider selling.

Again, be sure you know market value, and negotiate gracefully and politely—but hard.

Getting the Money

Usually the easiest source of financing on a foreclosed property is the lending institution that did the foreclosing. It will sometimes even bend the qualification rules a bit on a property it is anxious to find a new owner for.

Most lenders today are also very much aware of mortgage-assistance programs for low-income families in their communities. For example, the FHA's 203(k) program (see page 58 in Chapter 3) can be used to purchase housing in turnaround areas.

Sometimes, conversions and incomplete builders'

More, More, More

- **If you qualify for low-income mortgage programs, your local board of Realtors** can give you the names of lenders, mortgage brokers, home-purchase counseling agencies and home-purchase support groups working in your area. You can find the board's number in the phone book or call any local Realtor and ask for it.

- **The Fannie Mae Foundation** (800–665–0012) offers a free booklet, "Opening the Door to a Home of Your Own."

- **The Department of Housing and Urban Development** (HUD; 888–466–3487) will refer you to a HUD-approved counseling agency in your area.

- **Your state housing agency** will send you information on state-supported home-purchase programs. The agency is listed in the blue pages of your phone book, but if you have trouble locating it or finding information about financial assistance for low- and moderate- income housing purchases, contact the National Council for State Housing Agencies (listed on page 60).

tract houses can be a problem when applying for financing. Because the finished product will be different from what is currently standing, the lender usually hesitates to commit to an appraisal of future value. Some buyers have had to apply for construction loans (see page 206 in Chapter 9) and then refinance their newly converted or completed home.

A good mortgage broker can help you find the kind of specialized financing you sometimes need with riskier purchases.

Legal Help

Whenever you're dealing with contracts that involve five or more figures after the dollar sign, it's a good idea to check things out with a lawyer. When your goal is buying a better home via a risky purchase strategy, legal help is absolutely essential.

In some areas of the country, attorneys include contract review in their fee for closing title. But even in areas where title is closed by agents of the lender or specialized closing firms, you can always hire an attorney to review a contract. (See page 353 in Chapter 15 for information on how to protect your right to attorney review.)

Most lenders will not write a home mortgage without title insurance, so most homeowners have it. But even if you are paying cash for your home or if your lender does not require title insurance, you will want to buy it. Title insurance protects against loss from claims against the title. Without good title you may not be able to sell the property (see the discussion "Why Title Insurance?" in Chapter 15).

From One Gateway to Another

Although risk and work make this gateway intimidating to many people, it's one that buyers at almost any stage in life can and do access. Foreclosed properties are most available in lower-cost neighborhoods, but there are also midrange houses, houses in affluent developments, and even luxury

*Take calculated
risks. That is
quite different
from being rash.*

George S. Patton Jr.
(1885–1945),
American general

estates among the REOs in many lenders' files.

Foreclosed property with clear title can be a comfortable and profitable purchase for both movable and rooted people. Homes sold at tax sales, and any other property where there might be some cloud on the title, however, are among the highest-risk purchases in the marketplace. Only rooted people with time and good financial resources should take them on, and then only if they can ultimately afford to lose the property.

The process of converting a property from a non-housing use into a unique and satisfying dwelling usually appeals to buyers with some previous experience in the marketplace, especially those who enter through the Craft and Creativity or New-Construction gateway. Some astute and creative first-time buyers, however, do find a building that can be bought for very little money and successfully converted to "home."

Because of the time required for planning and implementation, conversion rarely appeals to movable people. Ironically, however, it is movable people, with experience in buying and selling many houses, who often choose a unique conversion when they leave their movable lifestyle to retire or establish their own businesses. And because of their home-buying experience, they have a high rate of success.

Creative people, both movable and rooted, sometimes acquire their vacation homes by conversion. This is where lighthouses, old mills, bait shacks, farm buildings and camps most often become appealing.

It's not uncommon for buyers to put in the essential working systems for livability and then work on the aesthetic and comfort elements of the conversion over several years. For movable people, the vacation home sometimes provides an anchor and a sense of rootedness.

Houses in turnaround neighborhoods can be the first purchase of the very young who want to get the tax and other financial benefits of ownership. But they can also be the first purchase of middle-aged people who want to stop renting and enjoy both the security of ownership and its equity-growing potential. Sometimes two generations pool their resources to buy a two- or three-unit multifamily.

Buyers might start out with a multifamily in a turn-around neighborhood, renovate, sell for a profit, and then go on to a single-family house elsewhere. Or they might not sell their first turn-around-neighborhood house, but keep it as an income-producing rental property and borrow on the increased equity (which was the result of appreciation due to the renovation and neighborhood turn-around) to buy another house.

Because of its high demands in almost every aspect of homeownership, the Risk-Taking Gateway is excellent preparation for most other areas of the marketplace. It shares challenges with the creative and shared-space gateways. It is like a graduate degree for the new-construction and additions-and-divisions gateways. And it can even be preparation for those who enter the independent-spirit gateway with thoughts of a bed and breakfast or an in-home child-care facility in mind.

Even more important than good preparation for future home buying, however, the risk-taking gateway is first and foremost the means to homeownership for many people who could not otherwise get into the marketplace. To enter it, home buyers must overcome their fears by learning the facts and getting good counseling.

- **Far-Out Locations**

- **Far-Out Farms**

- **Lost Lots**

- **Doing Business in the Neighborhood**

Pioneering Into the 21st Century:

The Independent Spirit Gateway

Pioneering? A lot of people think there's not much pioneering opportunity around nowadays. The West is won, the North and South poles and the bottom of the oceans aren't especially inviting, and the moon is out of the question—for most of our lifetimes, anyway.

No problem. We're talking about the pioneering *spirit*. That spirit is born of an exploring mind that seeks opportunities where others haven't looked or will not go. It's the spirit that achieves fulfillment through courage and perseverance. Pioneering at the turn of the millennium is meeting challenges and overcoming obstacles. The pioneering spirit can prompt buying a home off the beaten path or one that's designed for a special use.

You will probably notice times when home-buying opportunities accessed by the Risk-Taking Gateway are similar to those accessed by the Independent Spirit Gateway. And there is indeed some overlap. The differences arise from home-buyer personality: the willingness to take legal and financial risks on the one hand and the seeking of opportunity in unusual places and arrangements on the other.

What's Beyond This Gateway?

The properties beyond the Independent Spirit Gateway are rarely part of a planned development. Often they are one-of-a-kind locations, sometimes they are surrounded by very different types of real estate. Sometimes they are very near the road, and sometimes they are very far off the road. If you have the kind of personality that frequently takes you off the beaten path, let's see if there's something special in this marketplace area that will fit your needs.

Far Out

Many of these home-buying opportunities are located beyond the imaginary circle that is the boundary of the suburbs. Suburbs spread outward in rings around work opportunities, primarily in or near cities but sometimes surrounding corporate parks or large industrial complexes. The suburban house usually appeals to people who want to keep their commute under an hour and want to make use of the services a city can offer, or to the people who serve the commuters such as doctors, restaurateurs, hairdressers and real estate agents.

For home buyers who rate the size and comfort of a house above the conveniences available in a city, "far out" locations may be the answer. So, how far is far out? Where suburbia ends and exurbia begins depends on the city. "Far out" from Atlanta is different from "far out" from Washington, D.C., and "far out" may not exist in Los Angeles. Manhattanites may have to cross New Jersey to find it in Pennsylvania.

What's the bottom line? The farther you are willing to travel to work centers, the bigger and better house and the more land you can afford to buy. Generally, the farther residential property is from major business and industrial centers, the lower the prices.

In the far-out locations, you can find almost every type of property from every other gateway, with the possible exception of condos and co-ops. Shared-space housing is represented, however, by multifamily houses, which are not at all uncommon in remote towns. You can also find houses that need fix-up work, as well as foreclosures and added-to properties. And you'll find plenty of land at inexpensive prices if you want to build from scratch. What's missing or very scarce are upscale, planned tract developments, although you'll occasionally find vacation or retirement properties.

Why should the tract house, which is the housing style voted "most desirable" in survey after survey, be scarce in far-out locations? It's the old supply-and-demand theory again. The demand for housing diminishes as you travel away from sources of employment. With diminished demand come lower prices. When their products are bringing in less money, developers are less motivated to build.

Don't Assume

• •

Don't assume that the difference in mortgage payment between two similar houses in a close suburb and a far-out town is all savings. You must factor in the additional cost and time of commuting to work, including the value of your time, the wear and tear on your car, additional maintenance and car insurance costs, the cost of parking if you were previously taking public transportation, and the probability that your family will need to own more than one car, which can almost double all costs.

Another challenging feature of far-out areas is the roads, including dirt roads. Yes, there are still dirt roads in this country, and pioneering types can find houses on them. Getting to and from rural houses on these back roads can be slow and difficult, but these homes are usually less expensive than their suburban counterparts, and they do offer privacy.

The Far-Out Farm

A farm is another far-out housing opportunity that appeals to buyers with an independent spirit. Some owners actually work the farm as a primary or secondary source of income. Others live in the farmhouse (or have a new house built on the farm) and lease the use of the working farm to a local farmer or farming company. This land-leasing arrangement attracts some retirees because they get a home and a source of income, plus a potential caretaker for their property when they are traveling.

Lost Lots

Scattered throughout suburban, small-town and rural America, there are lots without any road frontage. As mentioned in the Ruth and Tom story in Chapter 1, they are called "flag lots." Often these properties are located behind other houses. (These lots are commonly created by subdivision of land by a private owner rather than as part of a development plan, although some developers do create flag lots. See Chapter 7.) Sometimes the houses stand alone in their off-road location, and sometimes they are part of a small cluster of homes.

More, More, More

● ●

The details of starting and running a farm have filled many a book as large as this one. If you are interested in becoming a farmer, however, the U.S. Department of Agriculture and the State Cooperative Extension Services offer a wealth of information and technical assistance. Check the blue pages of your local phone book for the number of your state's cooperative extension service.

Some houses that stand alone on flag lots get road access because the lot includes a small ribbon-like strip of land over which the driveway runs. Most houses on flag lots, whether in clusters or standing alone, however, get road access by an easement over a neighbor's land. (Read about easements on page 291 in Chapter 11.) Because their off-road location makes them less appealing to some home buyers, flag-lot houses are often priced lower than similar houses with road frontage. Home buyers with an independent spirit can often find more house for the money when they come upon a flag lot.

In some far-out locations, the streets or street names for some clusters of houses do not appear on local maps. The omission is not usually an oversight by the mapmakers. It results from a planned development, approved by the town, in which the developer creates a private road (or web of roads) and builds along it. Private roads do not usually appear on street maps.

Does having an unmapped road create problems for residents? That depends on the opinions of the residents. Do they mind that people trying to find them, sometimes including parcel delivery services, get lost? Do they mind giving explicit directions to the property (including odometer readings) to everyone who asks? Do they mind that all the country mailboxes for their "street" line up in a row at its intersection with the "real" street because the mail truck can't go on a private road? Or do they love the privacy?

Maintenance for the private road serving a community of houses falls to the homeowners who own the land and share the road usage, not the town or county. This means the town won't plow the road in the winter or add crushed rock and blacktop every year or two to keep the going smooth—at least not without charging the residents.

In most such developments, a condominium ownership of the road is established and a homeowners association collects dues for its maintenance. Many such communities are exclusive and expensive; some are gated. Others, however, are just clusters of a few homes with owners who enjoy being a little away and out of sight.

Doing Business in the Neighborhood

Some people choose home-buying opportunities in this marketplace area because their independent spirit prompts them to work alone or work for themselves. There are several appropriate housing choices available to these pioneers.

Living above the store

In the first half of this century, many young people started their businesses while living above the store. The practice was so common that the phrase became a synonym for starting out.

With the intense interest in self-employment today, many individuals are again turning to this mixture of housing and work space to get started. They choose houses in mixed-use (commercial and residential) areas, usually close to the center of a small town or in a well-established neighborhood of a city. The commercial space is usually on the ground floor and the family housing on the upper floor or floors. Some such properties also have a rental unit, creating overlap with the Shared-Space Gateway, too.

Once the young business becomes profitable, most of these property owners move out to other types of homes. They then either rent their former living space as an apartment or use it for an office or warehouse.

Telecommuting

Part of the growing popularity of far-out locations is attributable to the increase in telecommuting. What's that? A great arrangement in which an employee works from home, communicating with the office via computer, fax and modem, either installed by the employer or purchased by the worker. Electronic ties with the workplace allow the employee to do most of the work at home and come into the office only once a week or so. And you don't have to live far out to telecommute; some people do it from living space within a half hour or less of the office.

Some prognosticators say telecommuting is the wave of the future and an antidote to increasing traffic and commuting problems in our cities. Others point to it as another factor contributing to the disintegration of *esprit de corps* that plagues so many companies.

Telecommuting saves not only commuting costs but also the cost of office clothing and its dry-cleaning and laundry bills (you can work at home in jeans and a T-shirt) and the time needed each day for personal grooming for the workplace (some guys don't even shave). Then again, some telecommuters complain that they get lonely and miss the water cooler.

If finding a house from which you can telecommute interests you, be aware that telecommuting is different from running a business from your home. Rather than selling a product or providing a service that brings people to

It's the Law
● ●

Pay attention to zoning: If you plan to buy one building to house your retail business and your living space, you should be sure to check that the building you choose is in a commercial or mixed-use zone. If it is in a residential zone, you will have to get a nonconforming-use permit for the business from the local zoning or planning board. Requests are not always granted, however, so to avoid risk be sure your contract to purchase is contingent on approval.

and from your home, you're simply doing work at home that you would otherwise do at a desk in your employer's office building. Your contact with your employer's workplace is by phone and computer. For that, you do not need any special zoning changes or use permits from the town in which you live as long as you do not make your home part of your interaction with the general public.

In-home offices

If you expect to conduct a business in your home that will regularly bring clients or customers to your property (as opposed to one like freelance writing that probably won't), you may need a zoning variance or nonconforming-use permit from the town as well as permission from your homeowners association. Or you will have to find a home in an area zoned for mixed or commercial use.

The number of visitors (clients or customers), the regularity and frequency of their visits, and their need for extra parking are the most common factors that will determine whether the local authority grants you the use permits you seek. In some neighborhoods, regulations may not allow you to park a commercial vehicle out front or advertise your business with a sign. Other locations may allow you to post a sign, but have strict rules about its size, shape, appearance and location.

All in-home offices, however, have tax implications that result from splitting your property into home and business use. You should be sure to discuss them with your accountant to make certain you meet the letter of the law and get all the tax advantages you may have coming.

The add-on option

Would-be telecommuters and in-home business owners often find houses with additions (especially "in-law" apartments) appealing because they have extra space that is often somewhat separated from the original living space. Others look for a house they can easily add on to.

But go slowly here. Before you buy a house with an addition that you will alter to create an in-home office or buy a house that will require adding-on to make an office, remember that add-ons are permanent and that you are unlikely to recoup your costs in the near future (see Chapter 7 for more on the pros and cons of adding on). Are you sure you will stay in this business? Do you know how much and what kind of office space you'll need immediately and in the future?

Consider looking for an existing house with a space that may not be perfect as your home office, but that will work well enough until your business has stabilized and you can rent space elsewhere. You are much less likely to lose money.

Bed and breakfast

One of the most commonly considered ways of combining home and income is the bed-and-breakfast establishment. Houses in vacation areas, those with water views or other visual attractions, historic houses, and houses in or near major cities all have potential for success.

Zoning regulation regarding B&B inns differ from town to town, and in many towns they are not clear. Many people convert a room or two, go along running a B&B for many years, and then come up against the zoning laws in their community. Some zoning boards ignore the issue, some grant a nonconforming-use permit, and some towns and states actually require licensing.

If you need a license, your facilities will be inspected and you must comply with the fire codes. You may also have to change some plumbing, stairways and window access to comply with local building codes. If you offer more than five guest rooms, you must comply with the Americans With Disabilities Act.

In-home child care

An in-home child-care business is another commonly contemplated income source at home. Most styles of houses will work, even some condominiums. Certain features,

---

More, More, More

• •

Talking with some experienced B&B owners can be your best move in deciding to buy an existing B&B or convert a suitable property. To locate B&B's in your area, check your Yellow Pages under "Bed & Breakfast Accommodations," or look for national or regional directories of B&B's in the travel section of your local library or bookstore. Then contact the owners and have a chat.

If you'd like to read about creating a B&B, seek out *How to Open and Operate a Bed & Breakfast Home,* by Jan Stankus (Globe Pequot, 1995).

however, may be most desirable, such as ground-level access to the backyard, a fence around the yard or a playroom separate from your family's living area.

Before you do too much planning and set up, however, check with your state's health department to see which state or county agency regulates child care and what kind of licensing and bonding you must obtain. Some changes to the property may also be required for safety purposes, such as hand railings along all stairs (even on two-step front and back stoops), carbon-monoxide detectors, and a fire shield on the door that leads to the garage.

More, More, More
• •

If you have or are considering a home-based business, you can get tips on everything from getting started, to setting up space in your home, to separating business time and personal time: **National Association of Home Based Businesses** (10451 Mill Run Circle, Suite 400, Owings Mill, MD 21117; www.usahomebusiness.com; 410–363–3698;)

Why Enter This Gateway?

The Independent Spirit Gateway tends to attract rooted people more than turnover-oriented "movable" people because out-of-the-ordinary houses take longer to find and longer to resell. Let's look at some of the reasons to choose the unusual. (Weigh the following motives carefully. If this gateway seems like a good fit with your homeowner personality, confirm your hunch with the self-test beginning on the following page.)

To live in the country with more land, lower taxes and reasonable mortgage payments

If you hanker for horses or you want to raise Rottweilers, the call of the country might overcome the demands of almost any commute. Don't forget, however, that in addition to the commute, all your driving will cost you money.

To find a place that's really quiet, really private and relatively free from cranky neighbors

Although many people object to the long driveways

Continued on page 102

Self-Test Before You Choose This Gateway

The following, three-part self-assessment will help you evaluate whether you have what it takes to successfully pursue the homeowning options outlined in this chapter. It focuses on the ten important home-buyer personality characteristics introduced in Chapter 2.

PART I: RATE YOURSELF

In Part I, below, read each of the self-descriptive statements for each characteristic and decide how well it describes you. Grade your responses on a scale from 1, "Not me at all!" to 5, "That's me all the way!" Encourage your spouse or home-buying partner(s) to do the same.

Certain statements pertain to only one or two home-buying opportunities. If those don't interest you, just skip those statements.

If your ratings vary within a category, average them.

Turn to the following page and Parts II and III to see how you've fared.

Creative vision

___ I know that I can't get everything I want, so I choose the things that are most important to me and work to improve those that I find objectionable. (I'm already planning to plant this wonderful rose hedge called "Simplicity" all around the perimeter of our flag lot, and I just bought a car that gets exceptional mileage out of every gallon of gas to help with the long commute.)

___ The in-law apartment built by the seller will make an excellent place to begin my business. It's on the ground floor, it has a handy lavatory, and because it's an addition, there should be minimal noise exchange between the living area and the working area.

Time and skills for work and maintenance

___ It will certainly be a little more work (keeping a B&B clean all the time, mowing the two-acre backyard, sharing plowing of "our" road out to the county road, etc.). But I think it's worth it.

___ I'm pretty good about doing routine maintenance and doing it on time. I get the sidewalk shoveled first thing so customers (or clients) can get in safely. (For far-out people: I almost like snow-blowing the driveway at dawn and then four-wheeling my way to work.)

Self-confidence

___ *If you want to telecommute:* One of the best things about telecommuting is working at home in jeans. Some people say I'll lose high-profile visibility and get passed over for a promotion, but I think my work will speak for itself. I feel comfortable about working alone.

___ *If you will provide day care in your home:* I'm sure I can provide accommodations, education and fun for day-care children in my home. I'll talk frequently with parents, and if there is a need or something is lacking, I can attend to it.

___ *If you want to own a B&B:* Although I'm generally cautious, I don't fear taking strangers into my home as paying guests. There are always some problems, but we can handle them.

___ Friends and relatives are asking us why we don't just pick a "normal" house, which probably means one like theirs. But we're quite sure that our choice is the right one for us.

Flexibility and adaptability

___ *If you expect to work at home:* I need a large work space for my credenza, desk, computer, bookcases, worktable and chairs. I'm putting it all in the master bedroom and we're sleeping in the middle-sized bedroom.

___ *If you're living above the store to get started:* Our flower shop on Main Street has enlarged our food horizons. We can eat Indian curries next door and Japanese sushi across the street. Officer Goldberg often brings in a couple of bagels and takes a coffee break with us, and Kitty Woods (no relation to Tiger) likes to stop by with samples of the fabulous cakes she bakes.

___ *If you're a far-out pioneer:* There are two good routes to work, and besides that, if the weather's bad I can also pick up a commuter train or bus nearby. I'm not at all worried about the commute. If it looks too risky to go home and back, I'll just get a room for the night and show up tomorrow in wrinkled clothes.

Willingness to take risks

___ This house suits my needs so well now and in the foreseeable future that I'm willing to take the risk that it will not sell well 15 or 20 years down the line.

___ I'm going to need a nonconforming-use permit to open my dental practice in the space that is now the garage. But there's plenty of parking and the house is on a through street with considerable traffic. Although the neighborhood is still zoned residential, a

hairdresser has done pretty much the same thing four houses down, and an insurance agent has an in-home office across the street. I checked at the town hall and both neighbors have permits for nonconforming use. So my permit seems like a sure thing to me. I'm going to make an offer before the house sells to someone else.

Perseverance

___ They say the first year(s) of owning a B&B/farm/home-based business (and, in fact, many other businesses) is a money loser. It sure seems that way. But I'm going to stick with it because using my home to produce income beats working outside the home.

___ I found a hilltop that's just perfect for the house I want to have built. Trouble is, the custom builder I want won't come out that far out to build it. I'm exploring kit houses now; I understand the company will send the builder and the equipment.

Attention to detail

___ I really don't care if the ruffled curtains seen from the outside through the dining room windows don't match the draw draperies seen through the living room windows. This town doesn't have window police, for gosh sakes! And I'm comfortable with the way the rooms look from the inside.

___ We'll build a small shelter for the kids at the school bus stop because the driveway is long and the bus is often late in bad weather.

Planning and evaluation skills

___ We'll set up separate tax files the day

we buy the place. One is for ordinary expenses. The other is for expenses generated by the home business.

___ Before we buy our off-the-beaten path home, we're testing all the routes (or the public transportation) for getting where we will want to go.

Tact and communication skills

___ I enjoy plenty of spontaneous conversation with my neighbors and love to attend neighborhood gatherings. I even like to help organize them!

___ I can put together clear and accurate information in an oral presentation to a zoning or planning board if needed.

Negotiating skills

___ Since unusual properties are difficult to appraise, I'll get tax records to see how much the property cost the seller and how long he or she has owned it. Then I'll try to find out how long it's been on the market and whether there have been any price reductions. When I have decided on an ideal price, I'll make a first offer well below it.

___ In order to encourage the seller to take the house off the market and wait for a zoning-board approval that I need, I intend to accompany my request with some additional money on the second or third offer.

PART II: WHAT'S IMPORTANT AND WHY

Now let's turn the tables and look at the home-buyer personality characteristics from the point of view of demand—that is, how vital the characteristic is to success through this gateway, and why. Each characteristic is rated from 1 to 5 (1 being low demand, 3 being variable demand that might be high-er in some instances and lower in others, and 5 being high demand).

Creative vision: 4

Most people associate creativity with the arts, but creativity also allows one to solve problems and see new or alternative ways of doing things. If you choose unconventional housing and locations, you'll need creativity to make it work.

Time and skills for work and maintenance: 4

Houses that are off the beaten path may require more of your time and attention because it may be difficult to get maintenance and repair people at your location. Or because you simply have more property to look after. And, if you buy a property to farm, you're automatically assuming additional work and maintenance. Houses that are being used—sometimes used hard—to help make a living will need extra TLC.

Self-confidence: 5

This is the gateway for the pioneering spirit, and self-confidence is the ingredient without which it just doesn't work.

Flexibility and adaptability: 5

Ask outfitters or trekking guides and they'll all tell you that survival in unfamiliar circumstances often depends upon the ability to adapt and be flexible. It's the same with life in unconventional houses.

Willingness to take risks: 3

There is always some risk in buying where there is low demand. On the other hand, in ten years the very same location may be in high demand. So with the risk goes some opportunity. You can avoid risks regarding the need for zoning variances or nonconforming-use permits with careful planning and the addition of contingencies in the contract.

Self-Test, Cont'd.

Perseverance: 5

There's no pioneering for those who turn back at the first obstacle. Beyond obstacles, there are the barriers put up by law and convention. Getting beyond them takes perseverance, knowledge and sometimes professional help.

Attention to detail: 3

Being too attentive to detail can actually hinder success in this marketplace area, especially if it keeps you from focusing on the overall appropriateness of the property to your housing goals. Details can be dealt with, but major omissions can cost plenty to fix, if they're fixable at all. You will probably find the most important details in the zoning laws affecting the property. If you choose to live "far out," you should particularly note the costs and time required for commuting before you decide to buy.

Planning and evaluation skills: 4

Numbers are important in every housing purchase but more so in the area served by the Independent Spirit Gateway because resale is not always easy. Always consider how long you plan to own the property and the costs and benefits of special use.

Tact and communication skills: 2

Independent spirits who rate privacy high on their list of housing needs don't really need a lot of neighborly communication skills. But you will need to get along in your community, and that requires at least minimal tact and respect for the needs of others. If you have high communication skills and make it known that you enjoy using them, you'll have lots of opportunity to use them; look forward to being asked to join in this and that volunteer or civic activity.

Negotiating skills: 3

A round or two may resolve negotiations on unusual properties. But on some properties they can go on for days, sometimes weeks, because the buyers and sellers may place very different estimates of value on different aspects of the property. Petitions to planning or zoning boards can also require some degree of negotiating.

PART III: THE CRITICAL COMPARISON

Now you can compare your self-ratings with the importance ratings for each characteristic to see how likely you are to measure up to the demands of this gateway. In the left column of the graph, the characteristics are presented in descending order from highest to lowest demand for this gateway. The black bars show each characteristic's importance rating. Use the space allowed to draw in your and your buying partner's results.

- **If you rated yourself *most* highly on this gateway's *most* important characteristics** (at least 4 on characteristics rated 5, and at least 3 on those rated 4), this gateway may be the one for you.

- **If you *also* rated yourself highly on the gateway's *least* important characteristics** (4s or 5s on characteristics rated 3 or less), other gateways might provide additional options suited to your strengths.

- **If you rated yourself highly *only* on the gateway's *least* important characteristics** (those rated 3 or less), look to another gateway for your best home-buying opportunities.

- **Be sure to look at your partner's strengths and weaknesses.** Is your partner strong where you're weak? Is it realistic to expect your partner to pick up the slack?

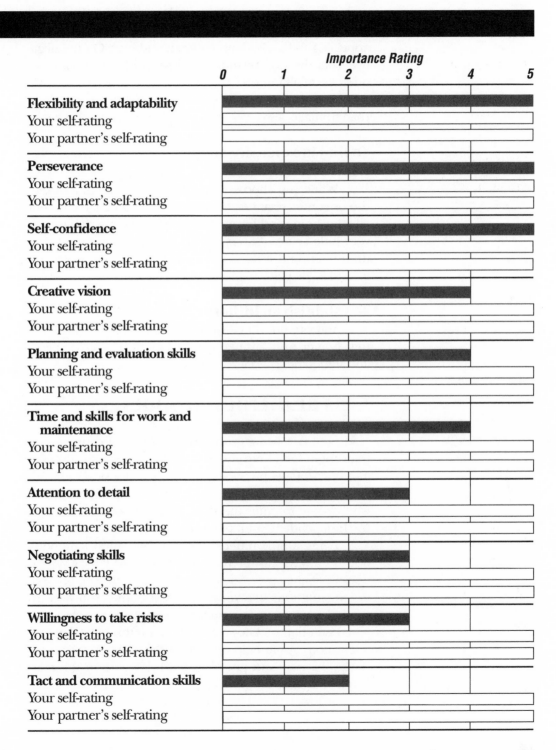

Importance Rating

Flexibility and adaptability
Your self-rating
Your partner's self-rating

Perseverance
Your self-rating
Your partner's self-rating

Self-confidence
Your self-rating
Your partner's self-rating

Creative vision
Your self-rating
Your partner's self-rating

Planning and evaluation skills
Your self-rating
Your partner's self-rating

Time and skills for work and maintenance
Your self-rating
Your partner's self-rating

Attention to detail
Your self-rating
Your partner's self-rating

Negotiating skills
Your self-rating
Your partner's self-rating

Willingness to take risks
Your self-rating
Your partner's self-rating

Tact and communication skills
Your self-rating
Your partner's self-rating

and easements of flag lots, these houses built off the road are safely away from traffic. That makes them particularly appealing to families with children and pets. On the negative side, the view from all windows is often the backs of other people's houses.

Acreage around the house, even if it does have main-road frontage, also gives many people the privacy they seek.

To find inexpensive shelter while starting a business

When you choose to live above the store in a mixed-use or commercial neighborhood, one mortgage payment pays for home and business. Unfortunately, there is usually very little sense of a residential neighborhood, and children often find it difficult to gather a group of playmates or find a safe place to play.

To establish an in-home business

You can put home space to work. Be aware, however, that homes with business aspirations need special spaces and sometimes special zoning laws.

Tips and Trouble Spots

"It's not easy being green," says Kermit. Of course green is just right for a frog, and Kermit lives on Sesame Street in a puppet-and-people society that is marvelously diverse. Yet he *feels* that he is different. So it is with many homeowners who choose to enter the real estate marketplace through the Independent Spirit Gateway.

Being a little different means the typical handbook doesn't always answer your questions and typical advice doesn't always apply. Sometimes you have to seek out others in situations like yours, and sometimes you have to think through your own situation and make your decisions based on what you know and can reason through. Here are a few more tips to help you with some of the common obstacles, barriers and just plain hard decisions in this marketplace area.

Far-out Futures

If you are a movable person or perhaps a young rooted person who plans on an uprooting in the foreseeable future, you may want to take note of factors that hint of imminent growth in one or more of the areas you are considering. If any of these factors enhance the desirability of an area, the demand will increase. With increased demand, you will have a better chance of making a genuine profit on the sale of your home someday. (Be sure to read about "appreciation" on page 10.)

On the other hand, if you're a rooted person who wants to stay in a home indefinitely and avoid all the hassles of growth in the backyard, not to mention the probability of rising property taxes, you'll want to avoid areas where growth and development are likely.

Read local newspapers carefully and keep in touch with national financial publications. Watch for:

Major highway proposed or under-construction

Better roads shorten the commuting time and can change an area once considered too far out to one that's considered just a long commute.

Industrial-park proposal or development

The building of huge campuses housing many different companies can create a whole new workplace center that completely redefines the commuting circle. The Research Triangle between Raleigh and Durham, N.C., stimulated the economy and transformed some rural areas into suburbs.

The new employer in town

Watch for announcements that a large company plans to relocate, either buying vacant existing buildings or buying land and putting up new construction. The location of AT&T's expanded corporate offices in Basking Ridge, N.J., for example, transformed a sleepy town into an upscale suburb. The development of huge casinos on Native American reservation land in Connecticut is creating a vacation-destination image (complete with factory-outlet shopping malls) in the southeastern part of the state.

Large shopping-mall construction

Developers do extensive research on site selection for new malls at costs that would often equal the combined annual incomes of a whole neighborhood. Consider that money spent on your behalf and ask yourself why that site was chosen. Draw a circle around where the mall will be, and investigate the desirability of all the nearby towns. Be careful, however, not to choose property too close to the mall site or you'll have to cope with increased traffic and noise during and after construction.

Private Road Maintenance

If you are considering a house on a flag lot that has a shared driveway, or in a cluster of homes on a private road, or on a dirt road that neither the town nor the county maintains, check to see how maintenance of the road is or can be handled. Plowing in winter, occasional resurfacing and regrading, and dust control if it's a dirt road, may be more expensive than you anticipated. If some owners don't pay their share, it can cause bad feelings in the neighborhood, not to mention extra costs for whoever winds up paying.

In private communities of ten or more homes, condominium ownership of the road—that is, shared ownership by a group—is usually the best arrangement because a levied monthly fee per unit can support maintenance.

Although smaller groups can create condominium ownership (even two parties can be condominium owners), many groups function well with individual owners holding title to pieces of the road with easements over the remainder of it. In condo road ownership, everyone who uses the road owns a share of every single stone and the ownership share cannot be separated. In individual ownership with easements, each owner holds title to a certain area and allows the others in the group to pass over that area to get to and from their property.

In cases of private ownership with shared use, it's best

to form an association of homeowners that will collect dues either monthly, quarterly or annually. If owners pay dues, the payment date should be late summer, so that the association will collect sufficient money to support the plowing necessary through the winter in most parts of the nation. Penalties for late payment and non-payment should be spelled out.

Two homeowners who share a driveway may make any arrangement they want for snow removal and maintenance, but they should make it in advance of the need. If you agree to shovel alternate snowfalls, keep a list of who shoveled when. If you agree to split the plowing bills, in the fall contribute an equal amount of money into a plowing fund from which to pay the bills.

It's the Law

• •

About driveway maintenance: The easement that allows one party to cross the land of the other doesn't require the owner to keep it plowed to anybody else's satisfaction. The neighbors should work out plowing and clearing arrangements, with or without a lawyer's help.

Whenever you are considering a house with a shared driveway, make whatever efforts are necessary to meet your prospective neighbor. Have a pleasant conversation, but don't leave without finding out how driveway maintenance has been handled. If the possibility of driveway noise and traffic concerns you, see if you can find out (during your chat or from other neighbors or the real estate agent) how many people live in the house, and the number and ages of children. If you can eyeball the property, look for potentially noisy vehicles like motorcycles or snowmobiles.

Buying With an Income in Mind

Above the store

If you are buying commercial property and plan to live above the store, ask yourself:

- **Does the living space include kitchen and bath facilities?** If not, how much will installation cost?

- **Does any converted living space meet building codes?** That's not an option—it must. Talk with the county or town building inspector before you even make an offer.

- **Will the existing heating and cooling systems support the living space?** If not, how much will upgrading cost?

- **Does the property meet the fire codes?**

- **Is there a separate exterior doorway and exterior staircase** so family members can come and go from the living space without walking through the business space?

- **Is there an off-street parking area** for the family cars?

- **Will the traffic from customers, and the sounds and smells of the business** interfere with domestic life?

Telecommuters and long-distance commuters

If you plan to telecommute, adequate wiring is essential to support your home-office equipment, but you can usually have additional phone lines brought in.

If you will have a long commute to work, try driving the route during rush hour. You might also check with state and local police to ask how many accidents have occurred during the past two years on the roads you will take. Some roads seem to get more than the average share of accidents, especially where hills and curves invite trouble. The reality of driving such a road five days a week may influence your housing purchase.

In-home office

If you are a professional who renders service to the public, such as a dentist, marriage counselor or beautician, and you are in need of office space, there's always the temptation to jump at the "perfect" house on a highly visible, easily found corner lot. Don't jump.

It's essential to gather information before you sign that purchase contract. Here are just a few of the questions you should be able to answer.

- **Does the property's zoning allow an in-home office?**

- **Is there a separate exterior entry door to the office area?** If not, can you have one installed? How much will it cost?

- **Can a lavatory be installed on the office level?**

- **How much will it cost to convert the designated space into an office?**

- **Is there adequate off-street parking?**

Paying guests

If you are considering buying a bed-and-breakfast inn, or if you want to take children in for child care, you should be sure that the building can routinely handle the extra people. Consider:

- **Is there enough water pressure** to support two showers running at once?

- **Is the hot-water supply adequate** for high usage?

- **Will wiring allow the use of two or more hair dryers at the same time** or will the circuit breakers (or fuses) shut down power?

- **Is the waste-disposal system adequate?** This question is especially important for properties that use septic tanks. Many towns restrict the number of bedrooms in houses to be built if the drainage on the lot isn't adequate to support a large number of people. They may also prohibit the change of use to an inn for the same reason. An inadequate disposal system can cause nasty backups that almost always occur when the house is full of happy people—who quickly become unhappy.

- **Are kitchen facilities adequate** for the preparation of food for large numbers of people?

- **Are closets and storage facilities adequate** for the extra china, linens and towels you will need?

Financing With a Difference

What kind of financing should you seek and how difficult will it be to get when a home and business share a location? Whether you apply for a commercial or home-mortgage loan depends on your intent: Will you primarily use the property as your residence, with a business that happens to be on site? Or will the property serve primarily as your business, over or behind which you happen to live?

From the lenders' point of view, they make more money on higher-risk commercial lending, so why should they make you a home mortgage when they could make a commercial loan? They may take the approach, "If it quacks like a duck, it probably is a duck." That is, if the property looks like a store, with a storefront, signage and customer parking, then it qualifies as a business or commercial property—even if it's in an area that's otherwise zoned residential or mixed-use. There will probably be no question if the property is in an area zoned commercial.

If your business will be your sole source of income for support of the property, you will have to jump through extra hoops to get a loan or a mortgage. Lenders will want to see proof of established, steady and sufficient income. Even if you're buying an established business, can you prove you have what it takes to keep it producing income? What can you put into the deal? Do you have other collateral besides the business itself?

If you'll have to do some remodeling to create a home office in the house you buy, one way to get the money is to make a smaller down payment. Use your extra cash to pay for supplies or contractors. In this way, you'll finance the cost of the remodeling over the entire length of your mortgage and at the first-mortgage interest rate rather than the usually higher second-mortgage or personal-loan rate.

If you are short on money, there are some loan programs that will finance the improvements. (Read about financing houses in a turnaround neighborhood in Chapter 4, contact your local FHA office for information on the 203(k) program (see page 58), and talk with mortgage brokers.)

Financing for a farm

If you want to buy a farm and you are unable to get financing from conventional sources, there may be government help available.

More, More, More

• •

You can start your quest for more information on home-business loans by consulting several mortgage brokers. Commercial real estate brokers also are familiar with the problems involved and may be helpful. An accountant can help you with any tax considerations.

If a business loan appears to be your best bet, you can get advice on procuring the loan and an overview of a variety of loan types in *How To Obtain Business Loans: An Insider's Guide,* by Addison Parker (PT Publications, West Palm Beach, Fla.)

The Farm Service Agency (FSA), a branch of what was once known as the Farmers Home Administration (FmHA), makes or insures mortgage loans to farmers and ranchers who can't get credit from other lenders. (Financing may have been denied because the applicant can make only a very small down payment, for example, or because of a recent bankruptcy or foreclosure, or a spotty credit report. Loans may also be hard to get because of an economic downturn in the area.)

FSA responsibilities include providing financing for:

- **the purchase and improvement of farms**
- **the building or rehabilitation of farm houses and outbuildings,** and
- **low-income farmers.**

Responsibilities of the **Rural Housing Service,** a branch of the Rural Development Mission (also formerly part of the FmHA), include:

- **rural housing for the elderly**
- **rural communities' housing rehab programs,** and
- **tenant farmers purchase programs**

FSA operates under the U.S. Department of Agriculture and is favorable to military veterans and married couples who wish to begin farming. Besides loans for the purchase of the farm, the agency also offers funds for purchase of farm equipment, seed and fertilizer. Generous credit terms are available from the Rural Housing Service for elderly people seeking rural housing.

Even if you can't get government-supported financing to purchase a farm, you might still want to give a nod of thanks to Uncle Sam and his cousins. There are tax benefits to farm ownership in many areas. These include tax credits, reduced tax rates, and reduced assessments both for farming and for preserving agricultural land (not developing it). You can often harvest these benefits even when you are using the farmland in nominal ways, such as planting a tree farm or renting your land for grazing.

**Penny for
Your Thoughts**

*Follow your
bliss.*

Joseph Campbell
(1904-1987), American
philosopher and writer

From One Gateway to Another

The decision to enter the real estate marketplace through the Independent Spirit Gateway doesn't depend on your level of experience in home buying or homeownership but upon personality and goals. The lower prices in far-out properties might well attract newcomers to the marketplace as well as experienced hands. And people in almost any stage of life can start an in-home business or seek a place where they could telecommute.

This marketplace area, however, works better for rooted people. Unusual properties that suit your personality and specific lifestyle needs are fewer and sometimes difficult to find. When the time comes to sell, the house appeals to a smaller prospect group and the selling time is often considerably longer than for the typical home.

Once they enter the Independent Spirit Gateway, most homeowners stay in that marketplace area by choice. If they sell and buy another house, it is often similar and appropriate to the same functions.

Living over the store, however, is usually the exception. Few people really want to live above a commercial establishment. This choice is usually a means of getting started. Once they get on their feet financially, many of these owners move into ownership of a multifamily house that is still close to their business, since multifamily houses require less qualification income. (Read about them in Chapter 6.) Some owners who start out above the store, however, wait until they are quite successful and can afford to enter the marketplace through the American Image Gateway (planned homogeneous neighborhoods) or the New Construction Gateway.

Housing is a personal choice that affects many aspects of our lives. Choosing to be "different" can be not only an affirmation but also a freeing experience. Just be sure to take the time to examine your motivations and think through the effects that your home purchase will have on both your day-to-day activities and your long-term goals.

Of People, Planning, & Profit:

The Shared-Space

Gateway

- **Multifamily Houses**

- **Condominiums**

- **Co-ops**

In the 19th century, the lure of free and abundant land motivated people seeking homeownership to, "*Go west!*" They staked out claims and built houses without a single neighbor in sight. But still neighbors gathered—to raise a barn, celebrate a birth, mourn a death, have a beer. Communities were established, laws were enacted.

At the end of the 20th century, many homeowners are separated from neighboring owners only by the walls between their bedrooms. Others are separated from their tenant-neighbors by ceilings, joists and floorboards. Communities gather their members from within walking distance. You can have a beer with your neighbor on the back steps that you share. You can meet to play bridge in a recreation building in which all four players own an undivided interest. Often you must share use of the land surrounding the place where you live. And, unlike in the early West where there were only a few laws to run the town, there seem to be rules for everything from where you can park your bicycle to how late you can play your CDs.

What happened between the mid 19th century and the mid 20th century to cause such a change? Essentially, desirable land became expensive. So people sought homeownership on less land and in closer communities. We know these "high density," 20th-century housing styles as condominiums, cooperative apartments and multifamily houses.

They are grouped in the marketplace area entered by

the Shared-Space Gateway, where they represent home-ownership opportunity for many Americans who don't fit the typical profiles for owners of single-family, suburban houses. Home buyers entering this gateway need to feel comfortable with planning, organization and good financial management. In the case of condos and co-ops, unit owners must also work for and be comfortable with good government because they must submit to a community-generated system of laws and rules. It's like living in a little city within a city.

What's Beyond This Gateway?

Twenty years ago, the Shared-Space Gateway attracted city dwellers almost exclusively. Today, however, ownership in high-density housing is very much available not only in large and midsize cities but also in suburbs, vacation destinations and retirement areas.

Prices range from the very lowest numbers in a Realtor's listing book to the highest. So there's something for everyone, theoretically at least. Let's look at the possibilities.

Multifamily Houses

The U.S. Department of Housing and Urban Development (HUD) generally considers buildings with four or more living units as apartment buildings, not multifamily houses, though at four units, there's some overlap in its definitions, depending in the specific dwelling. For our purposes, a multifamily house is a house with two to four living units.

The majority of such houses in the United States were built in the first half of this century, and most have a single living unit on each floor. Some multifamily houses are also conversions from huge, rambling 19th-century mansions.

Since 1950, new multifamily construction has been far overshadowed by single-family tract construction (covered in Chapter 8), but there are scatterings of newer units in many smaller cities and towns. Some of these follow the earlier one-unit-per-floor pattern, but many others use a "duplex" plan, where the two units each have two stories but share a common interior wall.

Some modern-day multifamily houses are the result of in-law apartments that were added by previous owners to houses in single-family residential zones. These houses usually have zoning variances or non-conforming-use permits. Some municipal governments hold the new owners to "in-law" use of the additions, while others look the other way, passively allowing rental to non–family members.

Don't assume that a house in which two or more families are living in separate units is legally a multifamily house. Across the nation since 1950, there has been considerable illegal subdivision of older housing stock into "apartments," some of which have neither adequate cooking nor toilet facilities. If you were to buy such a property expecting to collect rent, and if zoning were to be strictly enforced, you could be forced to revert to a single-family house—and you would lose the income that was supporting your purchase.

> # *Penny for Your Thoughts*
> •
>
> "..It seems to have been reserved to the people of this country, by their conduct and example, to decide the important question, whether societies of men are really capable or not, of establishing good government..."
>
> Alexander Hamilton (1757–1804), first
> U.S. secretary of the Treasury, in *The Federalist #1*

Condominiums

Would you believe that condominiums go back to ancient Rome? They do, and they have been a popular ownership style throughout most of Europe far longer than the third of the century they've been popular in the U.S. The condo ownership style can apply to almost any building type. Existing buildings can even be converted to condominium ownership.

Are you beginning to get sleepy? Or anxious at the thought of all the legal mumbo jumbo about ownership rights that might be coming? Don't worry. Condo ownership isn't as complicated as it sounds, and millions of home buyers have made it.

Condominiums are a form of shared-space ownership. You, the unit owner, own a designated area. That usually means the space enclosed by certain walls, floors and ceilings, but in some condominium communities it can mean an entire house and even the land it stands on. You also hold an *undivided interest* in the common areas of the community. Common areas are the shared-space part. They can include the building's walls, hallways, stairwells, elevators, roof, foundation and the land it stands on. In communities composed of more than one building, common areas can include roads, parking areas, recreational facilities and open spaces (land designated not to be built upon).

Words to the Wise

• •

Undivided interest is an ownership share that cannot be severed or separated from the whole. Your share is determined by the size of your unit or the number of units you own, and you own the same proportional share in all the common elements. In other words, if the value of your share is 3% of the whole, you don't own three hundred of the 10,000 tiles in the swimming pool; you own 3% of each and every tile. And 3% of the elevator cable and 3% of the roof. And you can never remove your particular 3% because, technically speaking, you actually own only 3% of each molecule in each of the common elements.

In a condo community, you have control of and responsibility for the space you own independently. If a faucet leaks, you fix it. Common areas, by contrast, are controlled and maintained by the association of homeowners run by an elected board of directors. If a water pipe breaks in a wall between two units, the association pays to have it repaired. You, as owner, are responsible for keeping your living space clean and functional; the homeowners association is responsible for maintenance of the building and all of its working systems, such as electrical wiring and plumbing. Funds for that maintenance come from the required monthly maintenance fee paid by each unit owner.

Condo styles

As mentioned, condos are now city, suburb, vacation and retirement living spaces. But you're not likely to find a townhouse community in the inner city or a high-rise in the country. Let's look at the most common building styles.

- **High-rise:** more than ten stories high. Usually found in large cities, this condo style is most like apartment living. Amenities such as an exercise room or community room are usually located within the building. Parking space—off- or on-street—is sometimes limited or nonexistent and may cost extra.

- **Mid-rise:** five to ten stories. Often found in groups of three buildings or more, and typically located in smaller cities or suburbs. Off-street parking space usually surrounds the buildings. Mid-rises may or may not have outdoor recreational space.

- **Garden-style:** one to four stories with parking areas and outdoor recreational areas surrounding the units. A suburban favorite, these condo communities can be very large and spread out over a web of streets, usually curved and sometimes circular.

Don't Assume

· ·

Don't assume that the laws governing condominium and cooperative ownership are the same in every state. Although the concepts are universal and there is a movement among states to adopt a uniform condominium code, the laws that protect consumers still differ significantly from state to state. For example, some states require that a reserve fund be maintained for future maintenance costs; others do not. For an overview of current law in your state, you can contact your state attorney general's office, make an appointment to talk with a local attorney whose practice deals primarily with real estate, or contact the Community Associations Institute, mentioned in the sidebar on page 131.

- **Townhouses:** two- or three-story units that are attached in groups of two to four townhouses per building. Usually found at the edges of downtowns and in close-in suburbs. Many have garages and storage space at the basement level. Some townhouse communities provide recreational facilities.

- **Patio homes:** one-story units with a patio or deck in the backyard, usually built in groups of two to four units per building. Common in the South and Southwest and a favorite with retirees. Many unit owners hold title to the land in front and back of their unit and share an undivided interest only in the roads and recreational facilities.

- **Detached houses:** communities that look just like suburban tract houses. These are most often found in the far suburbs and even in rural locations. Owners hold title to the land around their homes and an undivided interest in roads, open-space land and recreational facilities.

Cooperative Apartments

People talk about "buying a co-op," but in fact no one actually owns the co-op apartment he or she lives in. You buy *into* a co-op. When you do, you own shares of stock in the corporation that owns the building and you hold a *proprietary lease* on "your" apartment.

Although they've been around in this country since the 1880s, co-ops never caught on the way condos did in the '70s. You'll find them primarily in larger metropolitan areas, especially in and around Chicago, New York City, Washington D.C., and Miami. Many are converted rental apartment buildings, some built early in this century.

Co-ops are run, like any other corporation, by an elected board of directors. As in condos, maintenance is paid for by apartment owners' maintenance fees, but unlike in condos, *all* the space in the building is the responsibility of the corporation—not just the common areas. With this increased responsibility comes even more power. A co-op board can prevent an apartment owner from subdividing a large living room into two smaller rooms, for instance. Most co-op boards hold the right to approve a prospective purchaser, which means you may not be able to sell the apartment to whomever you choose.

Words to the Wise

• •

Proprietary lease is an oxymoron. *Proprietary* is associated with ownership, *lease* with rental. So which is it? Both. With an ownership share in a cooperative apartment building, you own the right to occupy the unit, but you don't own the unit. In legalese, a proprietary lease is sometimes called an occupancy agreement.

Why Enter This Gateway?

The Shared-Space Gateway is not for rebels, loners or free spirits. In this togetherness style of ownership, success often requires some degree of conformity and depends on a good deal of cooperation. Is it worth the extra effort?

People who choose it for the right reasons usually think so. (Weigh the following motives carefully. If this gateway seems like a good fit with your homeowner personality, confirm your hunch with the self-test beginning on page 119.)

To buy at a low price with a small down payment

Condos and co-ops can be found even at the one-room "studio" size and represent a low-price entryway into the tax-reducing and equity-building benefits of homeownership, especially for people just getting started in their careers. Developers of new condo communities sometimes offer mortgages with little (2% to 5%) or nothing down.

Multifamily houses in older and turnaround neighborhoods often sell at low prices for the available amount of living space and enjoy assistance with financing and closing costs from lenders and municipal and state governments. (Read Chapter 4.)

To qualify for a mortgage

Lenders will factor in rental income when qualifying prospective buyers of multifamily houses. That extra income can sometimes make the purchase possible. It also helps to make those mortgage payments each month.

When two parties (whether two generations of a family, siblings or just friends) buy together, the annual incomes of all the parties are considered in qualification.

For freedom from maintenance work

For young people on the go, dual-income professionals devoted to their jobs and retirees who've had their fill of home maintenance, one of the great attractions of condo and co-op ownership is having all building and grounds maintenance done by professionals. But remember, you pay for the service in the maintenance fee.

For recreational amenities

Swimming pools, golf courses, tennis courts, exercise rooms, walking trails—they're available in many condos and co-ops. These amenities are made possible by group buying power.

For convenience

Condo, co-op or multifamily ownership can provide homeownership close to the city workplace and urban attractions, especially cultural life. Owners save time and money by not having a long commute to work and sometimes, in very large cities, by not needing to own a car.

For retirement

Some retirees choose to own a multifamily home because the rents supplement their fixed income and don't count as part of the maximum earnings allowed before social security benefits are reduced. Other retirees choose condo living because they enjoy being in a large community where there are social programs and recreational activities with others like themselves. Some retirees who love city living choose co-ops or condos.

Tips and Trouble Spots

In real estate offices, there's a truism about buying and selling: *The more people involved, the more complicated the deal.* If we were to extend that to ownership, we'd get: *The more people involved, the more complicated the...*well, everything!

Yes, living in togetherness-style housing affects everything: the demands on your money, the amount of space you can occupy, your living patterns, security, comfort and, of course, resale value. But don't take that as a negative statement. There are both good and not-so-good effects.

And there are lots of things to remember. Let's look at a few you shouldn't forget.

Condos Under Construction

Some developers offer below-market, preconstruction prices on condos to be built and sometimes on occupied apartments in buildings that are being converted to condominium or cooperative ownership. The deals are usually tempting, but this is high-risk buying because:

Continued on page 124

Self-Test Before You Choose This Gateway

The following, three-part self-assessment will help you evaluate whether you have what it takes to successfully pursue the homeowning options outlined in this chapter. It focuses on the ten important home-buyer personality characteristics described in Chapter 2.

PART I: RATE YOURSELF

In Part I, below, read each of the self-descriptive statements for each characteristic and decide how well it describes you. Grade your response on a scale from 1, "Not me at all!" to 5, "That's me all the way!" Encourage your spouse or home-buying partner(s) to do the same.

Certain statements pertain to only one or two gateway options. If those don't interest you, skip those statements.

If your ratings vary within a category, average them.

Turn to the following page to see how you've fared.

Creative vision

___ *For multifamily houses:* I can come up with the most economical ways to keep a rental unit clean, attractive and well maintained.

___ *For condos and co-ops:* I don't much care about how pretty it is, I just want a comfortable, undemanding place to live.

Time and skills for work and maintenance

___ *Multifamily:* I wouldn't mind doing some maintenance work if I knew I would be getting paid for it in the rent. Besides, I would probably feel a little power and pride at my tenants' knowing that they can count on me for prompt and good repairs.

___ *Condos and co-ops:* I don't have time for house maintenance stuff. I'd rather pay someone else to do it.

Self-confidence

___ *Multifamily:* I think I'm pretty good at sizing people up, so I should be able to pick tenants that I can live with.

___ *Condos and co-ops:* I'm not an accountant, but I know I can do the job of treasurer for our condo board of directors.

Flexibility and adaptability

___ When my party-giving neighbors say, "Come on in!" I'll join them rather than complain about the noise.

___ *Multifamily:* I'll allow my tenant to chain his Harley to the lally column in the basement as long as he never starts it up indoors.

___ *Condos and co-ops:* If my Harley won't fit into the designated storage area, I'll petition the condo board and all nearby owners for permission to store it in another location, even if that means my maintenance fee will rise slightly.

Willingness to take risks

___ I'm aware that this housing style often takes longer to sell and means less profit than I might get from many single-family, detached houses, but for me the advantages outweigh the risks.

___ I know there's always some risk that my tenants (multifamily) or the other unit owners (condos and co-ops) won't make their monthly payments or won't call for repairs that will avoid damage to the property.

Self-Test, Cont'd.

Perseverance

___ *Multifamily:* If my tenants don't pay their rent, I will take whatever legal measures are necessary to collect it or to evict them.

___ *Condos and co-ops:* If members of the board of directors aren't doing their jobs well, I will make efforts to find others to replace them and even volunteer to hold office myself, if necessary.

Attention to detail

___ I will take the time to study the past two years' income and expense records for rental units (multifamily) or financial statements for the condo or co-op.

___ *Multifamily:* I will check the town's zoning regulations to be certain the house I want to buy is a legal multifamily dwelling.

___ *Condos and co-ops:* I will read the by-laws, the covenants, conditions and restrictions, and the house rules before I buy.

Planning and evaluation skills

___ I will consider what repairs and improvements will be needed during the coming few years and how those expenses will affect my living costs.

___ I've run the numbers several times and I'm satisfied that I can meet the mortgage payment, insurance and maintenance costs of this property even if a rental unit remains vacant several months or if special assessments are imposed in the condo or co-op.

Tact and communication skills

___ I can calmly tell my neighbor (or tenant) that the rules prohibit leaving tricycles in the middle of the driveway.

___ *Multifamily:* I'm not afraid to knock on my tenant's door and ask about the rent if he hasn't paid it by the due date.

___ *Condos and co-ops:* If I believe something must be changed in the community, I'm willing to circulate a petition or to stand up and speak at a homeowners association meeting.

Negotiating skills

___ *Multifamily:* I'm willing to lower the rent some months in return for my tenant shoveling snow or fixing that leaky faucet.

___ *Condos and co-ops:* There's a unit for sale by owner in a complex that I'd really like to live in. I've already checked out the other three units for sale there, so I know this owner is asking way too much. I'm going to offer him something less than the going rate but with an all-cash deal. And I'll emphasize that he will be saving real estate commissions by dealing directly with me.

PART II: WHAT'S IMPORTANT AND WHY

Now let's turn the tables and look at the home-buyer personality characteristics from the point of view of demand—that is, how vital the characteristic is to success through this gateway, and why. Each characteristic is rated from 1 to 5 (1 being low demand, 3 being variable demand that might be higher in some instances and lower in others, and 5 being high demand).

Creative vision: 2

In condo and co-op ownership, creativity may actually be a detriment to contentment. Most likely, you won't be allowed to paint your front door fuchsia or replace the sliders to the back deck with French patio doors. When dealing with rental units in multifamily houses, off-white is the best color for all the walls. Creativity does play a roll in saving money, getting work done efficiently, and socializing.

Time and skills for work and maintenance: 1 or 4

Condos and co-ops make no demands on unit owners, hence a rating of 1.

Self-confidence: 3

Being a landlord requires firmness, fairness, foresight, and sometimes the ability to forgive. All of those qualities are at least somewhat based on self-confidence.

Multifamily houses are more profitable if the owners can fix the clogged toilet, replace a broken window pane, and do other routine maintenance jobs themselves, so they get a 4. Remember, however, that money you pay for maintenance work on the rental unit is tax-deductible against its income.

Requirements for self-confidence in a condo or co-op are eased by the knowledge that you are not solely responsible for maintenance. However, there are self-confidence demands in the arena called "getting along with the neighbors."

Flexibility and adaptability: 3

In a multifamily house, you, the landlord, set the rules; in a condo or co-op, the rules are set out in the by-laws and house rules. But in both housing styles there's an important human factor that overrides theory. If people are to live their lives in close proximity to other people, the written rules cannot reach very far beyond what is conventionally acceptable in our society. And beyond the rules, neighbors need to allow

each other a little extra space, a little bending, to accommodate personality, family needs, and ethnic heritage.

Willingness to take risks: 3

The amount of risk in the Shared-Space Gateway often correlates to the amount of time and attention the buyer pays to available numbers. The major risk raisers are extraordinary maintenance expenses and empty units. By studying tax returns and financial reports for the past several years, a buyer can evaluate the demands of the investment. For added security, ask the local chamber of commerce or Realtor board what the rental-apartment vacancy rate in the area is. The lower the rate (5% is a low rate), the more secure your investment.

Perseverance: 4

It's often easy to give up on small stuff. But little things, let go, can snowball into discontent and sometimes anger. Anger in togetherness housing spells trouble. If something is bothering you, speak up courteously, and if you are ignored or refused, try another approach. The same goes for big things, like the rent or the running of the condo or co-op association.

Attention to detail: 3

Besides reading all the documents that surround your purchase, the details you'll encounter with this gateway's options often concern money and people. Good multi-family-home management means setting out policies on rent payment and other tenant responsibilities, and keeping accurate and thorough records of your dealings with tenants and money earned and spent. Even if you're not a natural record keeper, you'll need this information at tax time.

Contented condo or co-op living is enhanced by attention to details like taking care not to park over the dividing line and thus take up someone else's place, stopping your son's sleep-over friends from doing cannonballs into the pool at 10 P.M., and getting your clothes out of the dryer soon after they're dry.

Planning and evaluation skills: 5

Multifamily houses become high-risk investments without adequate planning for rental policies, repairs and maintenance, and without careful evaluation of cash flow and profitability. These are issues that you would be wise to discuss with your lawyer and accountant.

Whenever you assume that the board of directors is doing a good job, you put your homeownership investment into the hands of others. Successful condo or co-op ownership means participating in the running of the community or, at the least, carefully evaluating annual financial statements.

Tact and communication skills: 5

In high-density housing, communication is not just a matter of clearly expressing your needs and expectations and protecting your rights. You've got to do all that while keeping the needs, expectations and rights of your tenants or neighbors in mind, too.

Negotiating skills: 4

Negotiating in this gateway doesn't stop when the purchase contract is signed; it gets a new dimension. The focus changes from money to services and concessions.

How much of a rent concession do you offer if your tenant repairs and paints the back steps? What if the tenant wants more? Are you willing to go up? How much?

Are you willing to pay a fellow condo owner for use of his vacant garage while your sister visits? Or can you gracefully offer pet-sitting services for the garage owner's dog and cat while he's on vacation this summer?

PART III: THE CRITICAL COMPARISON

Now you can compare your self-ratings with the importance ratings for each characteristic to see how likely you are to measure up to the demands of this gateway. In the left column of the graph, the characteristics are presented in descending order from highest to lowest demand. The black bars show each characteristic's importance rating. Use the space allowed to draw in your and your buying partner's results.

- **If you rated yourself *most* highly on this gateway's *most* important characteristics** (at least 4 on characteristics rated 5, and at least 3 on those rated 4), this gateway may be the one for you.

- **If you *also* rated yourself highly on the gateway's *least* important characteristics** (4s or 5s on characteristics rated 3 or less), other gateways might provide additional options suited to your strengths.

- **If you rated yourself highly *only* on the gateway's *least* important characteristics** (those rated 3 or less), look to another gateway for your best home-buying opportunities.

- **Be sure to look at your partner's strengths and weaknesses.** Is your partner strong where you're weak? Is it realistic to expect your partner to pick up the slack?

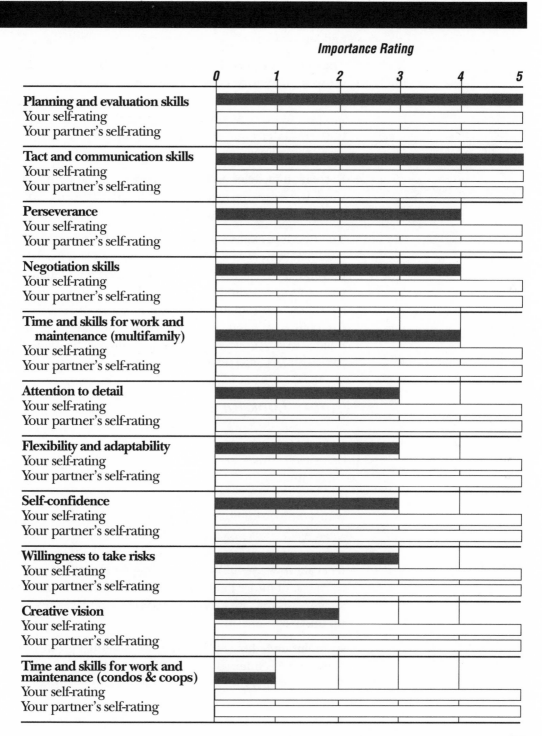

Importance Rating

	0	1	2	3	4	5

Planning and evaluation skills
Your self-rating
Your partner's self-rating

Tact and communication skills
Your self-rating
Your partner's self-rating

Perseverance
Your self-rating
Your partner's self-rating

Negotiation skills
Your self-rating
Your partner's self-rating

Time and skills for work and maintenance (multifamily)
Your self-rating
Your partner's self-rating

Attention to detail
Your self-rating
Your partner's self-rating

Flexibility and adaptability
Your self-rating
Your partner's self-rating

Self-confidence
Your self-rating
Your partner's self-rating

Willingness to take risks
Your self-rating
Your partner's self-rating

Creative vision
Your self-rating
Your partner's self-rating

Time and skills for work and maintenance (condos & coops)
Your self-rating
Your partner's self-rating

- **Statistics show** that the date you are promised is unlikely to be the date by which you'll get your unit. Most builders run late.

- **The builder or developer** could fail and abandon the development before completing your unit. This could mean the loss of all or part of the good-faith money that was put into escrow when you signed the purchase contract and interminable delays in bankruptcy or foreclosure proceedings.

- **Recreation facilities and other amenities** could be scheduled for completion only after all the units are occupied—and that could be years.

- **The builder retains** responsibility (and voting rights in the homeowners association) for to-be-built and partially built units. While this helps to keep your maintenance payments low, it also gives the developer control over all board and association decisions until more than 50% of the units have been sold. That control would allow the builder to vote down something the unit owners wanted, for example, paved sidewalks.

What to Look for in the Numbers

Once you have narrowed your choices to two or three properties in this marketplace area, you should crunch some numbers.

- **In condos and co-ops,** because the potential growth of your equity is interwoven with the *financial health of the shared-space community* into which you are buying, examining each financial statement carefully can help you protect your investment. You are looking for clues that would warn you of future jumps in maintenance costs or special assessments that are even more painful than taxes (more on this in a moment).

- **In multifamily houses,** because the potential growth of your equity is interwoven with the *desirability of the neighborhood* in which the property is located and the *desirabili-*

ty of your rental unit, inquiring about the vacancy rate in the neighborhood and the rents being charged by other landlords will help you to estimate the potential profit and the security of your purchase. Be aware that the vacancy rate for apartments in the town or city in which you live may be quite different from the vacancy rate in a particular neighborhood because of the desirability factor. Generally, real estate agents are a good source of information on the amount of rent being charged, how difficult or easy it is to get a renter, and how many apartments are vacant at any given time in a particular neighborhood.

Words to the Wise

● ●

Reserve fund, contingency fund and **emergency fund,** in the language of condos and co-ops, all refer to money set aside from collected maintenance fees to meet future maintenance needs. Reserve funds provide for planned improvements, while contingency funds cover unexpected expenses. In some cases, the documents that establish the condominium or cooperative mandate that such funds be maintained. In others, the owners vote to establish and maintain them. Generally, the maintenance of a healthy reserve and contingency funds is a sign of a well-run community.

Financial statements

If you are not comfortable with number-crunching, or if you get intimidated (or bored) by 30-page documents in fine print, you might want to hire an accountant or a real estate lawyer to help you review the finances. Try to get a local person, and ask him or her if there have been any new developments in the condo community itself (bankruptcy, law suits, refinancing) or in the town (zoning changes, a new highway) that might affect the value of your purchase. (You can ask these same questions of your real estate agent. The law requires him to answer honestly if he knows the information.)

Condos

A big jump in maintenance fees can make your monthly payments difficult to meet, but it's always a real possibility. The condominium must raise money for general maintenance and for all major repairs by contributions (maintenance fees and special assessments) from the unit owners because the common areas (everything other than the owner-held units) cannot be mortgaged. In a healthy condo community, there is a *contingency fund* for emergencies and a *reserve fund* for future improvements. These funds ward off sudden jumps in maintenance fees. How large these funds should be depends on the individual community and the circumstances in which it exists.

- **Check to see how old the condo community is.** Older communities may be susceptible to more frequent maintenance and repair problems.

- **Since its beginning, what repairs and improvements have been done and paid for?** How long ago?

- **What others are pending?**

- **Are there any likely or pending special assessments?** How much would they be?

- **Does the association pay a management company?** How much and for what services? Have these costs remained relatively stable over the past several years? Is the service satisfactory?

Co-ops

The corporation that owns the building can obtain mortgage loans to finance repairs and improvements rather than levying special assessments on the unit holders. This fact may sound like a plus, but it makes the financial statement more difficult to interpret because more than one mortgage and its statistics can be included, and multiple mortgages can be an added risk factor. That's because the type and amount of mortgage indebtedness is the most

Don't Assume

• •

Don't assume that next year's maintenance fee will be just about the same as this year's. If some apartment owners default on maintenance payments in a co-op, they can lose their ownership rights and be evicted. But who will make up for the lost money? The board of directors can levy higher maintenance fees on the paying apartment owners to cover the shortfall. This is a major difference from a condominium, where foreclosure proceedings can be started against a unit owner who does not pay maintenance fees but other unit owners cannot be required to pay extra to carry the unit.

important factor in estimating future increases and decreases in your maintenance fee.

There may be first, second and even third mortgages on the property that create a debt requiring the contribution of all owners. Some mortgages may be self-liquidating (the corporation's monthly payments completely pay off the loan over a given period of time); some may be interest-only notes (the principal will probably have to be refinanced, and the payment of interest and refinancing of principal could go on indefinitely). If your co-op has a self-liquidating mortgage, your maintenance fee may go down when the mortgage is paid off. Look for the date the payments are scheduled to end. If your building has an interest-only loan, it may be refinanced at a higher rate of interest that would result in higher payments.

As in condos, check to see how old the building is, how much the management company is paid, what repairs and improvements have been made, and what needs are anticipated. You are trying to find a building where maintenance costs will not significantly raise your monthly fees.

It's the Law

Required bookkeeping: If you purchase a multifamily house with at least one rental unit, you'll be taking on the responsibility for some record keeping. Federal tax law requires records of both maintenance expenditures and income. You'll also want to keep track of the cost of all improvements because they will affect your tax basis (the value of your home in the eyes of the IRS) when you sell the property. Your accountant can help you set up a record-keeping system.

Multifamily houses

Owners of multifamily houses don't publish annual financial statements. But they do file tax returns with the IRS. As a prospective buyer, have your attorney request that the owner supply copies of tax returns for the past three years. Because landlords can deduct the cost of producing rental income, you're likely to find an itemized list of the owner's tax-saving expenses. These could include the cost of repairs, utilities paid for the tenants, and wages paid to others to take care of the property, such as for cleaning or lawn maintenance. On a tax return, no one overstates income or understates expenses.

Note the repairs and improvements that have been done and how much they cost. Quality work can mean freedom from trouble in those areas during your period of ownership. Beware of surprisingly low-cost repairs, which might indicate substandard work or materials.

Consider the rental income against your estimated mortgage payment and tax and insurance bills. At least half the combined costs should come from tenants in a two-family house, more in a three- or four-family building.

About Those Laws and Rules and Stuff

The need for a group of rules for living in close proximity is the distinguishing feature of the Shared-Space Gateway. State laws govern procedures for establishing and running a condo or co-op community. Federal, state and municipal laws and the owner's rules affect the relationships between tenants and owners in multifamily houses. The following are some terms and documents you need to know. Your purchase contract may include your acknowledgment that you have received and read some of these documents. If you haven't, it's like buying a house without looking into the kitchen and bathrooms.

CC&Rs (Covenants, Conditions & Restrictions) or occupancy agreements

These are the restrictions placed on a property in its deed. (In some places, they are simply called *restrictions*.) They apply to condos, co-ops and multifamily houses, and stay with the property through all ownership changes. CC&Rs or occupancy agreements for co-ops might dictate the maximum number of occupants per unit, prescribe maximum or minimum size or height of the buildings, or describe certain lands to be designated as open spaces.

The Master Deed or the Declaration

This document creates the condominium community, legally establishes its name, sets out a plan for an association of unit owners, gives that association the power to govern the condominium, and establishes the percentage of undivided interest in the common elements that is assigned to each unit.

Find your unit number in the master deed and note how much voting power is associated with it. Often those units that were originally higher-priced carry more voting power. If your unit was originally one of the lower-priced units, carrying less voting power, and is now tagged with an asking price higher than some of the units with more voting power, you might well suspect that the asking price is inflated. Use the information about voting power to negotiate a lower price.

The Corporate Charter or Certificate of Incorporation

This document establishes the co-op corporation. It must include the name of the corporation and its location, and it must identify the state law under which it is being incorporated. Most important, it must state that the purpose of the cooperative corporation is the acquisition or ownership of a particular piece of property to be used to provide *residences* for its shareholders (as opposed to commercial use). Without that statement you won't be able to get financing to buy an apartment or deduct its interest on your federal tax return.

By-laws

No condo or co-op community could function without by-laws. These rules establish and describe the administration and working systems by which the community lives. They create and maintain order and harmony, and everyone who buys a unit must agree to abide by them. They cover everything from how the board is elected and how long each officer will serve to whether a management company will be hired and who will supervise it. Some by-laws decree whether pets may be kept, and if so, what kind and even how big. Often a unanimous vote is required to change a by-law. *Read the by-laws before you buy a unit and be sure you can live with their restrictions.*

Penny for Your Thoughts

When your neighbor's wall is on fire, it becomes your business.

Horace (65–8 BC),
Roman poet

House rules

Items not covered in the by-laws are usually written as house rules. They are often easier to change than by-laws, requiring only some stated majority of the unit owners' votes. House rules can keep you out of the swimming pool after 10 P.M.; prohibit gatherings after midnight; prohibit lawn mowing, hammering, or music before noon on Sunday; keep your dog out of the elevator; restrict the number of times per year you can rent your unit; and almost anything else you can think of that concerns community life.

Condos and co-ops always print their house rules and distribute them to all unit owners. As a prospective buyer, you should ask for a copy. The rules will give you an intimate glimpse of the community's personality.

If you expect to be the owner of a multifamily house, take a cue from this housing style's larger cousins and hand each tenant a list of house rules before the lease is signed. No law requires that you do this, but it will certainly keep your Tylenol bill down. Also ask the seller about deed restrictions. CC&Rs pass from one owner to another.

Financing Your Purchase

Multifamily houses and condos are financed exactly like single-family detached houses. All the government-supported programs—such as FHA and VA loans—are available, as are low-down-payment loans with private mortgage insurance. The only real difference lies in the rules for mortgage qualification. As discussed under "Why Enter this Gateway?" prospective rental income will help you to qualify for a mortgage on a multifamily house. Monthly maintenance fees for a condo unit, however, are *added* to your monthly housing costs on the debit side of the qualifying equation. (See also "The Nuts and Bolts of Home Financing," beginning on page 209.)

Co-ops are a slightly different story. Technically speaking, you cannot get a mortgage on a co-op because your apartment is not a separate piece of real estate. (Remember, you own shares in the corporation that owns the building.) You can, however, get a mortgage-like loan and deduct the interest you pay on federal tax returns as long as the building maintains its status as a residential cooperative. As with a mortgage, if you default on your loan payments, the lender will take possession of your apartment by taking over your proprietary lease and the ownership of your shares in the co-op corporation.

In cities where co-ops are prevalent, most lenders offer co-op loans. Down-payment requirements and interest rates, however, are sometimes higher than for conventional mortgage loans if the lender is unfamiliar with co-ops because many lenders consider co-ops a higher-risk investment. If you decide to buy into the one co-op in your area and have trouble getting financing, you might try contacting a mortgage broker, who can take your search to a larger pool of lenders.

There is often yet another hurdle in buying a co-op, and it involves down-payment money even though it has nothing to do with lenders. In many co-ops, the board of directors can set the minimum down-payment require-

More, More, More

Generally, local libraries don't shelve many books on property management or shared-space living, but most libraries are now hooked up by computer to state and regional library networks that facilitate interlibrary loans. Ask your reference librarian to help you find information that will guide you. Don't worry if the books aren't recently published. Most concepts in rental and shared-space housing are timeless. (Remember, condos go back to the Romans!)

To get you started, here are two excellent resources.

- *The Landlord's Handbook,* by Daniel Goodwin & Richard Rusdorf (Dearborn Financial Publishing Inc.) A 235-page oversize paperback that contains many of the forms you will need as a landlord.

- *The Buy & Hold Real Estate Strategy,* by David T. Schumacher with Erik Page Bucy (John Wiley & Sons). A 285-page hardcover book that covers everything from selecting your first property to managing your investment for maximum profit.

If you'd like to know about what a homeowners association can and cannot do, how to run one more efficiently, and how changing condominium laws across the nation affect life in a shared-space community, free booklets and information are available from: **Community Associations Institute** (1630 Duke St., Alexandria, VA 22314; 703–548–8600; http://www.caionline.org).

ments for purchase—sometimes as much as 50%. The board wants to be sure that everyone in the co-op can afford to live there.

"How can they do that?" you ask. "How can they control financing when they're not the lenders?"

In most co-ops, the board of directors holds the right to approve or disapprove every transfer of ownership. The board can turn an applicant down for any reason (except those prohibited by fair-housing laws). The size of the down payment a person can afford is one such reason.

How to Choose a Tenant

When you become the owner-occupant of a multi-family home, you can refuse a prospective tenant because, say, he or she has pets, but you can't discriminate on the basis of race or other protected status.

To select the right tenant, follow a standard procedure with each applicant. Have applicants meet with you for a personal interview. Create an application form and have every applicant fill it out. You are looking for:

- **Good credit history.** You can ask about outstanding loans or, as a courtesy, you can ask for permission to run a credit check though you're not legally obligated to get permission.

10 Questions to Ask a Prospective Tenant

Don't assume that you'll be able to remember which tenant applicant is which by looking at the written application forms. After an applicant completes your form, take out another sheet of paper with the following list of questions on it, interview the applicant, "chat" if possible and make notes on the applicant's answers. Staple the two sheets together.

- How did you hear about this rental?

- Where are you living now?

- How long have you lived there?

- Why are you leaving?

- What kind of work do you do?

- How long have you been doing that?

- What are you looking for in a place to live?

- Of those features, what is most important?

- Do you have any unusual hobbies or special needs?

- If you were the landlord, why would you choose a person like yourself for a tenant?

- **Good (steady) job.** How long has the applicant held the present job? Who were the previous employers? How long at each?

- **Good references.** Ask for three. Previous landlords are the best for your purposes.

- **No pets,** or pets limited to those you approve.

- **Long-term lease potential.** You want at least a year. Rental to transients cuts into your time and positive cash flow because you have to go through the process of finding new tenants again. During that time, your apartment will be standing empty and you'll be without the rental income. This may be less of a concern if you live in an area heavily populated with students or military personnel.

- **Positive vibes.** You should "feel right" about the person who will be your tenant.

More, More, More

Landlords can initiate credit checks on prospective tenants by contacting a credit information agency. Look for them under "Credit Reporting Agency" in the Yellow Pages. Costs average $20 per person, $40 for a couple. Once you fill out the necessary paperwork, the agency will contact a national credit bureau to which it subscribes and run the check.

One Gateway to Another

Many people in a more transient, "movable" phase of life make their first home purchase a condo, co-op or multifamily home purchase. They buy the homes with the intention of selling in the fairly near future and the hope of equity growth—all of which is possible as long as the owners view their goals without rose-colored glasses.

All three of these housing styles are particularly susceptible to the influence of both the national and local economies. In some parts of the nation, condo communities were far overbuilt in the '70s and early '80s, creating a surplus that makes them difficult to sell. The flip side, however, is that they are excellent bargains for buyers. Negotiating a below-market price today can mean a profitable and easy at-market sale a few years down the road. For example,

**Penny for
Your Thoughts**

*To fear the
worst oft cures
the worse.*

William Shakespeare
(1564–1616), in *Troilus and
Cressida, act III, scene ii*

let's say that all similar condo apartments are selling at $50,000. You find a tired owner who will let an apartment go for $40,000. What's to stop you from cleaning and decorating just a bit and selling at the market value of $50,000? And you can probably get a quick sale at $45,000.

Movable people committed to no-maintenance or minimal-maintenance homeownership often move from one condo to a larger, more luxurious condo or co-op on their next purchase. Those who wish more privacy and autonomy choose a patio home, townhouse or detached-house condo community.

Those who are ready to take on home maintenance with their homeownership usually choose to buy in a planned development where there is a sense of community without the formal organization and regulation of a condominium. This group likes the American Image Gateway.

Movement from a condo or co-op to the Craft and Creativity Gateway is a much bigger leap because shared-space housing affords very few opportunities for learning substantial home-maintenance skills.

People who buy multifamily houses are often in a marketplace area where there is an overlap of properties accessed by the Craft and Creativity, Risk-Taking, and Shared-Space gateways. Their next purchase is easily made through any of these gateways. The New-Construction Gateway requires a little more learning, but the Shared-Space experience with property management, rules and red tape, and people with authority will be helpful. And of course, the American Image Gateway is a common goal destination of many multifamily-home buyers who want privacy and no longer need the rental income to meet mortgage payments.

Because both movable and rooted people often choose the Shared-Space Gateway for vacation-home and retirement purchases, condominium construction in resort and retirement areas is booming. Some astute home buyers are finding condos in areas where they like to vacation and hope to retire eventually. They believe that prices will probably go up as more and more baby-boomers also look for retirement havens. These vacationer/investor/planners can then sell their vacation home for a profit and buy a better and bigger retirement home. Or they can simply settle down and enjoy the comfort and familiarity of a home they have had for years.

Many rooted retirees, however, prefer to remain close to family and friends. The multifamily house, sometimes needing renovation, sometimes calling for a historic restoration, gives them the opportunity to use the maintenance skills they have acquired over the years and develop an income-producing opportunity at the same time. Some retirees use the rental unit as a starter apartment for a newly married son or daughter.

Among retirees who choose a condo, some also buy a multifamily house as an income-producing investment property. And some retirees convert their large, many-bedroom, family home into a multifamily. Or they use it in a commercial capacity such as a bed and breakfast inn or a restaurant that becomes their second career (see Chapter 5, the Independent Spirit Gateway).

A final word of caution, however. Because properties in this marketplace area are not the ultimate goal of most home buyers, they sometimes take considerably longer to sell than single-family, detached houses. With that fact in mind, plan a conservative selling strategy. Evaluate the pace of the market and give yourself plenty of time to sell. And don't rush into another purchase based on what you think your present home will bring or how quickly you think it might sell. In fact, it's a good idea to have a signed purchase contract on the shared-space home you are selling *before* you commit to buying another.

Penny for Your Thoughts

Delay is preferable to error.

Thomas Jefferson
(1743–1826), in a letter to
George Washington

- **Added-to**

- **Add-On Potential**

- **Small Houses With Lots of Land**

- **Converting to Multifamily**

- **In-Law Apartments**

A House United:
The Addition
(& Division) Gateway

Who hasn't been out on a shopping expedition and come upon the "perfect thing"? Well, perfect *except for...* There's just this little addition, or perhaps an alteration that has to be made. It happens in house-hunting all the time.

The trouble is that in the real estate marketplace the little addition or alteration is almost never little and almost always expensive. To add more complexity, it's more or less permanent, too! Additions or alterations change the character of a house, the way it appears, the way it is used and sometimes the way its systems function. It follows, therefore, that they will also change your comfort level and your potential for equity growth. Every homeowner hopes those changes will be for the better. But sometimes they're not.

For example, one of the risks in buying a house with an addition, or in buying a small house and planning an addition, is the possibility of fragmentation. A house that looks patched together often loses resale value because it doesn't feel comfortable to most people. The resulting smaller pool of potential buyers often increases the time it will take to sell the house.

But when a house is "perfect except for...," it has some obvious appeal both to "movable" people, who think "we can fix the problem and sell for a profit," and to rooted people, who think "we can fix the problem and enjoy the house for a long time." Should you yield to that appeal?

At the Addition (and Division) Gateway, it's helpful to

remember three of the distinguishing character traits of the president who worked to hold our nation together. Think of Abraham Lincoln: his practicality, his stability and his desire for harmony. Additions to houses should be:

- **practical** enough to serve the needs for which they were done,

- **stable** in their construction and design so that structural elements and working systems are not stressed, and

- **harmonious** in appearance, both with other properties in the neighborhood and within themselves.

In order to meet those three objectives, the people who plan additions to houses, and often those who buy houses with additions, must be flexible, creative and quite good at both planning and rational evaluation. Let's see how that requirement affects you in the marketplace.

A house divided against itself cannot stand.

Abraham Lincoln
(1809-1865)

What's Beyond This Gateway?

The Addition (and Division) Gateway includes houses that have been changed or can be changed from their original use and structure, and houses with large lots that can be subdivided into two or more separate properties. Much of the advice found in Chapter 9 (do read it!), which focuses on creating new structures, is also helpful in this marketplace area. Like the Craft and Creativity Gateway and the Risk-Taking Gateway, the Addition and Division Gateway can lead to getting more space and comfort for your money or to making a profit when you sell. But there are *watch-out-for*s and *only-if*s aplenty.

Added To

Houses that have been "added to" are common in the real estate marketplace. An addition can go up or out, or both ways.

- **Going up** means living space has been increased, either by raising the roof or by adding dormers and creating rooms in the attic space.

- **Going out** means living space has been increased by building upon existing foundation that is currently under a garage or breezeway, for example, or by building upon a new foundation adjacent to the existing building.

It's the Law

• •

The limits of ownership: Ownership of real estate extends beyond the surface of the land. Theoretically subsurface rights go to the center of the earth, and air rights go to the limits of the atmosphere. It's the subsurface rights that allow for basements, wells, septic systems—and drilling for oil. It's the air rights that allow for additional stories—even skyscrapers. Zoning or deed restrictions, however, might limit exactly where and how far you can dig, or how high an addition or even a fence can go.

Just for the record, converting a basement to additional living space isn't usually considered an addition, and it rarely adds to property value.

Although houses with additions can be both tasteful and spacious, movable people should bear in mind that they are often slow to sell because they are unconventional. Rooted people, on the other hand, should be especially concerned with evaluating the livability of the floor plan because a source of discomfort unnoticed prior to purchase can pinch and pressure like a pebble in a shoe—one that you can't take off for a long time.

Add-On Potential

Some house-hunters fall in love with a location. They want that particular spot even though the house that stands on it is too small, too old or too ugly. They plan to add on (and, in the case of "old and ugly," to renovate) even before they move in. Sometimes they finance an addition in the mortgage (more about that under "Tips.")

Other house-hunters find a house that is right for their current stage in life and then, over the years, grow out of it. Movable people move; rooted people consider adding on. If you see yourself as a rooted person now or in the future, be sure to read "If You Might Add-on Later," on page 151.

The Small House With Lots of Land

Buying a small house on a large piece of land can sometimes be an excellent investment for rooted people with some experience in real estate and a good deal of perseverance and planning skills. There's usually a dream behind the purchase. It goes like this: *If we subdivide, we can create some new lots and sell them to a builder. Maybe we'll keep one for ourselves, finance the building of a new house with the proceeds from the sale of other lots, and then sell the original house for pure profit. Whoopee!*

Does that sound too good to be true? Well, it could be.

Small houses on large tracts of land suitable for residential development are very hard to find. Lots in cities and close-in suburbs are usually already as small as is feasible. Where they are larger, local zoning and planning boards are usually unwilling to grant subdivision approval, at least not without considerable hassle. Large tracts of land in rural areas or very far-out suburbs are not usually cost-effective for subdivision and development because there is not enough demand for new housing in the area. The best chances are in suburbs that were once considered far-out but are now increasing in popular demand.

Even when you do find the little gem on the big lot, the ability to subdivide does not happen just because the tract is large. The new lots must meet municipal or county zoning requirements for size, drainage and appropriate use. A proposal for subdivision usually means a hearing before a zoning or planning board. A plan must be drawn and presented showing the proposed lot lines. Such a plan can be sketched by the owners, but final drawings and surveys must be done to professional standards. That means paying a civil engineer and a surveyor. And not all requests are approved. Many planning boards do not want to change the character of a neighborhood by new development. Even the neighbors within a specified distance from your property (a quarter-mile radius is common) can object to your subdivision and have their objections heard by the board.

Okay, so maybe moonlighting as a property developer is a bit more than you want to take on. But what about a house on an oversized lot that is *just short* of being large enough to meet the zoning requirements for two lots? If the existing house is well-sited on the lot, you might still be able to subdivide and take the profit from the sale of part of your land. But first you must petition the zoning board of appeals for a *variance*. You'll probably want to consult with a local real estate lawyer to help you anticipate and answer all of the possible objections and to proceed according to all the rules and regulations. You'll also need to see a surveyor to have plans drawn for the proposed two-lot subdivision.

Words to the Wise

• •

A **variance** allows for a change in the zoning requirements for one particular piece of land without changing the zoning for the area.

Making a Multifamily

Some of the large, elegant houses built at the beginning of this century seem particularly unsuitable for today's lifestyles, and many have already been converted to offices. But others seem to cry out for multifamily use, both to young entrepreneurs who want to get started in investment real estate while also buying a place to live, and to the still-young retired people who see home buying as a source of both shelter and income.

Converting from a large, single-family home to a two-, three- or four-unit multifamily house means the possibility of rental income that will help to pay your real estate taxes, maintenance expenses, insurance and mortgage payment. Sometimes there's even money left over for some extra fun! (For more about multifamily houses, see Chapter 6.)

This type of investment is being undertaken very successfully in many small and midsize cities across the nation. But it's not easy. As in the subdivision of land, you must work through the red tape involved in zoning-board approvals. Neighbors may oppose the introduction of higher-density housing. Then, of course, building codes come into play as you start the conversion. Converting a rambling old house to a multifamily demands many of the same skills and much of the knowledge required to succeed beyond the Craft and Creativity and Risk-Taking gateways. You'll also need extra tact and perseverance to get through zoning-board approval, obtain building permits, hire and work with contractors, and pass building code inspections. Once you're finished, you've got to call in skills from the Shared-Space Gateway because you're going to be a landlord.

You'll also need money for new plumbing and wiring and renovation throughout. Fortunately, community- and government-supported financing is available in many cities (see Chapters 3 and 4).

In-Law Apartments

If you choose a house with the idea of adding an in-law apartment, be aware that you are taking on trouble. No, not the in-laws, the zoning board!

In-law additions require all the skills, time and money commitments of any other addition, with the extra factor that zoning variances must be obtained in order to change a single-family house into multifamily use. (As soon as you add another kitchen, you have a multifamily house even if you don't charge rent.)

The "trouble" dimension here arises from the permanence of additions. A sympathetic zoning board may be inclined to allow you to add a small apartment for your mother-in-law to the rear of your house where it is virtually invisible from the street. Okay, it won't disturb the neighborhood.

But what happens when your mother-in-law moves to an assisted-care facility or when you decide to sell your home? Do the new buyers absolutely have to have a mother-in-law to buy the house? No, but the house would be a lot

Don't Assume

Don't assume that you can cut corners with a total do-it-yourself and minimal changes in your conversion to a multifamily. You will be required to comply with all current building codes, and only licensed contractors (plumbers, electricians, heating contractors, and so on) will be allowed to install working systems. Total do-it-yourself home renovation is allowed only on houses occupied solely by the owners. Of course, you can still paint, sand, scrape, hammer, lay floor tiles, install cabinets, clean and do anything else that doesn't require licensed professional labor.

more attractive to them if they did. Unfortunately, this is a very limited market, and that's why many homes with an in-law apartment stay on the market for much longer than the average house.

Can the new owners ever rent out that apartment? Most zoning boards say "Absolutely not!" Some people rent them anyway, without asking. If someone complains, those people could be required to boot the tenants and re-move the addition. For all these reasons, most zoning boards are not inclined to grant permission for in-law apartments.

Certain housing styles such as the bilevel with a walk-out lower level are most conducive to adding a bedroom with closets, a bathroom and a living room in that lower area. That's fine, until you add kitchen facilities. If you add kitchen facilities without appropriate permissions, occupan-cy of that level becomes illegal. If someone complains, you can be required to remove all the additions on that level, re-store the area to its original use and evict your in-laws.

If you think you will be needing an in-law apartment in the near future, you would do well to explore multifami-ly houses; two condominiums in the same community; the legal conversion of a large, old single-family house to a multifamily house; or the subdivision of a lot with a small, new house added. (You can sell the house separately later.) Adding an in-law apartment is rarely a choice that will in-crease your equity. And before you buy a house with an in-law apartment, check its status with the zoning board. Will you be able to rent it out?

Why Enter This Gateway?

Choosing to permanently alter a house or the perimeters of its land takes courage. Mistakes are easily spotted and not easily erased. But there are both reasons and rewards that make the Addition and Division Gateway appealing. (Weigh the following motives carefully. If this gateway seems like a good fit with your homeowner personality, confirm your hunch with the self-test beginning on the following page.)

Continued on page 148

Self-Test Before You Choose This Gateway

The following, three-part self-assessment will help you evaluate whether you have what it takes to successfully pursue the homeowning options outlined in this chapter. It focuses on the 10 important homebuyer personality characteristics described in Chapter 2.

PART I: RATE YOURSELF

In Part I, below, read each of the self-descriptive statements in each category and decide how well it describes you. Grade your response on a scale from 1, "Not me at all!" to 5, "That's me all the way!" Encourage your spouse or home-buying partner(s) to do the same.

Certain statements pertain to only one or two gateway options. If those don't interest you, skip those statements.

If your ratings vary within a category, average them.

Turn to the following page to see how you've fared.

Creative vision

____ I can walk through a house and then imagine living there. What would the traffic pattern be at different times of the day? Where would people gather? Where would someone go to be alone?

____ I can picture the advantages and problems that would occur if we changed the interior and added more space. Where would the stairs go? Do we really want the master bedroom over the new family room? Do we want to have to walk through the dining room to get to the new family room?

Time and skills for work and maintenance

____ I not only have the time, I have the ideas, too!

____ I'm willing to spend time at planning or zoning board meetings to present my petitions and get them approved.

Self-confidence

____ I don't mind if my house looks different from the rest of the neighborhood.

____ I like the family room and the laundry facilities on the second floor, with the bedrooms, and I don't care if that's not exactly typical.

Flexibility and adaptability

____ We'll make it! We can live on the second floor while the first floor is being done and on the first floor while the second floor is being done.

____ It's a situation where you have to walk through one bedroom to get to the other, but we don't mind. We've just moved the girls together into the farther room and made the first room into their playroom. If they want to separate when they get older, they can draw straws for who gets which room.

Willingness to take risks

____ Comfort and the suitability of a house to my particular lifestyle are more important to me than profit potential.

____ I'm willing to pay a little more for that extra-large lot even though I'm not at all certain that I can get the zoning variance needed to subdivide.

Self-Test, Cont'd.

Perseverance
___ I won't give up on my petition for a variance even if the planning board postpones decisions several months running and requires soil tests, additional surveys or revised plans.

___ When I set down roots, I want to stay, and I'm willing to do whatever it takes to make this house comfortable for my family for the long-run.

Attention to detail
___ I will seek out whatever professional people I need to help me make the changes I want and make them the way they should be made.

___ When considering a house with an addition, I'd ask about construction dates, the plans, the bills, the materials used, the added cost of heat and electricity (because of the electric-baseboard heat they used in the addition), and any warranties that survive the transfer of title.

Planning and evaluation skills
___ Before I make an offer on a house I intend to enlarge or convert to a multi-family, I will determine exactly what will need to be done and get estimates for how much it will cost.

___ Realizing that the value of an addition is limited by the price range of the neighborhood, I will get the selling prices of recently sold houses and the tax appraisals for all the neighborhood houses in order to determine the real value (not the cost) of an addition. (See Chapter 12.)

___ This house is perfectly adequate for us now. By the time we have children and need more space, we'll have the money to add on or to sell it and buy another house. At that time, we'll be in a better position to make that decision than we are now.

Tact and communication skills
___ Our family often sits around the dinner table talking about what each of us would like to have in a house.

___ If I need to go to the planning board for a variance, I can organize my thoughts on why I want it, anticipate objections, present my plan both verbally and in writing, and answer whatever questions are asked of me.

___ I can "casually" talk with the seller, asking about the kind of work done on the addition, who did it, where the materials came from, and anything else I can think of that would help me to judge the quality of the work.

Negotiating skills
___ Even if town planning board's members are being unreasonably difficult, I will not lose my temper. I will continue, tactfully and courteously, to present valid data to support my plan.

___ I am not afraid to make my first offer on a house slightly below market value for the neighborhood, even though the listing sheet reads "two-year-old addition, cost: $48,000" and the asking price is $50,000 higher than the asking price of an unimproved but otherwise similar house down the street.

PART II: WHAT'S IMPORTANT AND WHY

Now let's turn the tables and look at the home-buyer personality characteristics from the point of view of demand—that is, how vital the characteristic is to success through this gateway, and why. Each characteristic is rated from 1 to 5 (1 being low demand, 3 being variable demand that might be higher in some instances and lower in others, and 5 being high demand).

Creative vision: 5

It's been said that architecture is inhabited sculpture. If that's the case, then perhaps we can say that changing the use and look of an already created building is like playing with the biggest Lego blocks in the world. This is your chance to play at being an architect.

Time and skills for work and maintenance: 4

Added-to houses have the potential for requiring not only the normal physical work of maintaining a property but also the thought, the paperwork and the "gofer" jobs involved in changing what was supposed to be permanent.

Self-confidence: 4

Perhaps "Dare to be Different" is the most appropriate motto for this homeowning gateway. On the other hand, an owner's satisfaction with an addition or subdivision often depends on the harmony achieved between the addition and the original, or between the added-to house and its neighbors.

Flexibility and adaptability: 5

Buying a house with an addition often means adapting to someone else's ideas of a good floor plan and traffic pattern. Doing your own addition means working with what you have and moving toward what you want.

Being able to see several ways of achieving the same goal is a major plus. And living with a work in progress takes a certain talent that allows you to step over piles of debris and not notice that you've lifted your feet higher than normal.

Willingness to take risks: 3

If you add on for comfort, not profit, there is little risk—you will get your comfort, and you didn't expect profit, anyway.

If you buy a house that already has an addition, there is little risk because through good negotiation you bought at a neighborhood market price, which means you paid little for the addition.

If you buy with the idea of making a profit by subdividing land or converting a large single-family house to a multifamily house, there is risk that the subdivision may not be approved or may not be as profitable as you had hoped, or that the multifamily conversion isn't approved or may not bring in as much positive cash flow as you had planned.

Perseverance: 3

If you start an addition or a conversion to a multifamily, you've got to finish it or live without a wall or floor of your home.

If you start a petition for a subdivision, the consequences of quitting are minimal, except the loss of the money you've invested in plans and professional advice.

Attention to detail: 4

Those property owners who dot every *i* and cross every *t* usually do better at planning-board meetings than those who gleefully wing it. Planning and building an addition demands as much attention to detail as building a new house—maybe more so from time to time because you have to

Self-Test, Cont'd.

make the new systems and structures fit with the old. Plumbing and waste-disposal systems, for example, must connect without a hitch. Attention to the details of construction when buying a house with an addition can save you from huge headaches, not to mention major repair bills.

Planning and evaluation skills: 5

This marketplace area requires planning and evaluation of almost every type:

- planning for future needs

- cost evaluation of proposed changes

- evaluation of costs against possible returns

- planning how best to use space and land

- evaluating price against neighborhood sales figures

- evaluating the effect an addition might have on property taxes

The list could go on and on.

Tact and communication skills: 4

Whenever you need approval or a permit, as in "subdivision approval" or "building permit," you are going to need all the tact and communication skills you can muster. There's something about asking for a change in land use that always seems to slow down the workings of local government. And then, of course, there are the contractors who will work for you on the addition. You will certainly need to employ firmness, tact and courtesy.

Negotiating skills: 4

Whenever you deal with anything that's different from the usual and customary, you need a little extra negotiating skill. It doesn't matter whether you're discussing a tangible building or a conceptual plan for land use. It also takes some extra negotiating skill to convince a seller that the $30,000 addition is not worth $30,000 in the marketplace.

PART III: THE CRITICAL COMPARISON

Now you can compare your self-ratings with the importance ratings for each characteristic to see how likely you are to measure up to the demands of this gateway. In the left column of the graph, the characteristics are presented in descending order from highest to lowestdemand for this gateway. The black bars show each characteristic's importance rating. Use the space allowed to draw in your and your buying partner's results.

- **If you rated yourself** *most* **highly on this gateway's** *most* **important characteristics** (at least 4 on characteristics rated 5, and at least 3 on those rated 4), this gateway may be the one for you.

- **If you** *also* **rated yourself highly on the gateway's** *least* **important characteristics** (4s or 5s on characteristics rated 3 or less), other gateways might provide additional options suited to your strengths.

- **If you rated yourself highly** *only* **on the gateway's** *least* **important characteristics** (those rated 3 or less), look to another gateway for your best home-buying opportunities.

- **Be sure to look at your partner's strengths and weaknesses.** Is your partner strong where you're weak? Is it realistic to expect your partner to pick up the slack?

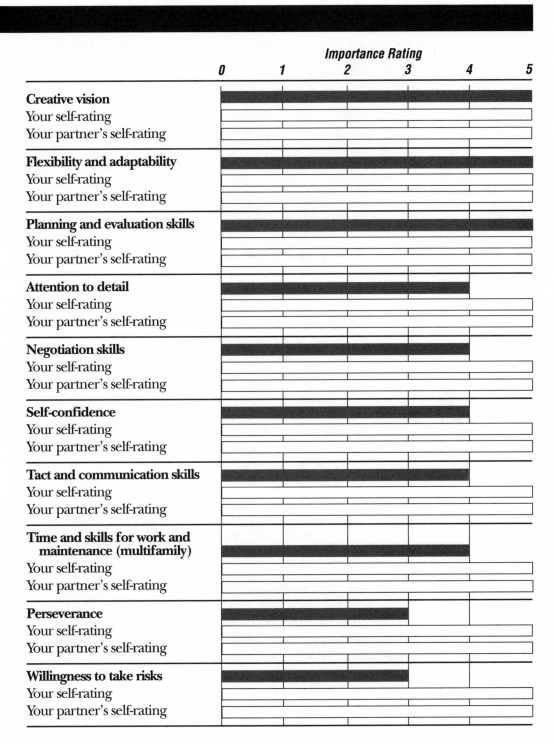

Importance Rating

| | 0 | 1 | 2 | 3 | 4 | 5 |

Creative vision
Your self-rating
Your partner's self-rating

Flexibility and adaptability
Your self-rating
Your partner's self-rating

Planning and evaluation skills
Your self-rating
Your partner's self-rating

Attention to detail
Your self-rating
Your partner's self-rating

Negotiation skills
Your self-rating
Your partner's self-rating

Self-confidence
Your self-rating
Your partner's self-rating

Tact and communication skills
Your self-rating
Your partner's self-rating

**Time and skills for work and
    maintenance (multifamily)**
Your self-rating
Your partner's self-rating

Perseverance
Your self-rating
Your partner's self-rating

Willingness to take risks
Your self-rating
Your partner's self-rating

To get more living space and amenities than would otherwise be available at your price

When you buy a house with a recent addition, you are often profiting from the seller's loss. Few sellers recoup their full expenditure because location is still the most important factor in determining the value of a house. This is especially true for added-to houses in tract developments. (Be sure to read the sidebar on page 164 in Chapter 8.) The buyer of an added-to house therefore gets not only extra space but also amenities, fixtures and appliances that are relatively new—at least in that part of the house—for less than what it would otherwise have cost you to replace them.

To buy a particular lot

If your "perfect" location has an unacceptable house standing on it, you must either tear it down and build from scratch or add on to the existing structure. If the lot is large enough, you might also be able to build behind or beside the existing house, which you promise the zoning board you will tear down when the new one is completed. Not all zoning boards will allow such creativity.

To buy now and build later

Houses with more land than is required by the zoning ordinance sometimes allow for future sale of subdivided lots or for construction of a new home for the owner and then the sale of the original house.

To create an income-producing property

By altering the interior of a large city house, a buyer can create up-to-date comfort in the owner's space and at the same time provide space for very marketable rental apartments. After a number of years, some homeowners use the equity and income in such a conversion to help qualify for the purchase and financing of a house in the marketplace areas accessed by the American Image and New-Construction Gateways.

Tips and Trouble Spots

Buying a house is stressful under any circumstances, but entering homeownership through this gateway adds a few stressors that are all its own. The first tip, therefore, is to think carefully through what you are doing. Can you deal with the following stress situations?

- **Feeling different from those around you.** Your house is likely to be the odd one on the block.

- **Making a major change.** You're going to have to make decisions that affect the way things appear and the way you live in the house, and then you're going to have to live with getting the change accomplished.

- **Presenting a request or petition before the zoning or planning board or the board of appeals.** You not only need to think well and speak well, you're also going to need the help of professionals.

- **Setting a goal that you can realistically achieve.** You will have to reconcile your dreams with the realities and limitations of the lot and the structure of the house.

Setting an unachievable goal is perhaps the most bothersome of the errors that can be made when considering properties that you intend to change. One of the most important keys to success in this marketplace area is the recognition and acceptance of limitations. Those limitations might be legal (zoning ordinances), physical (the building and the land), financial (your savings and income) or temporal (the amount of available time), or some combination of the above. You must identify your particular limitations and their probable effects on your plans before you take those plans too far. All of this boils down to the need for planning and evaluation. Be sure to allow enough time and to take all you need!

Eyeballing a Prospective Property

Before you purchase a house that has an addition, check the following points.

Structure

The worst nightmare is an addition that pulls away from the original structure. Seams at roof intersections seem to be the most vulnerable points. Go into the attic, find the intersecting areas and use a high-powered flashlight to check for evidence of leaks.

Working systems

Heating, air-conditioning, electrical, plumbing and waste-disposal systems must be tied into existing systems. The question is: Do they work? Is the addition as warm or cool as the original house? Does the toilet get clogged? Is there enough water pressure in the shower? Talk with your home inspector about the special considerations for additions (and read Chapter 14 carefully).

Traffic pattern

Does the house seem to serve the movements and needs of its inhabitants, or do they move or work around the immovable elements of the house? A stairway, for example, might jut into a room because of changes necessary for an addition or you might have to walk through the dining room to get from the kitchen to the new family room. The need to walk through one room to get to another—say, through a bedroom to get to the only upstairs bathroom—usually hurts resale value. Walking through the kitchen is an exception to this rule because it is often at the center of a house. Additions that necessitate the creation of long corridors without windows also put off buyers.

Zoning and building code compliance

Occasionally, homeowners put on an addition without getting a building permit and the town doesn't notice. The illegal construction is usually discovered when a new tax assessment is done. Even if ownership has changed hands since the illegal addition was done, the town can levy fines on the new owner or even require that the addition be torn down. Of course, the new owner will probably appeal this judgment. Before you buy, check the municipal or county inspections or tax records to be certain the addition is recorded.

If You Might Add On Later

If you see yourself as a rooted person, weigh the following factors when you consider the small house that might not be big enough later.

The size of the lot

Zoning ordinances decree how close to each property line a building wall can stand. Since the distances are expressed in feet and run parallel to the property lines, surveys show them as "setback" lines. (Read more about them on pages 199 in Chapter 9.) Does the space within the setback lines allow for an addition without a zoning variance?

Deed restrictions

Can you legally build another story? Can you have a fence? Can you paint your house purple with a yellow stripe here or there? Can you play catch on Sunday? Almost anything can "run with the deed." It is important to check, or have your attorney check, to be sure there are no deed restrictions that will keep you from fulfilling your plans.

Drainage

If waste disposal is by septic system, the number of bedrooms may be limited by the capacity of the soil to handle wastewater.

Property value

Read Chapter 12 on the price-versus-value question. Remember: Location limits value. Homeowners who put on an addition and then sell within a few years rarely get full return on money spent, much less a profit. A house can indeed be improved beyond the price that the neighborhood will support in the near or even the distant future.

Financing a House With an Addition

Houses with additions are financed through all the conventional sources with just about all the current mortgage instruments. The only "watch-out-for" concerns the professional appraisal that virtually every lender requires.

The difference an appraisal makes

Many altered properties are difficult to appraise accurately with the most commonly used appraisal methods.

The *market data* approach uses the sale prices of other comparable properties in the neighborhood to determine fair market value. Usually there *are* no properties comparable to a house with a major addition.

The *cost* approach evaluates the worth of the land, plus the current cost of constructing the building as it now stands, minus the depreciation factored in because of age and normal wear and tear or catastrophic damage. This figure is unreliable because it doesn't give enough weight to the limiting effects of location on value.

Appraisals on added-to houses therefore tend to be conservative (which means on the low side of what their replacement cost would be) and, funny thing, most appraisals come in at or very near the proposed purchase price. Sometimes, however, an appraiser will work with a figure closer to the actual cost of the addition and come up with an appraisal that is higher than the purchase price agreed to in the contract.

Such a "high-side" appraisal (which is probably closer to the replacement value of the house) can save you a lot of money in loan-procurement and even interest costs. To understand why, you need to understand how loan-to-value (LTV) ratio can affect your mortgage. (It's all explained in the tabbed pages, *The Nuts and Bolts of Home Financing.*)

Consider that the LTV ratio may determine your interest rate, your need for mortgage insurance and even your qualification for a loan. Let's say you thought you were putting $5,000 down on an added-to house that you agreed to buy at $100,000. But the appraisal comes in at $118,500. When you applied for the $95,000 mortgage, it looked like a loan for 95% of the value of the house. According to the appraisal, however, $95,000 is only 80% of

---

More, More, More

• •

If you buy with the idea of adding on or converting space, it's important to have a plan. These two books will help you explore your ideas.

Converting Basements, Garages & Attics, by R. Dodge Woodson (Sterling Publishing Co., 1993)

Adding On: How to Design and Build a Beautiful Addition to Your Home, by the editors of the Rodale Press (1995)

the value of the house. With an 80% LTV ratio, you don't need mortgage insurance and you may be able to get a better interest rate.

This scenario doesn't happen often, even when houses with additions are involved. But it *does* happen and it could make a difference for you. If you are buying a house with a relatively recent major addition, be sure to ask your lender for a copy of the appraisal or a statement of appraised value.

Financing to Build an Addition

If you buy a small house with plans to add on years later, you'll probably be able to finance that addition with a second mortgage or a home-equity line of credit. When the work is complete, you can either refinance the house with a new first mortgage that covers both the balance due on your first mortgage and the amount you borrowed for the addition, or keep both the first and second mortgages on the property. Which plan is preferable depends on the interest rates on the two loans, the length of time until each loan is paid off, and the appraised value of the house with the addition. Discuss the options with a financial adviser or have a mortgage company run the numbers for various financing alternatives.

If you buy a house with the intention of adding on before you even move in, you can find mortgage programs that will lend money based on the value of the completed project. You'll need professionally drawn blueprints, contractors' estimates of cost, and an appraisal estimating the probable fair market value from a lender-approved appraiser. To find opportunities for this type of financing, call several mortgage brokers in your local area (listed in the Yellow Pages of your phone book).

Subdividing Land

It's not exactly fair, but sometimes approval of a request to subdivide property at a planning or zoning board meeting depends on the quality of the presentation. Spend the money necessary to have professional drawings done of your proposed plan and lot lines. Then gather the data necessary to support your petition on clearly organized pages. Make copies and present a set to each member of the hearing board.

Whether you make the presentation yourself or hire an attorney or civil engineer to do it for you depends on the complexity of the project, your self-confidence and the prevailing practice in your area. If you go to the planning or zoning-board office in your town hall and talk with the clerk there, you might be able to get a set of guidelines for petitions. You will certainly be able to get the names of the planning-board members. In some areas, a separate board of appeals will hear your petition instead of the planning board itself.

Every petition has its own particular need for documentation and rationale. Among the most commonly required information is:

• **A clear summary of the zoning restrictions for the area,** including the minimal square footage of land that is required to build a particular type of building, minimal road frontage required (the number of linear feet that run along the street), and setback requirements.

• **Data on each proposed lot** that shows its conformity or nonconformity to the zoning requirements. Where there is nonconformity, state how the proposed lot will differ from the requirements, using exact measurements in feet.

• **A summary statement** telling why the proposed subdivision will be an improvement to the area and will not overburden municipal facilities such as local streets, storm sewers, water supply, municipal sewer systems and open spaces. If septic systems will be used for waste disposal, you'll have to show that drainage in the area is adequate for the size houses that will be built on the lots.

If you are subdividing one oversized lot into two lots, each of which will be just slightly undersized, spend some time in the town hall to see if you can gather data for other houses on slightly undersized lots in the neighborhood, and include the data in your presentation papers. The existence of other nonconforming lots will help your petition.

Being Practical

Occasionally, in a newspaper or magazine, you'll read about a homeowner who transformed an ordinary one-story house into one that looked exactly like a lace-up boot. ("There was an old woman who lived in a shoe...") Or perhaps a freighter complete with bridge and decks. Don't even think of it!

If you are planning an addition, try to stay away from anything that teenagers would call "weird." That includes four-story towers; underground media centers; all glass, "fishbowl" family rooms; and even garden-style bathrooms. Even if you are one of the most rooted of people, someday either you or your heirs will want to sell your home. Weirdness does not sell. And let's not even get into a discussion of how much strange additions will do for friendliness of the neighbors.

Don't Assume

• •

Don't assume, when you are making decisions about your addition, that expensive means "it's gotta be good." Price is not as important as appropriateness.

Harmony

Students who major in music in college all agree that "harmony" is one of the most difficult courses in the curriculum, full of mathematical formulas and complex rules. In nonacademic life, the concept of harmony is also hard to define. In its simplest form, we think of it as a kind of "going together comfortably without being identical." And it's just that kind of harmony that you should seek when judging a house with an addition or considering a house that may need some kind of an addition in the future.

And remember: Additions require harmony on two levels. The style of the addition should be harmonious with the original house, and the style of the finished house (complete with addition) should be harmonious with the neighborhood. Roof lines are very important, as are the materials used for the siding. For example, you really can't

Penny for Your Thoughts

He who hesitates is sometimes saved.

James Thurber (1894-1961), American writer and artist

put a hip-roofed addition against a New England saltbox. Conversely, a clapboard-sided addition would look foolish on a redwood and glass contemporary. A three-story addition of any style and siding would be offensive in a neighborhood of ranch style houses.

Judging harmony is really just a matter of exercising good taste. Still, it's smart to double-check your decisions by scheduling a one-hour consultation with an architect (for more on working with an architect, see page 185 in Chapter 9). That will be much less expensive than putting up a structure that you later dislike so much that you try to change it again or that compares so badly with its neighbors that you have trouble selling it when the time comes.

A Search for Quality

One of the risks beyond the Addition and Division Gateway is quality—or, more accurately, the lack of it. Since some or all of the work on many additions is done by the homeowners themselves, there is always the question, "How good is it, really?" Who chose the materials? Were they closeouts or seconds? The low end of the line? Were mistakes remedied with a tape-and-paper-clips solution and then covered over with wallboard?

Be certain to get a professional home inspection if you are buying a house with an addition. Accompany the home inspector through the entire process. Try to note the brand names on things you can see—a new furnace or air conditioner, for example. If good-quality brands and models were chosen on large items, the unseen materials may also be acceptable, but there's no guarantee. Ask whether any warranties still apply and whether they will survive the change of ownership.

Ask the real estate agent to get the dates for construction of the addition. How old is it? How long did it take to complete? (Professional jobs usually take less time than do-it-yourself work.) Ask whether professional plans were drawn—something had to be drawn to get a building permit. If the seller no longer has the drawings and plans, you may find them on file in the town hall with the records for the building permit. If there are no plans to be found, check again with the municipal tax records department to be sure the addition is recorded and legal.

If you are putting on an addition, try to choose a contractor from referrals by people who have had similar work done. Be sure to get at least three estimates, and have each contractor indicate what materials will be necessary, with the amounts of each, brand names and model numbers, where they will be purchased (or whether you can purchase them yourself), and the amount being charged for labor.

Try to be present when the work on the addition is being done. And don't be afraid to ask questions if anything seems "a little strange."

One Gateway to Another

Addition and Division is rarely an appropriate gateway for beginners. It calls for both foresight and good homeowner judgment, and those qualities are hard to come by without experience. It also appeals to rooted people far more than moveable people because its housing styles are often slow to sell and its opportunities long in coming to fruition.

Most home buyers come to this marketplace area from other gateways where flexibility and adaptability are important, especially the Craft and Creativity, the Risk-Taking, and the Independent Spirit Gateways. Sometimes, however, a homeowner who bought a starter house in a 40-year-old development that would still qualify for the American Image designation will choose to buy in another, perhaps newer, development but, seeking more space and comfort, will choose a house with an addition. Some starter homes in older developments also come with additions so longstanding that they are no longer noticed as additions.

Most Addition and Division Gateway purchases are for long-term ownership, but even rooted people do sell eventually. Once they have successfully mastered the challenge of changing the character of a house and gained experience working with a planning board, an architect, a municipal buildings inspector, and builders and subcontractors, most sellers head to the New-Construction Gateway.

Penny for Your Thoughts

No rose without a thorn.

English proverb

Others, however, have simply had enough of being different or working to make something "better." They very often buy a bigger, better and very conventional house in the American Image marketplace. Very few homeowners say that they would consider putting on an addition to another house.

Those home buyers who choose a house with an addition are usually choosing comfort over profit. They get more house for their money to start with, but the factors that created that bargain will probably still prevail when it's time to sell. Significant profit, therefore, is rarely the motivating goal in this marketplace area, except when subdivision of the land is possible.

People who subdivide their land usually take considerable profit from their venture, but they reduce the privacy that ample land affords and perhaps the aesthetic appeal of a house with a lovely yard. The newer house or houses built on the subdivided land and the smaller lot created by subdividing usually reduce the market value of the original house.

People who choose to put an addition on an existing house will probably increase their comfort level and may increase market value somewhat. The increase rarely equals the expenditure, however, and usually slows the selling time.

People who choose to convert a single-family house to a multifamily dwelling will generate income from their property. But they lose the privacy of single-family detached housing and take on the responsibilities of being a landlord.

Like every home-buying decision, determining whether to enter this gateway requires weighing positives against negatives and making choices. Finding a *perfect* house is just as difficult as finding a *perfect* mate.

Model Neighborhoods:
The American Image Gateway

- **Starter Homes**

- **Step-Up Homes**

- **Status Homes**

From the air, suburban America looks like no other nation. Its neighborhoods create a patchwork quilt, each "square" laced with street patterns in angles or curves and dotted with a rhythmic repetition of rooftops. On the ground, each rooftop covers a house cared for by its owner and surrounded by a patch of land similar to its neighbors.

Development, tract, subdivision, planned community, whatever you call it, the single-family detached house in a group of similar houses is the image you think of first when you hear the words "American home." But in fact, this housing style has existed only in the second half of this century. Earlier, houses were most often built one at a time on farms or on single lots along city streets. No one had heard of Levittown—the planned development that arose on former potato fields of Long Island, N.Y., in 1947.

This change in the character of American neighborhoods began after World War II in response to the overwhelming demand for housing that was stimulated by the return of American troops, the G.I. Bill and the economic boom that followed the war. Contractors bought up tracts of land to build whole communities of all-alike or very similar houses. Building the same house again and again improved both cost and time efficiency, just as assembly lines had improved auto manufacturing.

The character of these developments has changed from those first straight rows of look-alike Cape Cod style homes. Today's newly built neighborhood usually features a variety of styles that have been designed and built in response to the climate, character and needs of the geographical area. And they are comfortable!

New houses in a planned neighborhood often represent "the American dream" in the media. But, in fact, "the dream house" in the minds of buyers has as many variations as the proverbial snowflake.

So you'll have a lot of choices. You can get one bathroom or four. Single-story houses, split-level houses, two- and even three-story houses. Basement or no basement. No garage or up to "three-car" or more. And all in neighborhoods created in the plans of a developer. If property ownership among houses that are all approximately the same age and valued within a narrow price range is your dream, your challenge will be to find the particular house that fits your needs in a neighborhood that will harmonize with and enhance your lifestyle.

Well, actually... The *challenge* is finding all that in a price range that you can afford! Many would say *that* is a large part of the pursuit of happiness.

Penny for Your Thoughts
• •

"We hold these truths to be self-evident; that all men are created equal; that they are endowed by their creator with certain unalienable rights; that among these are life, liberty, and the pursuit of happiness..."

Thomas Jefferson (1743–1826)

What's Beyond This Gateway?

If you've driven about in suburban America, you've surely seen the signs mounted on gateways or stone pillars: Cactus Corners, Deer Crossing, Palm Estates, Stonewood, Happy Valley, Windsor Chase—the list could go on forever. These are the names developers chose for the communities they created.

Some names stay with their neighborhoods over decades, others are forgotten soon after the last ad for new construction is pulled from the newspapers. But with or without a name, the communities usually retain their identities because of the similarity in size, style, age, amenities, construction and lot size.

Single-family detached and *similar* are the key words at this gateway because no more specific description of the concept of subdivision development could possibly capture the range of character in all the planned communities that have been built over half a century. There are communities of small houses on small lots, small houses on spacious lots, huge houses on small lots, huge houses on huge lots, and medium-size houses on all kinds of lots.

The two primary motivators for purchasing houses in the American subdivision are:

• **investment security** created by clusters of similar properties supporting the value of all, and

• **the perception of lifestyle enhancement** created by living in a community that is socioeconomically homogeneous.

Words to the Wise

There are several words often confused when talking about American suburban neighborhoods. Let's set them straight.

• **Development:** a construction project in which the relationship of buildings (how they are located on a pattern of streets) is planned for. In residential housing, it is usually a community of houses similar in value. You may hear people say, "We live in the development just off Maple Avenue." A residential development is always a neighborhood, but a neighborhood is not always a development.

• **Developer:** (1) a builder; (2) one who gets subdivision approval, prepares the unimproved land for building, puts in the roads, and then sells lots or packages of lots to builders.

• **Tract:** a parcel of land. In common usage, however, tract has also come to mean a parcel of land that has been subdivided for a housing development. You might hear a real estate agent say, "We've just listed the Happy Valley tract."

• **Tract house:** one of many similar houses in a subdivision built from plans chosen by the developer. Its opposite is the custom-built house, often designed by an architect for a particular client and a particular lot. You may sometimes hear the term "tract house" used in a derogatory way but, in fact, most of the suburban housing now in use is tract housing.

• **Subdivision:** the creation of two or more lots from one parcel of land by filing a map describing the new lots and obtaining approval from city or county commissions. In common usage the term "subdivision" is used to mean the community of houses on a tract of land that has been subdivided. You might hear someone say, "The Johnsons live in the big subdivision on Blueberry Hill."

Given the fact that you can find subdivisions of Spanish haciendas, glass-and-stone contemporaries, New England saltboxes, Southern plantation houses and numerous other regional styles, let's organize our discussion of what's available through this gateway by price tag—that is, starter homes, step-up homes, and status homes.

Starter Homes

One of the biggest unfulfilled demands in today's housing market is the *new* small and inexpensive home. Builders make more money building larger, more luxurious, pricier homes. In areas where demand for inexpensive housing is high, they have found building condominium or townhouse communities more profitable. As a result, it's very difficult to find new or nearly new developments of single-family detached homes at the low end of the price scale. If you do find one in your area, consider it carefully. It may be a very good buy because demand far outpaces supply.

Most starter homes can be found in developments that are 25 or more years old. Usually they have three bedrooms and a total of five to seven rooms. These four housing styles are common:

Cape Cod

This was the style of choice for many of the early postwar building tracts because it was easy to build and the second floor could be left unfinished but available for future expansion, typically when the children came. The basic house was a square box of four rooms. Center-hall stairs led to an unfinished attic where, if the first owner paid for it, two dormer windows in front and windows on the two ends provided light. Most of those attics have now been transformed into two bedrooms with a bath between them. Unless full dormers have been added at the back of the house, however, upstairs ceilings are still slanted. With inadequate insulation under the roof, the rooms can be hot in the summer and cold in the winter.

Ranch

Popular with early developers and still popular today, the terms "ranch" or "ranch-style" house are applied to any single-story floor plan. Most ranches built in the '50s and early '60s have only one bathroom; those built more recently usually have 1½ baths or more. Many owners of '50s and early '60s ranches have added family rooms at the back of their homes; others have created basement "rec" rooms. The added main-level family room increases value somewhat; the basement rec room does not.

Words to the Wise
• •

A **starter home** is not always a first real estate purchase. In the marketplace, the term has come to mean a small, relatively inexpensive house in a subdivision of like houses. You'll often see advertisements in newspapers captioned **Ideal Starter Home!** Only very rarely will the text describe a condominium, a multifamily home, or even a fixer-upper.

Split-level

The split-level style came "in" as the popularity of the Cape Cod began to fade in the '50s. Like the Cape, it was built in huge, look-alike developments. The main level has a small kitchen, a dining area, and a living room. A half flight up are three bedrooms and a half flight down is a small family room. Some buyers complain that you're *always* going up and down stairs for *everything*. Others object to the lower-level family room. Most split-levels have more than one bathroom.

Bi-level, split foyer, or raised ranch

This style came into popularity nationwide with the call for large "family rooms" in the mid '60s. In the split foyer version, the entry foyer is between floors and the lower floor is sometimes partially below grade level. Upstairs is a traditional ranch floor plan; downstairs a large family room, laundry room, utility room, garage, and sometimes another bedroom. There is no basement.

Many buyers object to the split entry, and this style is often difficult to sell. Some buyers don't like an entry that feels suspended in space—when you walk in you're neither here nor there. Others don't like the formal living room near the kitchen and the family room "in the cellar."

Starter homes are most easily found in the early, close-in suburbs that first surrounded the central core of cities. Some small-home developments that were originally lower priced because they were considered to be in the farthest-out suburbs in the '60s, however, are now tucked in among desirable developments of larger and even luxury homes. Location among such up-scale neighbors usually raises their value, sometimes pricing them right out of the starter-home range.

Don't Assume

Don't assume that a house is worth $30,000 more than its neighbor because it recently had a $30,000 addition. No matter what improvements have been made, a tract house is not likely to sell for more than 15% above the average price in the neighborhood.

Because of their age, many starters are also fixer-uppers or candidates for renovation. If you want a house in this marketplace area but are a bit strapped for down-payment money, you may be able to break in through the Craft and Creativity Gateway. (Be sure to read Chapter 3.)

Step-Up Homes

Step-ups are homes purchased after you have grown some equity in the real estate marketplace. Although they can occur in any marketplace area, those beyond the American Image Gateway are newer (sometimes even new), larger and more comfortable than starter homes. The general standard today is eight rooms with four bedrooms and 2½ baths. A two-car garage is also expected.

The homes in these developments, built in the '70s or later, are usually designed with consideration for the local geography, economy and history. Many houses in the Southwest, for example, tend to have a hint of adobe. In the Northeast, you're likely to see a development featuring the colonial "saltbox." Step-up homes come in one- and two-story plans, with contemporaries sometimes featuring multilevels. Although you will sometimes find step-up developments in the near suburbs, most are located in the farther suburbs and require serious commuting.

Status Homes

The third area in the American Image marketplace comes close to the realization of a dream house for many people. These are the affluent developments built in the '80s and '90s. Most of these houses have 3,000 square feet or more in living area and feature four or five bedrooms, three or more luxury baths, three-car garages, and large decks, porches and patios.

Landscaping in these developments is far more extensive than in lower-cost areas, sometimes including stone pillars, arbors and "islands of greenery," and individual lots are usually larger. Larger, of course, is a relative term. If the average house in an area is on a postage stamp, then a quarter-acre might suffice for the status house. If mid-price houses can be found on an acre, however, then the typical status house might have three, or even five acres. Even though all the floor plans of the houses may be duplicates of three or four "models," the facades are made to look different enough to give the impression of custom-built housing.

Some single-family, detached, status homes are in communities that include condominium ownership of recreation areas such as golf courses, tennis courts, swimming pools, walking trails and clubhouses. In these communities, the homeowner holds title to the house and the lot it stands on and holds an undivided interest in the common areas. (If you're getting confused with the terms, read Chapter 6.) In some communities, the homeowner owns the house but the condominium community owns the land it stands on as well as all the roads within the community.

One of the distinguishing features of some luxury single-family developments with some form of condominium ownership is the use of controlled access for security. Commonly called *gated communities,* these developments feature privately maintained roads that all feed into one entryway, which connects to a public road. Visitors who wish to enter must have the owner's permission registered with the gatekeeper. These gated communities are attractive not only to business people who are often away from home but also to retirees who travel extensively.

Penny for Your Thoughts

Love your neighbor, but don't pull down the hedge.

Swiss proverb

Why Enter This Gateway?

Why is the American Image Gateway the most sought-after of all? Certainly it must satisfy many of the motives that make home buying so much a part of the American character. Here are some of the most common reasons homeowners cite for choosing to live in a neighborhood of similar, single-family houses. (Weigh the following motives carefully. If this gateway seems like a good fit with your homeowner personality, confirm your hunch with the self-test beginning on the following page.)

Privacy

This is number one! It seems virtually everyone would like a little earth and air around his or her living quarters. Many people feel that the shared walls, ceilings, and floors of multifamily housing let everything pass through but whispers. Outdoors, even the smallest lot allows for some measure of undisturbed enjoyment, a barbecue area, a play area, a garden and a place for pets.

Family matters

Young parents usually want to buy a house on a safe street where there is a likelihood of finding convenient playmates for their children. Many fathers and mothers also enjoy the proximity of other parents like themselves. The planned subdivision is especially appealing to "movable" people because it makes settling in and establishing a new social circle easier for these transient folks.

Security

In a nation where street crime is an ever-present concern, many people feel safer in the midst of a community of people like themselves. Neighbors tend to watch each others' houses and children. And strangers in the streets are quickly spotted.

Equity protection

Just as a school of fish enhances each member's survival, the planned community improves each owner's

Continued on page 172

Self-Test Before You Choose This Gateway

The following, three-part self-assessment will help you evaluate whether you have what it takes to successfully pursue the homeowning options outlined in this chapter. It focuses on the 10 important homebuyer personality characteristics described in Chapter 2.

PART I: RATE YOURSELF

In Part I, below, read each of the self-descriptive statements for each characteristic and decide how well it describes you. Grade your response on a scale from 1, "Not me at all!" to 5, "That's me all the way!" Encourage your spouse or home-buying partner(s) to do the same.

Certain statements pertain to only one or two gateway options. If those don't interest you, skip those statements.

If your ratings vary within a category, average them.

Turn to the following page to see how you've fared.

Creative vision

___ I do not like to stand out from the group (I like to belong to the group).

___ I like things balanced and harmonious.

Time and skills for work and maintenance

___ If paint is peeling on the shutters, I take them down and paint them.

___ To keep the neighborhood looking neat, I pull weeds and trim grass along the road in front of my house even though it isn't actually my property.

Self-confidence

___ I feel more secure when I can see lights on in my neighbors' houses.

___ When I have to hire contractors for repairs or improvements, I usually choose well and get my money's worth.

___ Though it's occasionally a bit tight, I'm confident that I can afford the mortgage payments. Next year I'll be getting a raise, with a promotion likely within a few years. We'll be just fine!

Flexibility and adaptability

___ The neighbors complained about Hamlet, our harlequin Great Dane. He's so friendly, and he'd never hurt a flea, and he was always loose in our old neighborhood. I don't believe in chaining a dog so we adapted to neighborhood custom and had an electronic, "invisible" fence installed.

___ A room for every purpose and a purpose for every room. I'm not interested in having to make do or force a room to accommodate several functions.

___ While bedrooms should be bedrooms, I don't mind if my kids use one for a sleeping room and one for a playroom.

Willingness to take risks

___ I want the market value of my property to be as secure as possible.

___ Before I make an improvement to my property, I check to see whether anyone else in the neighborhood has

Self-Test, Cont'd.

made a similar improvement and ask them how they like it and if they think it increased the value of their house. If there's been a tax reassessment since their improvement was made, I might even sneak a peek at the tax records.

Perseverance

___ I put down the fertilizer and weedkiller every spring, and then I go after the dandelions with the spot spray.

___ It will probably take me the whole summer to put a patio in the backyard, but, by George, I'll do it!

Attention to detail

___ When a faucet starts to leak, I change the washer. If that doesn't work, I call the plumber.

___ I would choose new carpeting in a neutral color so that it would flow from room to room without abrupt color changes at each doorway.

Planning and evaluation skills

___ I keep a maintenance calendar to remind me when to change the furnace filters, add salt to the water softener, clean the gutters, and, yes, even wash the windows.

___ I want to take a class on home landscaping and develop a five-year plan for our lot.

___ Every year or two, I evaluate our comfort level in this house. Are we happy here? Can we afford a bigger house? Do we want a bigger house?

Tact and communication skills

___ I can politely tell my neighbor that coming upon his child's Power Ranger figures buried in my garden is somewhat unnerving.

___ I can give clear directions to the people I hire to do work on my property.

___ The shutters on the house down the street were peeling badly and it made the neighborhood look really unkempt. So I organized a kind of joke/hint. Everybody on the street contributed to buy the owner two gallons of house-trim paint for his birthday! Great laugh and it got the job done.

Negotiating skills

___ I think price negotiations are difficult and I'm happy when they're over. But I definitely want a good deal.

___ Before I make an offer I always get the selling prices for similar nearby properties that sold during the past year.

PART II: WHAT'S IMPORTANT AND WHY

Now let's turn the tables and look at the home-buyer personality characteristics from the point of view of demand—that is, how vital the characteristic is to success through this gateway, and why. Each characteristic is rated from 1 to 5 (1 being low demand, 3 being variable demand that might be higher in some instances and lower in others, and 5 being high demand).

Creative vision: 2

The harmony and uniformity of builders' developments helps to set guidelines for appearance and function. Houses that are strikingly different from their neighbors often sell less quickly. An appreciation for and a willingness to conform with prevalent styles is a plus.

Time and skills for work and maintenance: 3

Good maintenance is an important factor in home value, and a certain amount of work must be done each week and each season in every single-family home. If you don't have the time or inclination to do this work, however, you can hire maintenance workers on a regular basis (lawn-mowing teams, for example) or when needed (plumbers and painters, for example).

Self-confidence: 3

A neighborhood of similar houses usually promotes a sense of security and belonging. Homeowners feel that they can get help when they need it because they are all dealing with similar problems, say, of family and career. Life is easier with this gateway's homeowning options if you feel confident that you can maintain a lifestyle similar to that of your neighbors.

Flexibility and adaptability: 1

If you choose a neighborhood and a house that is right for you, you will need but little bending to make it work. Problems come up when you try to make yourself conform to a new mold when you have bought in a neighborhood that is not right for you.

Willingness to take risks: 1

Houses in well-maintained developments are among the least risky real estate investments. What risk there is comes from factors beyond your control—the economy, for example, or natural disasters like earthquakes and floods.

Perseverance: 4

It's important to stick with problems and projects until they are resolved or completed. Problems that are "let go" tend to grow, like the lawn! Unfinished projects and untended maintenance items hurt resale value.

Attention to detail: 4

Sometimes the demands of a house in suburbia seem trivial and endless. How well you attend to them or have them attended to will affect the value of your investment, the comfort of your lifestyle, and sometimes the friendliness of your neighbors.

Planning and evaluation skills: 4

Evaluating how well a house is fulfilling your needs—whether comfort is worth the cost, and what maintenance work and improvements need to be done (and when)—is sometimes hard. You might rather spend the time and money on a much-needed vacation. But unless you take charge of planning, budgeting and saving—somewhat bothersome parts of homeownership—you are letting your investment control you. Planning when to sell and move on is always a factor for movable people.

Tact and communication skills: 3

Living comfortably in a community, any community, requires that you learn to deal with everyday issues such as other people's children and pets, a neighbor's habitual lawn-mowing at 7 A.M. on Sunday, and backyard barbecue noise and smoke. Sure, you can choose a development that you think will offer a maximum of privacy and quiet, but even if the neighbors are an acre and a half away, there will inevitably be issues of mutual interest or conflict, even on a limited scale, that you'll have to discuss.

Negotiating skills: 2

Any real estate professional will tell you that houses in homogeneous subdivisions are among the easiest to appraise because comparables are usually readily available. (Read Chapter 11 with care.) If you use comparables and determine an accurate estimate of fair market value, you will have strong guidelines for your negotiating.

Self-Test, Cont'd.

PART III: THE CRITICAL COMPARISON

Now you can compare your self-ratings with the importance ratings for each characteristic to see how likely you are to measure up to the demands of this gateway. In the left column of the graph, the characteristics are presented in descending order from highest to lowest demand for this gateway. The black bars show each characteristic's importance rating. Use the space allowed to draw in your and your buying partner's results.

- **If you rated yourself *most* highly on this gateway's *most* important characteristics** (at least 4 on characteristics rated 5, and at least

3 on those rated 4), this gateway may be the one for you.

- **If you *also* rated yourself highly on the gateway's *least* important characteristics** (4s or 5s on characteristics rated 3 or less), other gateways might provide additional options suited to your strengths.

- **If you rated yourself highly *only* on the gateway's *least* important characteristics** (those rated 3 or less), look to another gateway for your best home-buying opportunities.

- **Be sure to look at your partner's strengths and weaknesses.** Is your partner strong where you're weak? Is it realistic to expect your partner to pick up the slack?

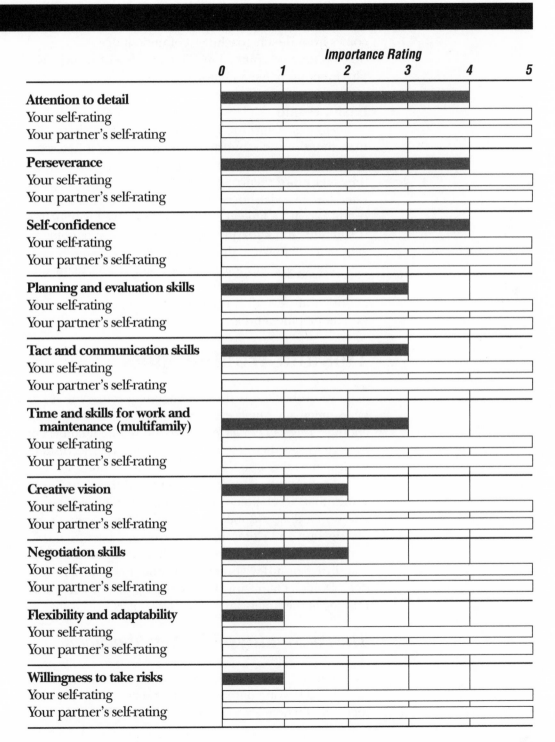

Importance Rating

	0	1	2	3	4	5

Attention to detail
Your self-rating
Your partner's self-rating

Perseverance
Your self-rating
Your partner's self-rating

Self-confidence
Your self-rating
Your partner's self-rating

Planning and evaluation skills
Your self-rating
Your partner's self-rating

Tact and communication skills
Your self-rating
Your partner's self-rating

Time and skills for work and maintenance (multifamily)
Your self-rating
Your partner's self-rating

Creative vision
Your self-rating
Your partner's self-rating

Negotiation skills
Your self-rating
Your partner's self-rating

Flexibility and adaptability
Your self-rating
Your partner's self-rating

Willingness to take risks
Your self-rating
Your partner's self-rating

financial safety. The market value of a house in a neighborhood of similar houses is protected against the loss that comes from the encroachment of undesirable commercial development or conversion. This investment security is a plus for both rooted and moveable people.

Easier resale

Houses within subdivisions are usually easier to sell than those of the same style, size and age in a heterogeneous community. Buyers seem to be attracted because they feel more secure in their ability to judge property value when similar houses just around the corner have recently sold. It's a little like the American love for franchise restaurants. You know just how much beef you're going to get when you pull into the parking lot.

The desirability and high turnover rate in many subdivisions is an attraction for movable people who are frequently transferred. But rooted people also do just fine with development living.

Tips and Trouble Spots

You've probably heard the denigrating remark that has been aimed at virtually every ethnic group at some time or another: *Yeah, but they all look alike!* And yet the members of the group see themselves as quite different and distinct from all the others. So it is with development houses.

Finding the right development and the right house within that development is often a matter of picking up and responding to subtle clues. And just as you don't notice the dust and clutter in your own home because it is so familiar, some home buyers miss these clues because they take living in a development as something "everybody" does. Don't let familiarity blur your judgment when house-hunting in the American Image marketplace area.

The Personality of the Neighborhood

You can learn a lot just by driving the neighborhood streets and looking out for clues that might affect your life there. As you note each factor, ask yourself, "Would I like to live next door?" and "Do I feel comfortable here?" Here's a list of clues to start you off. You'll certainly add others of your own. (And, you'll find plenty more on choosing a neighborhood in Chapter 11.)

- **Are there toys and bicycles** in the yards?

- **Are there basketball hoops** at the end of driveways?

- **Do weeds** grow along the curbs?

- **How many yards are fenced?**

- **Do you see any dogs** running about loose?

- **Are there extra cars** parked in the driveways? On the street? (More than two cars per house usually means teens or college students are part of the family.)

> # It's the Law!
> •
>
> **Local government standards:** Local zoning ordinances help to establish and maintain the character of subdivision neighborhoods. Besides restricting a development to single-family residences and setting out the minimum lot size, for example, zoning laws can restrict the maximum number of stories in a building, the minimum setback from the road, and even whether homeowners can keep horses, or chickens, on the property. (For more on zoning, see Chapter 11, "Your Piece of the Earth.")

- **Can you see recreational vehicles,** boats, snowmobiles or motorcycles parked on some properties?

- **Are there patios or decks** and barbecue grills on just about every lot?

- **Do you see adults walking** or bicycle riding for exercise?

- **Are residents friendly and willing to chat** about life in the neighborhood? Stop your car, get out, and ask someone who is raking or pulling weeds about the school bus stop or the distance to the nearest convenience store. It usually helps to tell prospective neighbors that you are considering purchasing the "Smiths'" house. Sometimes you get more information than you expected!

Watch Out for Steering

Despite decades of legislation to prevent racial discrimination, prejudice still exists. It can show itself with a "not-in-my-neighborhood" attitude from sellers in development communities.

The vast majority of agreements to list property for sale in this country state that the listing real estate agent must be willing to show the property to all financially qualified prospective buyers. But there are always the few agents who risk loss of their licenses to help support the prejudices of an owner or group of owners. The practice of showing some buyers only certain areas and not making them aware of some houses that are for sale is called *steering*.

If you are concerned that steering may be a factor in your house hunt, ask to see the printed listing book and spend some time reading through all the listings in your price range. If you see listings that seem right for you, ask the agent to show the properties. If you are not satisfied

Don't Assume

Municipal services

Don't assume that a suburban development will have the same municipal services you expect in a city neighborhood. In many parts of the country, subdivisions still get drinking water from private wells. Instead of sewers, waste disposal is handled by septic tanks or other private sewage systems. Refuse may not be collected by the town but by private haulers whom you must pay separately for the service.

You'll make the payment for refuse pick-up and well and septic-system maintenance out of pocket rather than having the services provided by the town and paid for by your property taxes. And unlike those taxes, you can't deduct the out-of-pocket cost of services on your federal income tax return!

Septic suspicions

Don't assume that those especially green spots in the lawn are places where the spring fertilizer ran out of the spreader too quickly. The grass is greener over the septic

tank. And you may even find the extra green extending out over the leach lines (the buried gravel trails under the surface of your lawn through which water is drawn away from the septic tank to drain or evaporate). If you look a little closer you may see swarms of tiny bugs hovering. Those bugs are probably breeding in standing water, and that could mean poor drainage and soggy land.

Same subdivision, different builders

Don't assume that all the houses in a subdivision are built by the same builder. Sometimes the developer who subdivides the land and puts in the roads sells packages of lots to different builders. Sometimes a developer/builder goes bankrupt or just quits before all the lots are built on, and another builder or builders finish the community. The town building inspector's office can give you the name of the builder for the house that interests you.

with the service your agent is providing, change agents! (You'll find more on this in Chapter 13.)

The Tales Taxes Tell

You can learn lots in the tax assessor's office. Property-tax information is public record and you can find out the tax assessment and property tax of every prospective neighbor with a quick trip to the town hall.

Why bother? Because the information will help you to judge the market value of a property you are considering. By comparing assessments, you can:

- **See how large the value range is** for the entire subdivision, and thereby,

- **Get a good idea of where "your" property's value stands** in relation to the others in the neighborhood;

- **Estimate where the value range of this subdivision lies** in relation to values throughout the town; and

- **Note which properties in the subdivision have been improved** with additions or major amenities.

Who Was the Builder?

When you are considering a purchase in a newer development, the builder is often still working in the area—either completing work on that development or perhaps on another one in the same town. Get the name of the builder either from the real estate agent or from town building-permit records, and find out where his (or her) newest project is. Then go there. You can learn a lot by taking a close look at buildings under construction.

- **What materials are being used?** Check for brand names that you might recognize. Windows, for example, will still have manufacturer's labels on them. Quality exterior plywood will usually have a name stamped on it. How is the foundation constructed—poured concrete? cinder blocks? Ask the real estate agent which is customary in the area and why.

- **How is the building being protected from weather damage during construction?** Are protective coverings used on roofless, windowless buildings or does the rainwater just dry? "Just drying" can cause warping.

- **Is the construction site clean and organized** or littered with debris?

Besides visiting a current construction site, you can also do a little detective work with your prospective neighbors. Ask them:

- **Are they satisfied with the new house they bought?** What do they like or dislike about the builder's work, the floor plan for their model or anything else?

- **Did the builder have to make a lot of return trips for "adjustments,"** like moldings coming away from the floor or a leaking roof? What were they?

- **Was the builder cooperative?** Did he return promptly to correct any problems?

- **Have they heard about anyone else in the neighborhood having problems?** People are often much more willing to talk about *other* people's problems.

In older developments, the builder is often long gone. But you can stop and talk with neighbors about recurring maintenance problems in the area that may be the result of faulty building practices.

- **Do basements flood?**

- **Is siding being repaired or replaced** in one house after another because of inadequate materials?

- **Inside, are nails popping in the wallboard** because green lumber was used in framing?

- **Are floors not level?** Do eggs roll off the kitchen countertops?

Plats and Plots

For every subdivision in town there is a map, called a *plat,* on file in the town records showing the position, boundaries and dimensions of each lot in the tract. When new houses in a development are being sold, the plat map is usually included with the marketing material.

Even if you are buying in a well-established development, long divorced from its builder, it's worth the effort to find the plat plan in the town records. By finding your lot on the plan, you can get an overview of its position in the development.

Some plats include topographical markings indicating changes in elevation. Designated wetlands and flood plains are also usually indicated. Try to avoid properties that are located at low points in the subdivision, which tend to collect water. Also try to choose properties above the grade level of the road rather than below it.

All proposed roads are indicated on a plat. If you come upon a cul-de-sac that seems somehow "funny" to you (it just ends suddenly), you can check the plat to see if it was originally proposed as a through street. The extension is called a "paper street." Be wary because it can be completed at a later date and that can completely change the character of a street.

The *plot plan* shows the location of improvements on the tract, including recreational improvements, community centers and any other buildings that have been constructed. The plot map for an individual lot will show the location of the house, the driveway and any other improvements, such as decks, patios, a shed or even a treehouse.

The plot plan of the development may be especially important to you if a dam has been built or extensive work has been done to divert the course of a stream or to drain a boggy area. By studying it you can determine where your property is in relation to the stream bed and storm drains.

Words to the Wise

• •

A **plat plan** or **plat map** is a drawing showing how a parcel of land is divided into lots. Don't confuse this term with **plot plan** or **plot map** which is a map showing the location of improvements (such as buildings, bridges, retaining walls, sewers and so on) on a parcel of land.

If the plat for your property does not show topography and you are concerned about your location in relation to the rest of the development, you can get topographical information on **U.S. Geological Survey** maps. They are available to the public. On page 289 in Chapter 11, there's an address and phone number to help you find the map for your area.

This is important because streams sometimes perversely like to return to their old beds.

If your property is located in an area designated as a special flood hazard area by the Army Corps of Engineers, you will be required by federal law to purchase flood insurance in order to get a federally insured mortgage. (Note that the law doesn't refer to flood plain. That's because all flood plains are not designated as special flood hazard areas. For example, a "100-year flood plain"—one that floods once every 100 years—might fit in this category.) Sellers and real estate agents are required by state disclosure laws to inform you about location in a flood hazard area. You can get more information on the federal flood insurance program by writing to: **National Flood Insurance Program** (P.O. Box 6468, Rockville, MD 20849; 800–638–6620).

Words to the Wise

• •

Eminent domain is the term for the government's right to acquire private property for the public good or public use. The enabling process is called **condemnation.** The government must pay the owner "just compensation" (usually interpreted as fair market value) for any property that is acquired by condemnation.

What's Coming?

A quick visit to the town's planning or zoning office before you buy might help to protect both your investment and your comfort level in the years to come. There you will find wall-size maps of the town showing not only roads and lot lines but also open land with its designated possible uses. If land near your subdivision is zoned for commercial or industrial use, future development could lower the value of your property, because most people prefer not to live close to such areas. This is also true of land zoned for high-density housing such as apartment buildings. Designated "open space" land, however, can improve the value of nearby properties because it protects privacy and quiet use.

Also on the planning-office maps look for indications of the projected paths of major highways that are scheduled for development. Be wary of buying property close to future roads even when "everyone" assures you that such development is "20 years away" or even that "it will never happen." If the highway is built, you could lose your home because the state claims *eminent domain,* condemns your property, buys you out, and forces you to move. Or, worse yet, the state could condemn some nearby properties but not yours, and you could find yourself with I–2001 in your backyard.

One Gateway to Another

More than any other home-buying option, the houses beyond the American Image Gateway represent the vast range of traditional middle America. From the practicality of the first Levittown, on Long Island, to the graceful elegance of a status neighborhood like The Woodlands, north of Houston, the planned community is a favorite choice of families. It is where we imagine the Cleavers and the Brady Bunch living. Single people and single-parent households are usually in the minority. There are, however, a good number of empty-nesters in most established communities.

Home buyers who can purchase their first home in this marketplace area often move up in size and luxury over the years by selling and then buying within another subdivision. Frequent corporate transferees will often consider only houses in planned developments. Many home buyers, however, come to this gateway after ownership of other types of housing, most commonly fixer-uppers, multifamily houses and condominiums.

The majority of home buyers who choose the American Image Gateway stay within its marketplace for most of their homeowning years. Divorce, retirement, working for oneself and newfound wealth are the most common moti-

---

Don't Assume
● ●

Don't assume that the zoning designations for undeveloped land are carved in stone. Consider them as guidelines or probabilities. Zoning comes under the auspices of the town's planning office and plans can be changed. The process of change involves notification of all surrounding owners. The protests of these owners, however, are not necessarily heeded, no matter how loudly or how urgently they are voiced.

vators for change. The shared common areas and community protection of the Shared-Space Gateway appeal to many divorced and retired people. These home buyers are especially attracted to the new townhouse-style condominiums. (Read about condos in Chapter 6.)

Self-employment sometimes sends American Image homeowners to the Independent Spirit Gateway. And some newly wealthy people decide to have architect-designed homes built and jump over to the New-Construction Gateway.

Although it is the goal of many home buyers, living in the American subdivision is not Heaven. Every neighborhood has not only an identifiable character but also identifiable problems and limitations.

Your investment dollar will be protected by the neighborhood, but you will have little or no opportunity to use your house to increase your income. You will be restricted to single-family usage and may have difficulty getting zoning-board approval to add even an in-law apartment.

Additions, outbuildings and even the pets you keep (remember, no horses or chickens!) will be restricted by zoning laws.

You will probably need a car for every adult family member because public transportation is virtually nonexistent and you simply can't walk to anything in or near most subdivisions. And you will chauffeur or car-pool your children to their after-school activities.

On the other hand, you may well enjoy a progressive dinner party on New Year's Eve. You can send your son or daughter over to your neighbor's house to do a little "borrowing" if you discover you're out of coffee one morning. At vacation time, you may be able to swap pet-sitting duties with another dog- or cat-loving neighbor, and you'll probably have little trouble getting someone to "watch the house" and take in the mail. You may even be able to find a simpatico group to walk the development's streets every morning at 6.

So much for "the American Dream" neighborhood. Can you do it? Do you want to? Remember: Success is finding the neighborhood you can afford with a character that lets you fit in and problems you can handle.

Being the First:
The New-Construction
Gateway

- **Spec Houses**

- **To-Be-Built in a Development**

- **Architect-Assisted**

- **Custom Construction With a General Contractor**

- **Being Your Own General Contractor**

- **Factory-Built Homes**

Whether it's the first president, the first human being to set foot on the moon, or the first family member to graduate college, being the first is an accomplishment. There is a bit of awe in the air. People take notice. The achiever of the "first" gains a new status. That aura also surrounds the owner of a brand-new home on a once vacant piece of real estate.

As is typical in the real estate marketplace, however, new status must be earned. A new home is not only a source of pride, a potential haven of comfort and convenience, and an aesthetically pleasing addition to the neighborhood, but also a tangible expression of time spent, decisions made, attention paid, and commitments honored.

Although there's certainly excitement and satisfaction at starting with a clean slate and choosing colors and styles in everything to suit your own taste, buying new is not easy. Of all the attractions at the Great Real Estate Carnival, this one's the fun house. When you pay for this ride, you climb into a rickety little car on a single track and go through a doorway into the dark. Before you come back into the light, a myriad of *things* jump out at you. Some new-construction homeowners even call their experience a horror show.

You can decrease the impact of the fun-house ride by becoming aware of what's in store for you. Surprise is a key factor in fright and intimidation. Once you know what makes the tyrannosaurus jump out of the walls, it becomes more fascinating and less frightening. Once you understand the steps in the process of buying new construction, they become less bothersome. Even the surprises can become manageable.

Because most new construction takes place today in builders' developments, the American Image and New-Construction Gateways share many common factors. Buying new, however, adds many complexities. Rather than repeat the advice in Chapter 8, this gateway will focus only on aspects of *newness* in buying a home in a development. If this is your choice, be certain that you read Chapter 8.

Advance thought, planning and careful attention to detail are the essential tools for success in this marketplace area. It also helps to approach complex situations or even apparent chaos with a calm, problem-solving attitude.

What's Beyond This Gateway?

Unless you peeked ahead, you may be thinking, "Well, this will be a nice short section. New construction is new construction, right?"

Surprise! You probably didn't realize that there are so many ways to become a first owner. You can buy a house:

- **built on "spec"**

- **"to-be-built" from a builder's plans in a development**

- **custom designed by an architect** who will also supervise construction

- **built by a general contractor** you've hired for custom construction of a home from plans you have selected

- **built by subcontractors under your supervision,** with you acting as your own general contractor

- **factory-built and transported to your site** and assembled there by a maker of manufactured, modular or panelized homes.

Whew! Small hub—lotta spokes!

The Spec House

Today, buyers will find most of the houses being built on speculation in builder's developments. A small number of independent builders, however, still look for the single lot for sale and build a house they intend to sell either during construction or soon after. Many buyers say the builders who do one house at a time are the most attentive to their work and therefore produce a finer house. On the other hand, independent builders do not have the big developers' buying power to get materials at lower prices and keep the cost of a new home down.

Buying a spec house takes a lot of the uncertainty out of being the first. Once the foundation is in and building has begun, the paper plans are gradually transformed into three-dimensional reality. Many buyers feel more comfortable being able to see what they are buying: How big is it? How does it sit on the lot? How does it feel to walk from the kitchen to the family room? What is the view from the dining room? And a hundred other homeowning concerns.

When the closing date is important, a completed or nearly completed spec house may allow a buyer to choose a new house without worry over completion date. Buyers can usually put to rest concerns over safe and adequate drinking water and waste disposal because the systems are

Words to the Wise

- **Builder and developer** are defined in Chapter 8 on page 161.

- **A general contractor** is the person or company that contracts for the construction of an entire building or project. The person for whom the house will be built pays the general contractor the agreed-on price for the home.

- The general contractor hires and supervises all **the subcontractors**. Framers, roofers, electricians and plumbers are just some of the subcontractors who will work on the construction of a home. The general contractor is responsible for negotiating the price for each job and paying the subcontractors.

- **Spec house** refers to new construction built on speculation by a general contractor. Without a buyer in sight, the builder chooses a lot and a plan and begins construction. The buyer might come along when only the framing is complete or not until the house has stood completed for many months.

already functioning and must meet or already have met local building codes. In short, you can see and test what you are buying before you must commit your money. This choice poses the least risk and is the least headache-inducing of any of the home-buying opportunities within the New-Construction Gateway. On the other hand, by choosing the spec house you may relinquish one of the primary incentives for buying new—the chance to make the many choices that are a part of building your own home. Depending on the stage of construction at which you decide to buy, you may or may not be able to choose:

- siding materials and color

- exterior trim color

- roofing materials and their color

- window type, style and brand

- alternate floor plans

- flooring materials (eg., hardwood, ceramic tile or carpet)

- plumbing and electrical fixtures

Don't Assume

More than one builder to a development

Don't assume that every development is controlled by just one builder. If you do, you might give up on a great location because you don't like the builder who's in control.

Some developers get subdivision approval, put in the roads, and then sell all or some of the lots to builders or home buyers.

Even when one developer-builder does control an entire tract, he might sell a single lot (usually on the fringe) to someone who wants to hire another builder or wants to act as his or her own general contractor. You'll never know if the builder will do this unless you ask.

Real estate agents can help you locate tracts where several different builders are working and lots are for sale.

The model: Is it the real deal?

Don't assume that the house you contract to have built will look exactly like the model. Many builders change the facades of their houses to give the development a "custom" look. They also fit and furnish most models with upgraded materials and maximum extras.

Ask exactly what the home you are buying will look like, what the price includes and how that list of features, systems and appliances compares with what you have seen in the model home.

- the type of heating system to be installed

- central air conditioning, if desired

- cabinets

- hardware

- the materials used to build the fireplace

- the size, style and location of a deck or porch

- the style of the front door

- and even the colors of the walls

To-Be-Built in a Development

Some spec houses are used as "models" for the houses to be built in a development project and are not for sale until all or most of the other available lots have been improved and sold. Salespeople show prospective buyers through three to five models and then ask them to choose a lot from a plan of the development (called a plat plan). Sometimes the builder has assigned certain models to certain lots; in other cases you can choose both the lot and the model you wish to have built on it.

Architect-Assisted

Most people are a bit intimidated by architects. They see these professionals as the engineer-artists who put up skyscrapers and churches, museums and famous houses like Frank Lloyd Wright's Fallingwater. Ordinary people think, "How could they possibly have time to redesign this magazine-clipping floor plan for me?" or "I couldn't even afford the shake-hands-how-are-you session, much less pay an architect to *work* on a house for me!"

Actually many architects do design individual, moderately priced houses, and many work with prospective homeowners who are considering new construction. With a little care and planning, a good architect can often *save* a client some money while adding considerable comfort and grace to a home.

Penny for Your Thoughts

Architecture begins where engineering ends.

Walter Gropius (1883-1969), founder of Bauhaus style of architecture; professor and chairman, Graduate School of Design, Harvard University

The most luxurious—and the most expensive—way to work with an architect is to put yourself totally into his or her hands. The architect will help with site selection, design the dwelling, advise in the choice of all materials and systems, and supervise the construction. Fees for this type of service can be a percentage of the final cost of the home, a flat fee based on the architect's proposal, or even an hourly rate.

But you may neither need nor want this Rolls-Royce style of service. If you have a sketch of what you want or a folder of magazine clippings that you've collected over the years, you can hire an architect to design your home and make a complete set of blueprints. You pay only a design fee. Once you have the plans you can hire a general contractor to execute them on the lot you choose, or you can act as your own general contractor (more about that in just a bit).

If you simply want advice or some minor changes on a off-the-shelf plan, you can also hire an architect by the hour. Don't be afraid to call several offices and ask what the hourly fee is. Compare what you will have to pay for design work and what that includes.

Custom Construction With a General Contractor

Custom construction usually means that you find and buy a lot and then hire a builder to put the house you want on it. The house may or may not be like others around it. After studying the plans and specifications that you provide, a general contractor will make a bid—the price for which he would build the house you want on your lot. To protect your current bank account, your future financial security and your sanity, experts all agree that you should get several bids. Comparing bids will often help you anticipate problems, not to mention keep you from hiring someone who's $50,000 more expensive than the average. The real challenge in hiring your own general contractor, however, is often in finding builders willing to bid.

The builders we easily recognize in our communities are usually running large subdivisions where several houses are going up simultaneously. Often the development of a large tract is being done by a corporation, and the builders in charge are the equivalent of corporate executives. It is difficult, usually impossible, to get those builders to consider building a single home on a lot far from their construction site. From a business perspective, they say, it just doesn't pay.

So what do you do when you've found the perfect lot and have the plans for the perfect house to go on it?

You hunt for an independent general contractor, also called a builder, who builds one house at a time on a single

More, More, More

Organizations

- **The American Institute of Architects** (1735 New York Ave., N.W., Washington, DC 20006; 800–242–9930; www.AIA.org) will supply you with a list of member architects who design private dwellings in your area. The AIA also has an assortment of booklets available to prospective new-construction homeowners—most of them free. Topics include: guides to architectural services and costs, what to ask an architect, how the architect will help, remodeling or additions, and how to evaluate a home site. Call or write for the current list of titles.

- **The Manufactured Housing Institute** (2101 Wilson Blvd., Suite 610, Arlington, VA 22201; 703–558–0400; fax, 703–558–0401). For more information on the possibilities of manufactured housing and the names of retailers in your area, contact the MHI, the national trade organization.

- **The National Association of Home Builders** (1201 15th St., N.W., Washington, DC 20005; 202–822–0200 http://www.NAHB.com) is the major trade group of North American home-building professionals. More than 50

years old, the NAHB now has more than 850 affiliated state and local associations. Local associations will provide you with names of their member builders. You can find your local group listed under "Associations" in your phone book, or you can get a list of associations in your area by contacting the NAHB at the address above. The NAHB's Internet site also lists local associations. Booklets on hiring and working with a builder are available to the public.

Books

Before you commit your money to do-it-yourself building, commit a little time to some in-depth reading. Check your library for specialized books such as:

- *Homing Instinct: Using Your Lifestyle to Design & Build Your Home,* by John Connell (Warner Books; out of print, look for it at your public library)

- *Building Your Home: An Insider's Guide,* by Carol Smith (Home Builder Press)

- *How To Plan, Contract and Build Your Own Home,* by Richard M. Scutella and David Heberle (TAB Books)

lot. If you are a rooted type and have been in the community for many years, you may well find such a person through the grapevine. You will hear of people who have successfully had custom homes built and you will begin to make calls. And of course, you'll ask them if they were satisfied with their builder.

What if you don't have deep ties to a community yet, but want to settle down and stay a long while in a house designed and built just for you? Where do you go to find the builder who can turn your dreams into tangible living space? Hang out at town hall. Chat with the folks in the planning office and the building inspector's office. These people work with local builders every day. Gather the names of the builders they know and respect, and names of the owners of recently built houses. Or ask your architect for the names of recommended builders.

It's the Law

The ultimate do-it-yourself project: Generally in the U.S., you can still build the home you will live in without having to use licensed contractors such as plumbers and electricians. But you'd better know what you're doing! All residential construction must meet local and state building codes. The local building inspector will evaluate each stage of the work, and you can't proceed with the next phase of building unless you pass!

Being Your Own General Contractor

In the tradition of the men and women who settled America, you can still build your own home. Well, maybe not exactly, but you can still supervise and participate in the building process by acting as your own general contractor. If you are committed and knowledgeable, you can succeed at saving many thousands of dollars.

Be aware, however, that you will not save time. When you decide to build your own home, you effectively take on a full-time job. And that's a job in addition to the full-time job that will pay the costs of building!

The biggest problem in do-it-yourself home building is not the do-it-yourself parts—it's finding subcontractors to do what you can't do. Subcontractor is the catchall marketplace term for the various specialists who contribute skills or services necessary to home building. Among them are excavators, masons, framers, roofers, carpenters, plumbers, heating contractors, electricians, painters and haulers (to cart away the debris).

Unless you have construction "connections" in your local area, you will spend a great deal of time just trying to find people who can and will do each job, not to mention persuading them to work at a reasonable and fair price. Once you find the subcontractors, scheduling them becomes the next challenge.

A subcontractor's failure to show up, or his slow or poor workmanship, usually causes a domino effect in the entire construction schedule because certain tasks or levels must be completed before others can begin. If you choose to act as your own general contractor, you'll spend untold hours on the phone and use every bit of communication and negotiating skill you've ever acquired.

Don't Assume

Don't assume that your subcontractors will show up when scheduled. Independent contractors generally follow the scent of money, and the homeowner-builder has relatively little money to offer. Given the choice between a job offered by a large developer and your job, most subcontractors go to the developer. After all, that job holds the promise of more jobs in the future. It's not nice, but that is the way it is.

Factory-Built Homes

Homes constructed in huge factories and delivered on wheels to the owner's site come in a tremendous variety today. This is a growing industry that has gone on the offensive and coined the somewhat derogatory term "stick-built" for those old-fashioned houses constructed from scratch on site.

Factory-built houses, in a direct ancestral line from the rounded-corner, shiny shoeboxes of the '50s and the not so "mobile" homes of the '60s and '70s, now are called *manufactured homes* and bear very little resemblance to their forerunners. Manufactured homes come in virtually every price range. But were you to drive by one, you probably wouldn't differentiate it from its stick-built cousins.

Manufactured houses can be ranches, split-levels, contemporaries, colonials or just about any style that is currently being stick-built. They are built to stringent federal standards that meet or exceed local building codes. Most will sit on permanent foundations. (Between 5% and 10% of manufactured homes are ever moved from their first location.)

Choosing this type of new construction eliminates the difficulties of finding materials and subcontractors and of scheduling construction work. The manufacturer will deliver everything, from the doorbell to the carpeting, at one time. Only water, waste-disposal, heating source and electricity need to be hooked up, and final grading and landscaping completed. The price is often lower than for an equivalent house built by a general contractor, and time required for delivery is usually shorter. There are, however, some limitations on choices of materials and features. You can't get a stucco house, for example, and you may not be able to have an attached garage.

In the marketplace, the word *modular* also refers to housing that is built in factories. Manufacturers who call themselves modular builders usually claim relationship to what used to be called "prefab" houses (short for prefabri-

More, More, More

For information on what's available in factory-built housing and the names of retailers in your area, contact the **Building Systems Council** of the **National Association of Home Builders (NAHB),** at the address on page 187. You can ask for information specific to the type of housing that interests you. Some of the larger manufacturers, listed by type, are:

Domes
- Oregon Dome Inc. (541–689–3443)
- Timberline Geodesics (510–849–4481)

Log Homes
- Alta Log Homes (914–586–3336)
- Lok-N-Logs (800–343–8928)

- Timberlog Building Systems Inc. (860–537–2393)

Modulars
- Chelsea Modular Homes (914–236–3311)
- Haven Homes (717–962–2111)
- Nationwide Homes Inc. (540–632–7100)

Panelized
- Deck House Inc. (617–259–9450)
- Deltec Homes (704–253–0483)
- Lindal Cedar Homes (206–725–0900)
- Timberpeg (manufacturers of post and beam homes; 603–298–8820)
- Yankee Barn Homes (603–863–4545)

cated). Like manufactured homes, sections of the modular home are delivered and then assembled on site using cranes and other heavy equipment. Be aware that modular and manufactured housing are shades of the same color. The term *manufactured housing* is commonly used to include both.

Kit, or panelized, homes

A step away from these manufactured houses are the so-called *kit homes* (more correctly known as *panelized houses*). Despite the nickname, however, kit homes are not recommended for do-it-yourselfers (unless, of course, you have considerable building expertise).

When a panelized home arrives at its site, the manufacturer has already cut, partially assembled, numbered and labeled all the construction materials. Then the house is put together like a puzzle, usually under the supervision of a company representative who acts much like a general contractor.

Log homes and dome homes are well-known kit styles, but you can purchase almost any style of house in panelized form. Advocates say panelized building saves time, money and stress for the home buyer. Traditional builders say there is no advantage. Often it depends on the situation. Panelized construction is sometimes the answer to finding a builder for the unusual lot (one outside a development). These houses compete favorably with traditionally built houses in both comfort and equity-growth potential.

Why Enter This Gateway?

Even though the New-Construction Gateway does sometimes earn the nicknames *fun-house ride* and *horror show,* thousands of home buyers each year continue to choose it. And many more thousands wish they could. What's the attraction? Certainly the pride and status of owning "new" (being the first) is a factor. But there are other considerations, too. (Weigh the following motives carefully. If this gateway seems like a good fit with your homeowner personality, confirm your hunch with the self-test beginning on page 193.)

self-test beginning on page 193.

Penny for Your Thoughts

The most beautiful house in the world is the one that you build for yourself.

Witold Rybczysnki,
Canadian author and
architect

Penny for Your Thoughts

Everyone has, I think, in some quiet corner of his mind, an ideal home waiting to become a reality.

Paige Rense, Editor,
Architectural Digest

To have control and make choices

Many new-construction buyers stand with Frank Sinatra to proclaim "my way" as an essential ingredient of happiness. To the last detail, they want the power and pleasure of creating a home that's entirely their own. Unlike Sinatra, however, most home buyers have jobs that keep "my way" tied to budget limitations.

To fulfill unusual housing needs

Many of us just don't fit into "typical" or "standard" profiles, and some home buyers prefer to adapt a building plan to fit their lifestyle rather than alter their lifestyle to fit an existing building. A word of caution, however: Unusual houses are often difficult to sell. For rooted people who expect to stay awhile and don't anticipate selling in a hurry, unique, creative or unusual designs may not be a problem; for turnover-oriented "movable" types, they could be a major mistake.

To buy for maximum appreciation

For approximately the first five years, the value of a newly built house keeps pace with the price increases of new construction in the area, an appreciation rate that is usually somewhat faster than that of older homes. When home values are on the rise, buying one of the first houses in a development can mean a significant bump up in resale value every six months or so. This investment enhancement is especially appealing to movable people.

Be aware, however, that the price of new construction also sets a cap on the value of existing houses. You may not recoup money spent on extraordinary landscaping or top-of-the-line comfort and convenience enhancements with short-term ownership. For example, say you buy a new home in a development for $200,000. A year later the same model new is being sold just down the street at $210,000. But you spent $7,000 on professional landscaping, $4,000 on custom window treatments and $2,000 on a ceramic-tile backsplash in your kitchen. Your purchase price plus your improvements comes to $213,000. If you tried to sell your home at this point, you probably wouldn't get more than

Continued on page 198

Self-Test Before You Choose This Gateway

The following, three-part self-assessment will help you evaluate whether you have what it takes to successfully pursue the homeowning options outlined in this chapter. It focuses on the 10 important homebuyer personality characteristics described in Chapter 2.

PART I: RATE YOURSELF

In Part I, below, read each of the self-descriptive statements for each characteristic and decide how well it describes you. Grade your response on a scale from 1, "Not me at all!" to 5, "That's me all the way!" Encourage your spouse or home-buying partner(s) to do the same.

Certain statements pertain only to one or two gateway options. If those don't interest you, skip those statements.

If your ratings vary within a category, average them.

Turn to the following page to see how you've fared.

Creative vision

____I can look at a floor plan and imagine myself in that house having a holiday family gathering, helping the kids take off their boots on a winter day, getting everyone up and out in the morning, finding a quiet and private corner, or pursuing a particular hobby.

____I think it's fun to look through a hundred racks of carpet samples to consider fiber, texture, color and price!

Time and skills for work and maintenance

____I enjoy planning and planting flower beds, borders and foundation plantings, and take pleasure in choosing a tree and watching it grow over time.

____There's both challenge and satisfaction in making 1,001 decisions about paint, wallpapers, draperies, hardware, lighting and accessories, and sometimes even in doing the work of installation or application myself.

____I have the time to visit the site regularly during the construction process, and I'm knowledgeable enough to know what I'm looking at.

Self-confidence

____I know I can manage the hundreds of decisions required of a huge project by taking them one at a time.

____I'm good both at juggling and at doing jigsaw puzzles. That is, I can keep a lot of things in the air simultaneously, and I can see how little things fit together into the whole.

____If something looks a bit odd, even if I'm not sure that I know what I'm looking at, I won't hesitate to speak with the builder.

Flexibility and adaptability

____If the special-order tub for two arrives in French vanilla instead of white, I can choose a toilet and sink in French vanilla rather than wait another six weeks for the white tub. (Large tubs must be put in before the walls are completed because there is no other way to get them into the house. A delay

Self-Test, Cont'd.

in tub delivery means a delay in house construction.)

____I'm willing to live without closet doors indefinitely until we can get around to hanging them.

____The builders hit a rock ledge where the foundation under the main section of the house should be. Rather than pay for blasting, we could flip the house plan right to left and put the garage (which doesn't need a deep foundation hole) over the ledge.

Willingness to take risks

____The builder says he can finish in 90 days and I'll go with that, even though we absolutely must be out of our current house by the same date. Of course, it would be a little less risky if his completion date were a few weeks earlier.

____We bought the first house built in the development. I see that as a chance to get some good appreciation since prices will surely go up as the neighborhood takes shape. But I recognize that there's always the risk that the builder will go bankrupt, and then we'll be stuck here in the only lived-in home on a street of skeleton houses.

____I'm not much of a risk-taker so I'm going to make absolutely certain that everything is in writing in the purchase contract. I figure if we spell it all out we'll get exactly the house we want.

Perseverance

____No matter how many times I hear "that's impossible," I'll persevere until I find a way to accomplish my goals.

____If I want special cabinet hardware or a particular style of transom window for the front door, I'll search stores, catalogs, and other sources until I find it.

Attention to detail

____Yes, it does matter that the plans show the kitchen counter six inches longer than it was built!

____I'll take the time to check that the products used in construction are exactly those promised in the contract and shown in the plans. I'm unwilling to accept substitutions without good reason.

Planning and evaluation skills

____Before I would consider building, I need a list of all the possible costs involved, an accurate evaluation of my current equity and spendable cash, a list of all my wants and needs in the house, and a tentative schedule for the completion of each major step in building.

____I have a contingency plan for where we will live in the event that the builder does not complete the work on time.

Tact and communication skills

____When I stop by the building site and discover that the "autumn russet" roof shingles I ordered look more like "sunset sizzle" and the roof is already half finished, I can keep from screaming at the general contractor.

____I make my wishes known clearly. When they are ignored, I restate them and follow through to see that I get what I ordered.

Negotiating skills

____Even though the builder says the price is fixed and firm, I'm willing to negotiate for upgrades and extras or for price reductions in return for doing some of the work myself.

____I believe there should be price concessions for lots with easements, corner lots, below-grade lots or even the last available lot—and I will ask for them.

PART II: WHAT'S IMPORTANT AND WHY

Now let's turn the tables and look at the home-buyer personality characteristics from the point of view of demand—that is, how vital the characteristic is to success through this gateway, and why. Each characteristic is rated from 1 to 5 (1 being low demand, 3 being variable demand that might be higher in some instances and lower in others, and 5 being high demand).

Creative vision: 5

Except for spec houses, buying new means visualizing what will fill an empty space. It also means coordinating colors and textures that will cover large spaces by making choices from hand-held swatches or samples.

Time and skills for work and maintenance: 3

Home buyers who choose to save money by participating in the building process will find high demands in this category. But even those who choose "new" because they want to avoid repairs and renovations will have to spend some time on finishing work, landscaping, decorating and maintenance (or find someone else to do the work).

Self-confidence: 4

Buying new construction can make you feel as though you're taking a battery of "how do you measure up?" tests. Realizing that every little decision will tangibly affect life in the house intimidates some people.

Flexibility and adaptability: 2

One of the reasons for buying new is to get what you want and not have to be especially adaptable. But the need to be flexible never disappears completely, especially when completion dates and scheduling come into play.

Willingness to take risks: 3

Most new construction turns out to be a good financial investment. This gateway's risks concern the skill and integrity of the builder and the likelihood of completion on or near the target date.

Perseverance: 5

Once you enter the New-Construction Gateway, you can't afford to give up, ever. You can't even afford to assume that everything is going along smoothly. Once you start the buying-new process, you must stay aware of what is happening and be willing to follow through to the end of each project or decision. If you don't, your house will cost you a great deal more money than necessary—and a great many headaches.

Attention to detail: 5

Way back in the Craft and Creativity chapter, we said that quality work is the result of care at each step. Here in the New-Construction area, expand that concept from repairing or renovating to building from scratch. A quality home is the result of attention to every detail in every step.

Self-Test, Cont'd.

Planning and evaluation skills: 5

Building a house is like planning a presidential inauguration or perhaps a five-generation family reunion. So many variables, so many diverse and changeable elements, must all be made to fit together.

Tact and communication skills: 5

Whether you're buying a spec house or acting as your own general contractor, buying new requires the ability to express not only what you want but also where and when you want it. And when things go amiss (something always does), you must be willing and able to fight for your rights while trying to maintain the goodwill of those who are working to build the house. You might win a point with a tantrum, but you could pay for it with a hundred inconveniences created by the negative feelings of workers.

Negotiating skills: 3

Don't expect to negotiate a steal when buying new construction. Your best objective is good value for the money. Be suspicious of bids that are far below the average. There is usually some negotiating space in extras and allowances, however.

PART III: THE CRITICAL COMPARISON

Now you can compare your self-ratings with the importance ratings for each characteristic to see how likely you are to measure up to the demands of this gateway. In the left column of the graph, the characteristics are presented in descending order from highest to lowest demand for this gateway. The black bars show each characteristic's importance rating. Use the space allowed to draw in your and your buying partner's results.

- **If you rated yourself *most* highly on this gateway's *most* important characteristics** (at least 4 on characteristics rated 5, and at least 3 on those rated 4), this gateway may be the one for you.

- **If you *also* rated yourself highly on the gateway's *least* important characteristics** (4s or 5s on characteristics rated 3 or less), other gateways might provide additional options suited to your strengths.

- **If you rated yourself highly *only* on the gateway's *least* important characteristics** (those rated 3 or less), look to another gateway for your best home-buying opportunities.

- **Be sure to look at your partner's strengths and weaknesses.** Is your partner strong where you're weak? Is it realistic to expect your partner to pick up the slack?

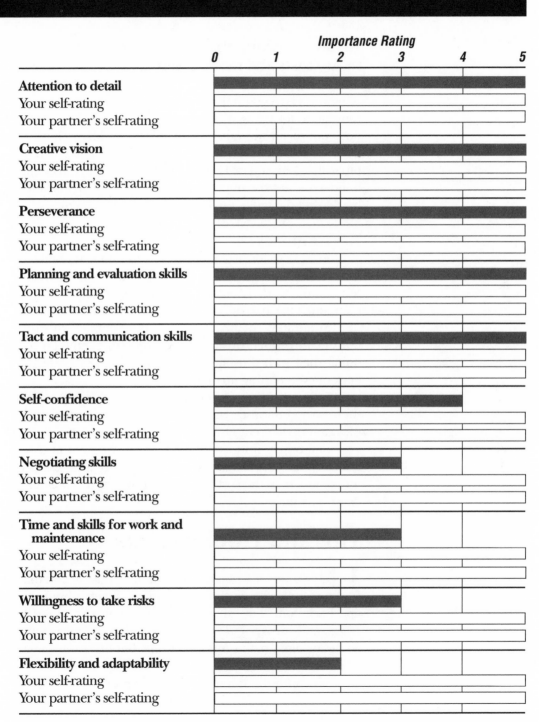

Importance Rating

	0	1	2	3	4	5

Attention to detail
Your self-rating
Your partner's self-rating

Creative vision
Your self-rating
Your partner's self-rating

Perseverance
Your self-rating
Your partner's self-rating

Planning and evaluation skills
Your self-rating
Your partner's self-rating

Tact and communication skills
Your self-rating
Your partner's self-rating

Self-confidence
Your self-rating
Your partner's self-rating

Negotiating skills
Your self-rating
Your partner's self-rating

Time and skills for work and maintenance
Your self-rating
Your partner's self-rating

Willingness to take risks
Your self-rating
Your partner's self-rating

Flexibility and adaptability
Your self-rating
Your partner's self-rating

$210,000 because the new house down the street will appeal to buyers' dreams of "being the first."

To have freedom from fix-up costs and requirements

For some home buyers, a major factor in the appeal of newness is freedom from even the thought of repair and renovation for many years to come. But remember: "New" does not mean without fault or problems. Many "buying-new" owners complain of a myriad of problems, such as pipes that leak or cracks at the doorjambs. Of course, the builder should fix all these problems. But sometimes it's hard to get the builder to come when you need him.

To save money

Most new construction exceeds its estimated budget, so how can anyone save money by buying new? By doing some of the work. It's much like the sweat-equity principle mentioned in Chapter 3.

Some new-construction buyers negotiate with the builder to reduce the purchase price in exchange for doing their own finishing work, like painting, building a deck or even putting up drywall.

Others with experience in homeownership act as their own general contractor and subcontract the work they cannot do themselves.

Still others find a suitable lot and choose a factory-built or panelized house at a price 10% to 30% less per square foot than the cost of a similar property in a builder's development.

Tips and Trouble Spots

Tell almost anyone who has bought new construction that you're planning to do the same and you'll get a shower of tips. Each home buyer has war stories to tell, a list of *I-wish-I-had*s, and ideas for *the-next-time-I-do-this*. Listen carefully. Someone else's path cannot be yours, but there will always be common experiences.

When buying new construction, all the generic rules

of house-hunting apply (be sure to read Part II), but you'll encounter some extra complexities. Those arise from buying a house that hasn't yet been lived in or that isn't even standing. The following tips will help you deal with some of the uncertainties, but don't stop here. Prepurchase research pays off in this marketplace area. Contact trade groups, check libraries and bookstores for guidebooks, and gather some current home-building magazines. Your reference librarian can also help you locate magazine articles on new-home construction in personal-finance and general consumer magazines.

About the Land

Read Chapter 11 and commit it to memory! Nothing is more important on the New-Construction Gateway than the lot. Your choice of land, whether it's a lot in a builder's development or a huge parcel of *raw land,* will affect not only the value of your home but also the ease and cost of construction. It may even determine the kind of house that you can build. Watch for:

Lot size and shape

Is the lot adequate for the house you want to build? Consider *setback lines.* Will there be any room for improvements in the future, such as an extra garage, a larger deck, a swimming pool, a children's playhouse or perhaps a shed for lawn and gardening tools? Will there be adequate privacy? For resale considerations, regular shape (rectangular) is usually best.

Zoning

Your investment in new construction will be most protected if zoning ordinances for the surrounding area limit current and future construction to houses similar to yours. If you are building a single-family home, for example, you do not want to buy a lot in or near an area zoned for high-density housing, such as apartment buildings and multi-family houses, or for commercial use.

Terrain and drainage

Does the topography lend itself to the kind of house you want to build? A lot that falls away from the road, for example, may allow for a walk-out basement or a garage underneath, but what if you want to build a contemporary without a basement? Also, consider what's under the surface of the land. A clay soil or rock ledge that results in poor drainage may mean water problems in your basement. You can make the purchase of a lot contingent on a satisfactory *perk test* by a soil scientist or testing laboratory. Some cautious lot buyers also have the soil tested for contaminants, such as oil leaked from a once-buried oil tank, or paint, coolant or other toxic waste left by the land's previous user.

Access to utilities

Find out what utilities are available at the road front. Electricity, gas, water, sewer? How far is the building site from the utility access point? When you build, you must pay to hook up to utilities, usually charged by the running foot of pipe or wiring required. Most utility installers use the shortest possible distance, but if they must work around obstructions, you will have to pay for the extra length. The shorter your setback, therefore, the lower the cost of hookup.

Siting

Consider where you might place a house on the lot. How far back from the road do you want it? Do you want it centered on the lot or off to one side? Whether it faces east-west or north-south will make a difference in heating and cooling costs and in the play of natural light inside. If

---

Words to the Wise

• •

Raw land has not been subdivided into building lots. It lacks roads, water, utilities and sewers.

Setback lines, as set out in local zoning ordinances, determine the minimum distance between the lot line and the point where the wall of a building may be constructed. Setback from the road usually determines how houses line up along a street and therefore how deep the front yards will be. Setback from the sides of a property determines the minimum space between houses.

To do a **percolation test (perk test),** the testing company digs a hole with a backhoe, pours in water, and times its drainage. The test determines the ability of the soil to absorb liquid. It is absolutely essential if waste disposal will be by septic system.

you like morning sunshine in your kitchen, face the kitchen east. Try to stand where a house might be and imagine the view from different rooms.

Purchase Contracts

Be sure to read Chapter 14. Then begin making lists of everything you want in the house. Your contract should name every working system and installed appliance, with brand name and model, and state that you'll allow no substitutions without prior approval. It should specify all the materials the builder will use and state *allowances* for cabinets, lighting, hardware, fixtures and floor covering.

Even if you have a wonderful relationship with your contractor at the outset and everyone is in agreement about changes to the plans and special features, put everything in writing. Building takes many months and much can happen during that time. There could be a fire, flood or materials shortage. You could change your mind and have the builder write a change order.

Words to the Wise
• •

An allowance in a purchase contract for new construction is the amount of money allocated in the purchase price for a certain item. For example, you may have a kitchen-cabinet allowance of $5,000. You then go to a cabinet manufacturer (either one you choose or one recommended by the builder) and choose the cabinets you want. If you stay under the allowance (hardly anyone does), you can apply the extra money to buying something else, like a more expensive dining-room chandelier. If you go over the allowance, the builder will add the extra money to your purchase price.

Make the delivery date firm and ask the contractor to give you a schedule of approximate completion dates for each stage of the building process. You'll want to know when the foundation will be poured, the framing will be complete, the roof will be on, plumbing and electrical work will be done, interior finishing will be done, and the appliances will be installed.

Then keep tabs on what's happening. It's good to visit at least once a week if you can, preferably during daytime hours when work is under way. Even if you don't know *what* you're watching, the fact that you *are* watching will keep some workers honest. If construction begins to fall behind, speak to the builder immediately. Don't wait to see if he can catch up!

Once you've signed the contract, hold the builder to it, but don't expect extras or favors. Home building is a business transaction. On the other hand, reply promptly when the builder asks you for a decision. Home-buyer indecision or changes of mind can seriously affect completion time.

Words to the Wise

• •

"Time is of the essence" is a clause used in real estate contracts to indicate that specific dates are essential to the contract and that the builder must perform the contract's terms by those dates. If the builder fails to meet the dates specified, the buyer can void the contract. Most builders do not want "time is of the essence" written into their contracts. Many contracts contain clauses allowing for extensions of time commitments for reasons of weather, acts of God or even materials shortages.

If there is something you must have changed, speak to the builder about a change order. Depending on the stage of construction, it may be just a slight inconvenience or a major project. In either case, it will cost you, though less if it's a small item. Change orders are known in the marketplace as "killers." Builders usually make a bundle for the inconvenience, and buyers feel the pain in the purse—all of which is another reason for very careful planning, in advance rather than along the way.

When Will It Be Done?

Compared with buying a spec house, contracting to have a house built from paper plans increases both the buyer's decision-making and progress-evaluation requirements and the risk factors for on-time completion. In hot markets, builders often take on more orders than they can actually handle and their promised completion dates have little relationship to realistic expectations.

Some buyers write *"time is of the essence" clauses* into their contracts. This legal verbiage has little effect unless the buyer will want out of the contract if the builder doesn't finish the house by the date agreed on. More effective for stimulating the builder's drive to finish is a listing of per diem fines for every day, until closing, that the builder fails to meet the contract date. The total fine reduces the price the buyer must pay. The trick is to get the builder to agree to have a clause written in that delineates the fines *before* the contract-to-purchase is signed.

Are There Really Any Guarantees?

One of the nightmares of every person who has a house built is the builder who completes the project and then leaves town (or declares bankruptcy). What if the roof caves in? Or, never mind the big disaster, what if all the faucets and the traps under all the sinks leak? Who will fix it? And who will pay?

Warranties, or more correctly the lack of them, are one of the hazards of new construction. Some builders give a written warranty for the structural soundness and working systems of the house for a year, and others give two years. Some give nothing in writing. Most states and local courts, however, hold builders to an implied warranty that their houses are safe and habitable. (Implied warranties originate in common law and they do hold up in court.)

Most builders return to do any necessary repairs for a year or two, anyway, because they want to protect their reputations. When a builder refuses to fix a flaw and lacks warranty coverage, however, you have no alternative but to take him to court. In other words, you must sue. If the builder has left the state, you may have no recourse at all.

Continued on page 206

More, More, More

Most new-home warranty corporations have brochures that describe their coverage. If your builder subscribes, he will give you one, or you can write to several companies and compare the replies you get. There aren't many competitors in the business. Your builder is likely to subscribe to one of the following plans.

- **Home Buyers Warranty** (1728 Montreal Circle, Tucker, GA 30084; 800–488–8844)

- **Professional Warranty Corp.** (P.O. Box 800, Annandale, VA 22003; 800–850–2799)

- **Quality Builders Warranty** (325 N. 2nd St., Wormleysburg, PA 17043; 800–334–9143)

- **Residential Warranty Corp.** (5300 Derry St., Harrisburg, PA 17111; 800–247–1812)

What Do You Really Want?

When contracting to have a house built, you have a multitude of opportunities to consider your personal comfort. It's important, therefore, to spend some time planning and evaluating features that you can finance with the mortgage rather than add later and pay for out of pocket.

Just reading through this checklist will probably make you think of a dozen other items that would enhance your home. (Read Chapter 10, "The Comforts of Home," too.) Keep a list. Then get prices from your architect or general contractor or from whatever discount source you can muster. Consider whether the extra money spent will improve livability or help resale (especially if you're a movable type).

Plan for light & electrical needs

Think of where you want windows, their number, size and style.

- Do you want double-glazed windows that do not require storm windows in the winter?

- Would you like them with thin venetian blinds permanently installed between the panes (you never have to dust them)?

- Would you like recessed ceiling lights installed?

- Would you like certain electrical outlets controlled by the wall switch?

- Do you want extra electrical outlets in the den or home office to meet your computing needs?

- Will you require 220-volt outlets in places other than your laundry room—say, in a workshop?

- Other desires or needs?

_____

_____

_____

Plan for security

- Would you like an alarm system? Do you want one that sounds sirens at a break-in?

Or do you want one that reports to a central station, which, in turn, calls the police?

- Do you want dead-bolt locks? (Dead-bolts are usually standard on front doors, but not on other doors.)

- Have you considered fencing? Is it to keep unwanted animals and people out, or to keep children and pets in? Is it also for privacy?

- Would you like fewer outside doors? Would too many doors mean possible security problems?

- Would you prefer hinged doors to glass sliders?

- Other desires or needs?

_____

_____

_____

Plan for comfort

- Would you like a whirlpool tub? For one person or two?

- Would you like a separate shower stall?

- Do you want multiple showerheads?

- Can you have a garbage disposal, or does a septic system prevent you from using one?

- A trash compactor?

- Would you like an extra sink in the kitchen? Or perhaps a wet bar in the family room?

- A center work island or a center-island cooktop?

- A breakfast bar?

- A desk in the kitchen?

- Built-in cabinetry in the dining room?

- Built-in bookcases? Where?

- How about air conditioning?

- A fireplace? Or two?

- A central vacuum system?

- Where would you like cable-television hookups?

- Where should telephone jacks go? Do you need more than one line in your den or home office for computer use?

- A built-in (usually brick) outdoor barbecue?

- Gas lines to a fireplace or outdoor gas grill?

- Other desires or needs?

_____

_____

_____

Plan for space

When a house is still in the blueprint stage, it's very easy to take down or put up a wall. If you have special needs (maybe your triplets would like to share one large bedroom rather than be divided up between two rooms), talk with the builder before framing is complete.

- A reading alcove in the master bedroom?

- A music room?

- More windows in the basement?

- An extra eight or ten feet on the width of the garage to accommodate all the outdoor things that live there (like lawn mowers, not raccoons)?

- Flooring in the attic for storage?

- Would you like a walk-up attic, with a door and real stairs as in houses of old?

- A vanity or dressing area with good lighting and plenty of mirrors (with at least one full length)?

- A cedar-lined closet with both hangers and shelves for off-season storage?

- A mud room at the back door?

- The laundry room adjacent to the kitchen (rather than in the basement or upstairs in a hall closet)?

- A pantry or butler's closet (for china and so on) off kitchen or dining room?

- No wall between kitchen and dining room to make for a more casual arrangement?

- An extra bathroom in the basement?

- More closets?

- Other desires or needs?

_____

_____

_____

Penny for Your Thoughts

The palest ink is better than the best memory.

Chinese proverb

That's why it's always a good idea to choose a builder who has been in town a while and plans to stay. Some builders also offer home warranties from insurance companies.

There are several national corporations that offer home-warranty insurance on new construction. Be aware, however, that plans differ from one another and that none really guarantees that everything will be done and paid for as you might like it to be. You don't buy this insurance; you get it automatically if your builder subscribes. There's no way to say whether a builder who subscribes is more or less likely to stand behind his product, but with the insured warranty, you have at least some recourse if the builder fails to perform. Generally, housing professionals feel that a builder's reputation is a far better recommendation than an insurance policy.

Most warranty plans guarantee that the builder will repair almost all defects during the first year. During the second year, they guarantee the builder will repair the major systems of the home, such as heating or electrical problems and any structural problems. After the end of the second year, the coverage is usually limited to structural problems. If the builder fails to show up, the home warranty corporation will pay your claims, usually through an insurance agency.

Many of these warranty programs cover structural defects for ten years and can be transferred from one owner to another. There is usually a deductible for each claim. Again, the warrantor will ask the original builder to do the repairs if he is available. If not, the warranty will pay another builder to do the job.

Getting the Money

Not many years ago, you could not get a mortgage from a conventional lender for a vacant lot because banks know how difficult it is both to appraise and to resell raw land. So you had to pay cash for the land or convince the seller to take back a mortgage. Today, however, there are programs that will let you borrow to buy the land and then take a reasonable amount of time to find a builder. Most mortgage brokers can help you to find financing to buy land for new construction.

Once you decide to begin building, you will need a construction mortgage. In this type of financing, you establish the total amount of loan you will need and then draw against that amount to pay the contractor or the subcontractors as their bills become due. In this way, you are paying interest only on the money you have spent.

Once the house is complete, you pay off the construction loan by refinancing with a conventional home-mortgage program.

It's important to shop for financing before you sign a contract to have a home built for you because new-construction financing is often somewhat more difficult to get than conventional mortgages. You will need to prove creditworthiness and dependability. Read "The Nuts and Bolts of Home Financing" (beginning on page 209) carefully, then talk with local lenders and mortgage brokers.

One Gateway to Another

Upon introduction to the New-Construction Gateway, a movable-type person is likely to think, "Well, that's for those rooted people." Not so. Buying a new home works equally well for either type home buyer. Well-rooted people will find it satisfying because they can make choices that suit their lifestyles. Those who are likely to move will enjoy the potential for appreciation and the usually easier and quicker resale of newly constructed houses.

Because of the added complexity in making a purchase that must develop from paper plans into a building, the New-Construction Gateway is usually easier for home buyers who have had some previous experience in the marketplace. First-time home buyers who really want "new" usually do better on a spec house where they can *see* what they are buying. Unfortunately, most spec houses today are in the higher price ranges and therefore unaffordable to those who are just starting out. Factory-built homes, however, can be a lower-cost opportunity if the home buyer is willing and able to put in the time to find an appropriate building lot.

> ### Penny for Your Thoughts
>
> *There can be no greater error than to expect or calculate upon real favors.*
>
> George Washington (1732–1799), in his farewell address, Sept. 17, 1796

The New-Construction Gateway doesn't progressively lead you from an entry point through several "stations" toward your goal. Instead, the different ways to build from scratch are all means to the same goal—being the first to own a newly built home. Some home buyers enter this gateway only once in their lives, either settling into their homes with satisfaction or preferring to avoid its many demands in future purchases. Some home buyers prefer it to all other buying opportunities and are the first owners of several homes during their lifetimes, carrying the learning from each experience to the next.

The Nuts and Bolts of
Home Financing

Have you ever considered postponing home buying until you had *saved* the entire price of a home that you wanted? Even with the most stringent savings program, most of us would be well into middle age before we could venture into the real estate marketplace. And many of us would never get there.

Borrowing money and using the home we want to buy as collateral (better known as *mortgaging*) makes it possible to own and live in a home while saving for and working toward a better home or a more financially secure future. That buy-earn-save opportunity makes home financing an essential element in your plan to improve the comforts of your life and increase your wealth through homeowning.

In this special section, we'll go over the basics of borrowing to buy a home. At this point, you may be tempted to skip ahead to the meat-and-potatoes home buying topics that will help you get the home you want. Don't do it—especially if your only reason for reading this book is to learn strategies that will help you to make money in your home buying ventures.

"But I pretty much know the basics," you're thinking. "Pretty much" isn't good enough when you're considering an investment that usually goes well into six figures. There are financing tips included at appropriate points in the home buying strategies in Part I and in the basic elements review in Part II. But those tips won't make much sense unless you understand the *what, where, why, when, how,* and *how much* of home financing. So take a little time to get the basics now; they'll help you use the strategy-specific financing tips more effectively later.

The Art of the Money Deal

Mortgage lending is a business. Most people who enter the real estate financing arena forget that fact and earnestly apply for the favor of a loan. Loans are not favors. They are business ventures. Lenders intend to make money whenever they write a mortgage—in fact, they *must* make money or they'll soon be out of business. And they very much want *your* business.

Like the lender, you should view your mortgage loan as a business transaction. Your objectives are:

- **to spend as little as possible** for the use of the money that you will borrow

- **to get repayment terms that are suitable** to your particular needs

- **to be certain that the mortgage contract protects** your ownership and financial interests.

Warm Bodies in a Cold World

While financing your home may be all numbers and terms, home buying is a business venture with an undeniable emotional factor. Unlike real estate you buy as an investment, you *should* love the house you're going to be living in, at least a little. (If you don't, you may be motivated to move before the optimum time for your investment's growth.) That emotional attachment to the place you want to call home can be a tremendous motivating factor in the search for financing.

But your strong motivation to find financing should not drive you to accept the first financing opportunity that opens to you. Financing for your home purchase should be searched for and agreed to with absolutely no emotional influence.

If you don't already know it, mortgages are a part of the adult world, right up there with sex and taxes. By the time you're looking for a mortgage, Santa Claus and the Tooth Fairy are things of the distant past and you've had plenty of time to get over your disappointment at finding out that nothing's for free. On the positive side, however, you no longer have to wait until morning to accept what you got. You can go out and get what you need and want.

In the world of home financing, you certainly don't have complete control, but you probably have more than you think. In every type of borrowing, you can make choices that will influence whether you'll get the loan, how much you'll get, when you'll get it, how long you'll have to pay it back and how much it will cost you.

Penny for Your Thoughts

"Money, which represents the prose of life, and which is hardly spoken of in parlors without an apology, is, in its effects and laws, as beautiful as roses."

Ralph Waldo Emerson (1803–1882),
American philosopher and essayist

What Do Lenders Want?

Let's look at home buying from a lender's point of view. Every application for a mortgage is a transaction that represents a potential source of income for the lender. Because we're talking about mortgage lending, every one of these money deals must begin with the land and the buildings on it, and each is evaluated by exactly the same factors.

"How can that be?" you ask. "How can an application for a loan on a new luxury condo be evaluated in the same way as a loan on a three-family house in an urban-renewal area?" Because every real estate transaction has the same three major components: the *parties,* the *collateral* and the *terms.* When considering a mortgage application, the lender will always evaluate all three. These three components of your home purchase will be factors in the mortgage you apply for next week, next year, next decade or next century. You must understand them.

Here's your primer:

- **The parties are the people involved,** the sellers and (much more important to the lender) the buyers. The lender will want answers to questions like: Who are the people involved? Do the sellers have clear title? What is the current financial position of the buyers? What is the buyers' financial potential in the short and long terms?

- **The collateral is the piece of property in question.** The lender will want answers to questions like: What is its current market value? What is the condition of its structure and working systems? What is its age and potential for continued use? What is its potential for future appreciation or depreciation?

- **The terms are the arrangements for exchanging money.** The lender will want answers to questions like: How much has the buyer agreed to pay? How much cash are the buyers bringing to the transaction? How will closing costs be covered? How much will the buyers need to borrow? For how long?

> ## Words to the Wise
> •
>
> **Certitude of performance** is a banking term that boils down to an evaluation of how much risk is involved in making a mortgage loan. You'll probably never hear or use the phrase outside of a bank building, but it is the standard by which every mortgage lending decision is made.

These three components all contribute to the essential question in property financing, the *certitude of performance*. Every lender considers the people, the property and the terms of the deal when evaluating the question "How will this loan be paid back?" Certitude of performance, therefore, is the major factor in deciding who gets how much money on what kind of property. The lower the risk for the lender, the more likely the loan will be approved.

How to Get a Good Deal

To give yourself the best possible chance at the best possible loan for your current situation, *you* must take control of your loan-application decisions. This requires knowledge and effort on three fronts extended over a period of time. Some of the work and learning should begin well before your first house-hunting expedition.

Here's the key:

- **Know yourself,** your housing needs, your goals and your financial capabilities. It's a good idea to go to a lender or mortgage broker and get prequalified (for more on pre-qualification, see the discussion beginning on page 320). There is no obligation to return to the lending source who did your prequalification to get your mortgage loan.

- **Know the property you are planning to buy,** its fair market value, its condition, and its potential for appreciation or depreciation. Use the resources of real estate professionals to do a comparative market analysis of your property and its like competitors in the marketplace. Lenders particularly favor houses surrounded by houses of similar value.

- **Know the mortgage marketplace,** the kinds of loans that are available, the current interest rates, the lenders who are competing for your business, the usual and customary terms, and the standards by which lending decisions are being made. Spend a little money, if necessary, to use the mortgage-lending reporting systems that are now available (more later in this section).

That sounds like a lot, doesn't it? Especially when you consider that the typical mortgage applicant is still dizzy from the house-hunting process when he or she suddenly realizes that it's time to find the money to actually *buy* the house. And what happens? Too many home buyers leave financing in the hands of either their real estate agent or a mortgage broker to whom they are referred by the agent.

Most often some kind of financing arrangement is worked out. Usually, however, the mortgage deal that is recommended is the one that will cause the least stress at the lender's office. If you prefer to go for the best possible deal for *your* interests and goals, you must actively participate. And that means you must know what you're doing.

What's a Mortgage, Anyway?

The word *mortgage* comes from the old French meaning *dead pledge*. Strange association? Well, when it comes right down to it, if you don't make the promised payments on your mortgage, your ownership interests in the real estate that has been pledged are in fact *dead!* The promissory note that accompanies a mortgage is a lien—a legal encumbrance (see further definition on page 357)—on the property. If you can't make your payments, the mortgagee can assume ownership.

Promissory note and trust deed

In some states, there are no mortgages, as such, even though residents think of their loans as mortgages. These states use a *promissory note and trust deed* system of financing property. In a trust-deed arrangement, the ownership of the property is held by a fiduciary for the benefit of another party. You, the owner, don't actually take title (that is, possess the deed that gives you ownership of the property) but rather have the title held for you by a *trustee* until you finish paying off your loan. You, therefore, are called the *trustor.* The lender is called the *beneficiary.* The advantage of this arrangement is all in the camp of the lender because foreclosure procedures are much simpler, quicker and less expensive. For purposes of understanding home financing, everything that is said about mortgages can be applied to trust deeds. (If you want to find out whether the state where you're purchasing a home uses trust deeds, ask your real estate agent or a mortgage lender.)

Words to the Wise

• •

Mortgagor and **mortgagee** are often confused, probably because most people think the lender gives the mortgage and is therefore the mortgagor. But that's not so. The lender makes the mortgage loan. You, the borrower, *give* the lender a mortgage on your property. You, then are the mortgagor. The lender who receives and holds the mortgage is the mortgagee.

Mortgage Alphabet Soup

At mid century there were *conventional* mortgages (those not insured or guaranteed by the government) and FHA-insured and VA-guaranteed mortgages. That was it—not many letter combinations to remember. Today lenders promote so many acronyms, many unpronounceable, that some home buyers feel as though they need coaching in a foreign language.

FINANCING

It's not quite that bad, but it certainly is confusing. So let's sort out the soup. We'll start with the types of mortgages that are available. They fall into two major categories, differentiated by how *interest* is determined, whether by a fixed or adjustable rate. Then we'll go on to explore those other mysterious words and letters in the mortgage-money ads. (Part I introduced you to some of the lending programs that are specific to particular home buying strategies.)

Fixed-Rate Mortgages

When you choose a fixed-rate mortgage, the interest rate on your loan will remain the same for the life of the loan, and you will make the same *principal* and interest payment at regular intervals (usually monthly). Your total housing expense may fluctuate slightly if homeowners insurance premiums or property taxes go up or down, but the *fixed* interest rate of your mortgage assures you maximum stability throughout its *amortization*.

Adjustable-Rate Mortgages (ARMs)

With interest rates free-floating upward in the 1980s, many lenders flirted with manic-depressive syndrome. They watched enthusiastically as interest rates for new mortgages went higher and higher and despaired over the long-term loans they still held at the low interest rates of the '60s and '70s. Suddenly, committing to a fixed rate for 30 years seemed like a bad deal, and some lenders virtually shut down their home mortgage departments—but not for long. ARMs came to the rescue.

Words to the Wise

● ●

Principal is the amount of your mortgage debt. **Interest** is the fee charged for the use of money. **Amortization** is the gradual paying off of a loan in equal installments over the term (length of time scheduled to repay the debt) of the mortgage. Each month, part of the payment is interest and part is principal. In the early years of the mortgage, the payment is applied almost entirely to interest. As your payments reduce the interest, less of each scheduled payment amount is needed to pay the interest, and therefore more is applied to paying out the principal. In the later years, the scheduled payment is almost entirely applied to principal.

Today's ARMs allow interest rates to adjust up or down, within certain limits, at regular intervals that are set forth in the loan agreement. Depending on which direction rates are going, this can work to the advantage of the *mortgagee* or *mortgagor* (see page 214). The interval may be as short as three or six months, but a year is most common. ARMs are also commonly available with three- and five-year intervals.

Words to the Wise

• •

An **index** is a statistical composite that rises or falls in response to changes in the economy. For example, the consumer price index, the benchmark of inflation, moves up or down as the cost of a typical "market basket" of consumer goods and services changes. Other indexes measure the ups and downs of the stock and commodities markets. None of those will affect your ARM. Adjustable-rate mortgages are linked to specialized rate indexes, described in the accompanying text.

The rate index

The interest rate that applies during each interval is determined by a rate index. Mortgage lenders currently use more than 20 different indexes. Among the more widely used are the one-, three- and five-year Treasury indexes, the six-month Treasury bill index, the Cost of Funds Index (COFI) as published by the Federal Home Loan Bank System, and the Federal Housing Finance Board's national average contract mortgage rate.

The margin

The index, however, is only a starting point for determining your rate. Every ARM includes a margin. The margin is a number of percentage points added to the index to make the loan more profitable to the lender. Two percentage points is common, but anything is possible. The margin is written into the loan contract and remains the same throughout the life of the loan.

Caps

"So what happens," you ask, "if interest rates skyrocket and my index plus the margin add up to 17% or worse?" That was the nightmare of early ARMs. Today all ARMs have safety features called caps, which set limits on interest-rate changes. There are two kinds:

- **The interval cap** sets the maximum interest rate change, up or down, on any given rate-change date. Two percentage points is a common figure. But that doesn't mean that your rate will change two points each interval; it merely establishes the most it can change. If you have a one-year ARM, for example, and your initial interest rate is 7.5%, the highest your rate could be next year is 9.5%. Your rate, however, could also remain the same, or go up or down one percentage point or just a fraction of a point, all depending on the position of the index for your loan on your rate-change date.

- **The life-of-the-loan cap** sets the maximum interest-rate range. Caps of five or six percentage points are now common. That means the rate can never go higher than five or six points above the original rate. For example, with a five-point cap on that 7.5% initial rate, the highest rate you will ever be required to pay is 12.5%, even if market interest rates climb to 18%. Theoretically, with this cap your rate also can't go more than five points lower than the initial rate. But if rates go that low, you can just rush off to refinance, and with that great a difference, it would probably be worth the cost of doing so.

Don't Assume

● ●

Don't assume that one index is just as good as another. Some are more responsive to changes in the financial world than others. Being tied to an index that doesn't rise at every fluctuation can save you money. When considering an ARM, you should ask how the index being used has compared with other indexes during the past several years. You are looking for the index that would have given you the lowest mortgage rates during that time. Lenders are required by law to have ARM disclosures readily available and to answer your questions. Make comparisons before you choose a loan.

Teaser rates

Unusually low introductory rates, called teaser rates, are sometimes used to attract borrowers to an adjustable-rate mortgage. The low initial rate can help qualify some buyers who would otherwise be turned down for a mortgage. The rates almost always increase at the first adjustment period, however, and responsible lenders warn borrowers to expect the increase.

Convertibles

Because interest rates today go *both* up and down, some home buyers, anticipating a drop in rates, are reluctant to choose a fixed-rate loan. Other home buyers, anticipating rising rates, are reluctant to choose an ARM. In response to these concerns—and for a price—lenders offer options for converting from one loan type to another.

Conversion always costs something, but the fees can be structured in many ways. Sometimes just putting the conversion clause into the mortgage can cost you a higher interest rate or an up-front fee. Some conversion agreements specify that borrowers pay the fee only if they exercise the conversion option. And some lenders allow conversion with little or no out-of-pocket cost but only for a fixed-rate loan that is slightly above the going fixed rate (often one-half percentage point). Sometimes the opportunity for conversion is limited to certain dates or time periods specified in the loan agreement.

Fixed-rate convertibles

Fixed-rate convertibles are also called Reduction Option Loans (ROLs) or Reducing Interest Loans (RILs). They allow you to exchange your fixed-rate loan for a new fixed-rate loan with a lower interest rate. What these opportunities boil down to is a kind of insurance policy against the cost, time and trouble of refinancing your mortgage if rates fall.

Loan agreements vary, but converting typically requires at least a stated minimum change in rates (two full percentage points is common) and the loan agreement sets a time frame for making the change, usually between the second and fifth years.

To have the convertible option written into your fixed-rate mortgage, you must usually pay an up-front fee of $100 to $200. If rates do go down and you exercise your option, there is usually another charge of 0.25% to 0.5% of the loan amount.

Convertible ARMs

Borrowers with adjustable-rate mortgages are usually warm and contented when rates have fallen. Some of them, however, fear another upswing and want to latch on to a lower fixed rate for the remainder of their mortgage term. Enter the *convertible* ARM.

Some ARMs that have been sold into the secondary mortgage market (explained below) can be converted to fixed-rate 15- or 30-year mortgages by paying 1% of the original loan plus an additional fee of $250. (Convertible ARMs not sold into the secondary marketplace can sometimes be converted, but there are no general guidelines because each lender sets its own policy.)

Graduated-Payment Mortgage (GPM)

Graduated-payment mortgages are designed for home buyers whose income is likely to increase significantly over the term of their homeownership. They specifically help young people whose incomes do not qualify them for the traditional mortgage payment at the outset.

Scheduled monthly payments at the beginning of the mortgage period sometimes do not even pay the interest due. The shortfall, if any, is added to the principal, creating a period of *negative amortization*. The amount of the sched-

Words to the Wise

Negative amortization is a condition created when scheduled loan payments are less than the interest due on the payment dates. The amount of principal and interest owed then increases every month. (If, for example, your scheduled payment was $20 short of the actual amount owed for interest, the $20 would be added to your principal. When the next payment is calculated, your loan balance would include the additional $20 debt and you would pay interest on it.) If negative amortization continues, you could come to the end of the term of your mortgage and discover that you still owed many thousands of dollars.

You are most likely to encounter negative amortization in ARMs that have a cap on the monthly payment rather than on the interest rate. If you are choosing an ARM and are uncertain about the fine print in the loan agreement, simply ask, "Are there any circumstances under which negative amortization can occur in this agreement?"

uled payment increases each year for an agreed-upon number of years, however, allowing the borrowers to catch up on the shortfall and pay out the principal during the term of the mortgage.

In this financing arrangement, a problem can occur if the property is sold in the early years of the mortgage term, especially if the purchase was made with a minimum *down payment*. The owners might find that they actually *owe* money at the closing. Unless there has been significant appreciation in the home's value, the real estate commissions and other costs of selling the property, combined with the negative amortization, can devour equity. The sellers find their down payment money has vanished and they need to dig deep into their pockets (and bank accounts) for more cash just to be allowed to transfer title to another owner.

Graduated-payment mortgages are available through conventional sources and through FHA and VA programs (discussed below). If you are a "rooted" person and certain that you will remain in this house for many years, or if you're just starting out in your career and quite certain that your income will increase, a graduated-payment mortgage may be the home-financing vehicle for you. Turnover-oriented "movable" people, however, should be very wary of the "you can qualify—look how low the payments are" appeal.

Loan-to-Value Ratio (LTV)

The closer the loan amount approaches the fair market value of a piece of property, the greater the risk to the lender. Lenders refer to this financial relationship as the *loan-to-value ratio* and express it as a percentage. For example, if you were buying a $200,000 home with a down pay-

Words to the Wise

The **down payment** is the portion of the purchase price that comes from the buyer's own funds—in other words, the portion that is *not* financed. It's correct to say, "We have a down payment of $45,000." In everyday usage, however, the term is often abbreviated to "**down**" and combined with a percentage. For example: "We can put 20% down." It's also correct to say, "We can put $45,000 down."

ment of $40,000 and a $160,000 mortgage, the LTV ratio would be 80% ($160,000 loan ÷ $200,000 value = 80%). Many lenders become anxious when LTV ratios exceed 80%—that is, when a borrower's down payment is less than 20% of the appraised value—because if the borrower defaults, the costs of foreclosing and selling the property to liquidate the debt can easily exceed the cash the borrower has put into the deal. That means the lender stands to lose money. And it probably stands to lose even more money because many foreclosed properties with high LTV will sell *below* the loan amount. Without some guarantee against borrower default, these loans are simply not a good business option for the lender. Lenders are also reluctant to write high-LTV mortgages because they can't sell them into the secondary mortgage market (more about that beginning on page 227, "The Power of the Secondary Mortgage Market").

The loan-to-value ratio therefore affects the kind of financing available to you and, often, the interest rate you'll be offered. The higher your down payment and the lower the LTV, the better your chance of negotiating favorable concessions such as waived application fees, reduced points (defined on page 234) or the opportunity to apply for a "no documentation" or "low doc" loan (more about these on page 245).

So what makes for a lower LTV ratio? A larger down payment helps, of course. A bank appraisal of the property (done to determine approximate fair market value) also lowers the LTV if the appraised valuation comes in above the purchase price.

Let's look at how that works. If you are putting $5,000 down on a house you have contracted to purchase at $100,000, you have an LTV of 95% ($100,000 value – $5,000 down payment = $95,000 loan; $95,000 ÷ $100,000 = 95%). But if the appraisal comes in at $120,000, you have an LTV of 79% ($120,000 value – $5,000 down payment – $20,000 value over the contracted price = $95,000 loan; $95,000 ÷ $120,000 = 79%). It's as though your down payment increased by magic, and it means that you no longer have to buy private mortgage insurance.

Remember, however, that a bank appraisal *below* the purchase price will *raise* the LTV. On that same $100,000 house, if the appraisal comes in at $97,000, you will not be able to get a $95,000 mortgage because that exceeds 95% of the value of the property ($97,000 − $5,000 + $3,000 = $95,000; $95,000 ÷ $97,000 = 98%). You will, however, be able to get a $92,150 mortgage (95% of $97,000). If the seller holds firm to the $100,000 price, you will have to put $7,850 down ($100,000 − $92,150) to get that mortgage.) In the case of a minimum down payment and an appraisal below purchase price, the increased LTV ratio could cause a prospective lender to turn you down if you couldn't come up with the extra cash needed. Sometimes anxious sellers will lower the sale price to meet the appraisal price.

Low- or No-Down-Payment Alternatives

Private Mortgage Insurance (PMI)

If you can't lower your LTV ratio by increasing your down payment, you may have to purchase private mortgage insurance. PMI makes low-down-payment loans safe and appealing to lenders and therefore available to borrowers. Generally, mortgages with PMI can be written with a down payment as low as 3%.

If a mortgage insurance company approves a loan, it insures the lender against loss due to the borrower's default. The borrower pays the insurance premium, usually by paying a monthly amount with each mortgage payment.

Fees are set by each company, but a typical borrower would pay 0.5% to 0.75% of the loan amount. That translates to between $40 to $65 a month on a $100,000 loan depending on the size of the down payment. Sometimes PMI fees are reduced as the principal balance decreases. And sometimes the buyer can petition to have PMI removed once a certain level of equity is reached (often 20% of the fair market value of the property).

FHA (Federal Housing Administration) Insured Loans

Many hopeful home buyers think of their Uncle Sam as a friendly, low-down-payment lender who runs a nationwide business called the FHA. That might make a great Norman Rockwell poster, but it's not reality. The Federal Housing Administration doesn't make loans, it insures them.

The FHA insures both fixed-rate and adjustable-rate loans. Its down-payment requirements are low, generally as little as 3%. It does, however, have maximum loan limits that keep FHA-insured loans feasible only for moderately priced housing. These limits change periodically with regional economic conditions. You can learn the current limits in your area by calling the nearest Housing and Urban Development office, checking online at

More, More, More

There are eight private mortgage insurance companies operating in the U.S. They will send information about their approval guidelines and fees upon request. You can ask the lenders that you are considering which of these companies they generally work with. Compare their fees and qualification guidelines to see if you can save some money or get better terms (an automatic drop of insurance, say, or a lower insurance rate when you have reached a certain level of equity in the house).

- **Amerin Guaranty Corp.** (200 E. Randolph Dr., 49th Floor, Chicago, IL 60601; 800–257–7643)

- **Commonwealth Mortgage Assurance Co.** (1601 Market St., Philadelphia, PA 19103–2197; 800–523–1988)

- **GE Capital Mortgage Insurance Corp.** (6601 Six Forks Rd., Raleigh, NC 27615; 800–334–9270)

- **Mortgage Guaranty Insurance Corp.** (P.O. Box 488, MGIC Plaza, Milwaukee, WI 53201–0488; 800–558–9900)

- **PMI Mortgage Insurance Co.** (601 Montgomery St., San Francisco, CA 94111; 800–288–1970)

- **Republic Mortgage Insurance Co.** (P.O. Box 2514, Winston-Salem, NC 27102–9954; 800–999–7642)

- **Triad Guaranty Insurance Corp.** (P.O. Box 2300, Winston-Salem, NC 27102; 800–451–4872)

- **United Guaranty Corp.** (P.O. Box 21567, Greensboro, NC 27420–1367; 800–334–8966)

http://www.hud.gov/fha/sfh/sfhhicos.html or calling any participating lender. At this writing, the maximum loan is $160,950.

Besides loan limits, LTV guidelines and financial qualification requirements for borrowers, the FHA-insured loan application process includes an evaluation of the property's structural and working systems. If a house does not meet FHA standards, repairs must be made before closing. Sometimes the seller will pay for these in order to make the sale. Sometimes the buyer agrees to pay.

Unlike PMI companies, which insure against any *loss* incurred by the lender if the borrower defaults (which means the lender has to foreclose and sell the property before calculating the loss), the FHA promises to repay the *balance* of the loan in full if the borrower defaults. This added security is paid for through a mortgage insurance premium (MIP). At this writing, the MIP includes an up-front fee of 2.25% of the loan amount and an annual insurance premium of 0.5% of the loan balance, divided over monthly payments. (The buyer or seller can pay the up-front fee in cash at the closing, or the buyer can finance it and have repayment included in the scheduled monthly payments.)

More, More, More

•••••••••••••••••••••••••••

The FHA is part of the U.S. Department of Housing and Urban Development, which has regional offices throughout the country. You can write, call or stop in at the office nearest you to obtain lists of FHA publications, which cover subjects including home-financing guidelines, mortgage shopping tips, and every loan program the FHA offers. Most of the material is free. To locate the office nearest you, check the government blue pages of your phone book or online at HUD's Web site (http://www.hud.gov/local.html).

The exception: direct loans

Having said that the FHA doesn't make direct loans to borrowers, it's necessary to mention the exception to the rule. Under specific circumstances involving the resale of foreclosed property that it owns, the FHA will consider making a direct loan to a homebuyer. Even then, however, the FHA will check first to be sure that the buyer has been unsuccessful in obtaining financing elsewhere.

VA (Department of Veterans Affairs) Guaranteed Loans

Americans who are serving or who have served in any branch of the armed forces (including National Guard or Reserve members with more than six years of service) can obtain no-down-payment home financing through loans guaranteed by the Department of Veterans Affairs (formerly the Veterans Administration). This agency oversees the federal program that guarantees against loss by a conventional lender. Like the FHA, the VA does not make the loans.

Before applying for a VA loan, a prospective borrower must obtain a *certificate of eligibility*. To apply for one, call 800–827–1000.

More, More, More
• •

The folks at the **VA regional offices** are ready, willing and able to help with both questions and procedures. They also have a number of booklets and pamphlets available for the asking. Contact the office nearest you (check the blue pages of your phone book or call 800–827–1000). For on-line information about the VA's home-loan programs, check http://www.va.gov.

Unlike the FHA, the VA does not set a top limit on the amount of the loan or the purchase price for properties financed through the program. Rather, it sets a limit on the amount it will pay in case of default. As of this writing, the maximum guarantee is $50,750, which in the eyes of a lender is the equivalent of a 25% down payment on a $203,000 house. To get a VA loan, the borrower must be qualified to make the payments on the entire $203,000, or whatever the principal is, and must live in the house as his or her primary dwelling.

The VA guarantees both fixed-rate and adjustable-rate loans and supports a variety of loan types.

The VA also requires a certified real estate appraiser to submit a formal estimate of the property's value and then issues a certificate of reasonable value (CRV). What if the CRV comes in below the purchase price on a no-down-payment loan? The buyer can make up the difference, the seller can accept the appraisal figure as a new sale price, buyer and seller can compromise, or the sale can be canceled without penalty to the buyer.

Community Home Buyer's Programs (CHBP)

Commonly referred to as Cherubs, these mortgage programs allow for very-low-down-payment, fixed-rate mortgages on urban and small-city properties. On paper, qualification guidelines require that the borrowers' combined income not exceed the area's median household income. This income cap is waived in about 600 cities, however.

Down payment requirements are as low as 3%, and debt-to-income qualification guidelines are generous (more about those under "How Much Can You Get?" on page 230). Because loans are subsidized by community organizations, local agencies or state governments, interest rates can be set at below-market levels. Borrowers also need less cash at the closing because these programs often waive the usual two to six months' worth of mortgage payments required to be held in escrow. However, these loans do require payment of a monthly mortgage insurance premium.

More, More, More

Here are a few more sources of information about mortgage shopping to add to those that have already been mentioned.

- **Consumer Information Center** (P.O. Box 100, Pueblo, CO 81002; 719–948–4000; http://www.pueblo.gsa.gov/). The federal government offers a number of pamphlets on mortgages and home buying, free or at minimal cost. Send a postcard to request a catalog.

- **Fannie Mae** (Consumer Education Group, 3900 Wisconsin Ave., N.W., Washington, DC 20016–2899; 800–688–4663). Ask for: "Choosing the Mortgage That's Right for You," or "Opening the Door to a Home of Your Own." (For more on Fannie Mae's HomePath online feature, see page 239.)

- **Federal Trade Commission** (Bureau of Consumer Protection, Pennsylvania Avenue & 6th Street, N.W., Washington, DC 20580; 202–326–3650; http://www.ftc.gov). Request: "Getting a Loan: Your Home as Security"

In bookstores and libraries

- *The Common-Sense Mortgage,* by Peter G. Miller (Harper Collins Publishers)

- *The Mortgage Kit,* by Thomas C. Steinmetz and Phillip Whitt (Dearborn Financial Publishing)

- *Tips and Traps When Mortgage Hunting,* by Robert Irwin (McGraw-Hill Publishers)

The Power of the Secondary Mortgage Market

In the sleepy 1950s (or so the decade seems looking back from today), a would-be home buyer went to a nearby savings bank or savings and loan association for a home mortgage. Most people thought it was helpful to have a savings account well established in the institution of choice. Then, the reasoning went, the lender "knew" who you were and you were more likely to get a mortgage even if you were stretching a bit. And often the strategy worked.

Things got a little tighter in the '60s and '70s, but essentially home-mortgage lending for the first three-quarters of this century was a local business. Most s&l's and savings banks limited their mortgage writing to properties within the state, or sometimes within a 50-mile radius of the lending office. Most of these mortgages were held by the lender until they were paid off or the property was sold.

But the days of truly personal, local banking are over. Today the independent s&l's and savings banks, once found on virtually every Main Street in America, are an endangered species. They have been replaced by huge lending corporations that seem oblivious to state boundaries and by commercial banks, some of which have home-mortgage departments that need to be housed in multistory buildings. Their lending practices—what they can do for you and what you must do for them—are determined not just by corporate policy but by other powerful forces as well.

Despite the millions of dollars the banking industry giants and the remaining savings institutions lend to home buyers each year, these lenders actually *hold* very few mortgages. Although they *take* plenty of mortgages (remember the lender is the mortgagee), they then quickly *sell* them.

"Who would buy a mortgage?" you ask. "And why?" You've certainly heard the names: Fannie Mae, the biggest player in the secondary mortgage market, Ginnie Mae and Freddie Mac. These corporations *invest* in mortgages. They make money by buying loans, usually at a discount (below the actual amount of principal); collecting interest on the entire principal; and sometimes reselling the mortgages or selling securities with the mortgages as backing.

Begun as a federal agency in 1938, Fannie Mae (formerly The Federal National Mortgage Association) is now a private corporation with the benefits of government "sponsorship." By buying mortgages, it replenishes primary lenders' financial resources, which allows them to write more mortgage loans, and thus keep the home mortgage market going.

But a question comes to mind. If primary lenders are selling off their mortgages at less than face value, how do they make any money?

The primary lenders make a profit from loan-origination fees and from the loan-servicing fees that Fannie Mae and other sources in the secondary mortgage market pay. (Most home buyers never know that their loan has been sold because they still make their monthly payments to the loan originator. That's called loan servicing.)

Ginnie Mae (formerly the Government National Mortgage Association), a wholly owned government corporation under the direction of HUD, is responsible for the operation of mortgage-securities pools. (A pool is a collection of mortgage holdings that one can buy an interest in through a securities dealer.)

Freddie Mac (formerly the Federal Home Loan Mortgage Corporation) is an independent stock company in direct competition with Fannie Mae and under the supervision of HUD.

Money Sources

• •

Who are the primary lenders in today's mortgage market?

- **Mortgage companies:** 55%

- **Commercial banks:** 27%

- **Savings and loans:** 14%

- **Other:** 4%

Source: U.S. Department of Housing & Urban Development

The essential need-to-know nuggets

But you don't really want a short course in American banking policy, do you? And you're wondering why you need to know all this. Well, you can't get along very well in the home-financing marketplace without recognizing the names of the chief players, their positions and their power. Once you recognize why the secondary mortgage market is important, your next logical question is: How does this secondary mortgage market affect *my* home financing goals?

The essential need-to-know nuggets are these:

- **The major source** for home-mortgage funds is investment money in the secondary mortgage market.

- **These investors and their corporations** want their investments to be as safe as possible.

- **Primary lenders** want to continue to tap the source of funds in the secondary market and therefore will conform to standards that will protect the corporations and their investors.

Add those three facts together and the equal sign points to an immensely powerful force in determining the character of home financing in the United States. In other words, how much *you* can get!

Secondary mortgage–market guidelines virtually dictate the following:

- **maximum loan-to-value limits**
- **maximum loan amounts** for various types of real estate
- **down-payment requirements**
- **private mortgage insurance requirements**
- **perhaps most important, income requirements for borrowers.**

If you don't fit the profiles established by Fannie Mae or its competitors, it doesn't necessarily mean that you can't get a mortgage. But you're going to have to work a bit harder or pay a bit more. For example, loans over Fannie Mae's $214,600 limit for single-family-house mortgages (called "jumbos") are usually written at higher interest rates and are often sold to groups of private investors rather than the secondary mortgage market giants. Loans to applicants who don't quite meet Fannie Mae's income standards are sometimes made by primary lenders who are willing to tie up their money for the term of the loan. And sometimes loans that don't conform to secondary mortgage–market standards are supported by community, state or federal government programs.

How Much Can You Get?

Back in those sleepy 1950s, people talked about the home-financing "rule of doubles." It was said that you could get a mortgage of approximately double your family's annual income. Like a childhood nickname, this "rule" is still heard in the real estate marketplace, but it's about as appropriate as calling an adult "Junior" or "Sissy."

Today the secondary mortgage market and government and private mortgage insurance companies, seeking to limit risk and protect the interests of lenders and investors, dictate very specific ratios for loan qualification. Determining factors for those ratios include:

- **the type of loan**
- **the amount of down payment**
- **the amount of long-term debt,** which is any debt with scheduled payments extending beyond 12 months
- **the credit history** of the prospective borrower
- **the nature of the property** to be financed, such as single-family residences or multifamily residences.

And if that's not complicated enough for you, these ratios are subject to change because the financial marketplace itself is ever-changing in response to the availability of money and the fluctuations of interest rates.

The age of knowing a friendly banker who might stretch a bit for you is just about over. (Some people even say "friendly banker" is an oxymoron.) So the very best thing you can do is sit down with a competent real estate professional, a mortgage rep from a convenient banking office, or a mortgage broker or banker (more about them in just a bit) and get *prequalified.* Within half an hour, you'll have a ballpark figure (based on numbers rather than feelings) for how much mortgage you can carry.

Now, Prequalify Yourself

Human nature being what it is, however, you probably want that ballpark figure *now*, without asking anyone for help. Okay, here's the set of guidelines that Fannie Mae most commonly uses as of this writing. Just remember that they are subject to change and that there are other qualification guidelines for other programs. (You can get current guidelines simply by calling any lender or mortgage broker.) After you finish your own quick qualification, you should still get prequalified by a professional as a safety check against something missed or miscalculated.

How to figure qualification with 20% or more down (which means you won't need mortgage insurance):

> ## *Words to the Wise*
> •
>
> To **prequalify** a prospective home buyer, a real estate professional, a mortgage broker or a representative of a lender examines the pertinent financial data and determines the maximum loan amount that any lender will likely approve. The lender makes no commitment and the home buyer is under no obligation. The term **preapproved** is used for home buyers who have a financing commitment from a specific lender.

Step A

Take 28% of your gross (pretax) monthly income. That is the maximum amount you can pay for total monthly housing expenses. (That total must cover monthly mortgage payments of principal and interest, property taxes, homeowners insurance, homeowners association fees, utilities and maintenance.)

Step B

Take 36% of your gross monthly income. Put that figure aside for a minute.

Step C

Add up all the other monthly installment-debt obligations you are currently making and add them to the figure from Step A. (Your debts might include car loans, personal and student loans, credit cards, and lines of credit.)

Subtract your Step C result from your Step B result (the 36% figure)

You must be left with at least $1 to qualify for a conventional mortgage loan.

(With some Cherub-supported nothing-down programs, described on page 226, that debt-obligation limit can go as high as 42%. This is a way into homeownership that leaves little money left over for "extras" like dinner out or a vacation at the beach.) Many home buyers find that they must pay off a car loan and reduce their credit card debt to meet mortgage qualification guidelines.

About Down Payment Money

What is the most money *you* could pull together for the down payment on a home? To figure the amount, start by adding up your *liquid* net worth—that is, the value of your savings and investments that you could readily sell for cash without a noticeable loss of value or penalty. (If you presently own a home, include the equity you'll get from its sale.) From your net worth subtract: savings for emergencies, educational expenses or retirement; settlement and moving costs; and cash you'll need to improve, decorate and furnish your new home. The difference is the amount you *could* put down if you chose to use it all.

A down payment is cash that *doesn't* come from the lender. But lenders often want to know where it does come from. They are, of course, protecting their investment in you, the borrower. In most cases, therefore, down-payment money cannot be borrowed money. (The lender doesn't want you paying off more loans than the qualification guidelines indicate you can afford.) Gifts (from family members only) are generally allowed, with some restrictions imposed by Fannie Mae and Freddie Mac.

When gifts of down-payment money are used for a mortgage loan with an LTV ratio higher than 80% (usually a down payment of less than 20%), at least 5% of the purchase price must come from the borrower's funds. For loans with an LTV of 80% or less (down payments higher than 20%), all of the down payment can come from gifts from relatives.

The lender must verify that all the gift funds were in the donor's account well before the mortgage application was filed. That's to ensure the relative isn't borrowing money that the home buyer must pay back. Verification is also required for evidence of withdrawal of the funds by the donor, receipt by the home buyer and deposit into the home buyer's account.

Be aware that some specific borrowing programs do not allow gifts for down-payment money.

Penalty-free IRA withdrawals for a first home

Thanks to changes in the tax law, you have another possible source of funds for a down payment. You can withdraw up to $10,000 from your IRAs at any age—though just once in your lifetime—to help pay for a first home for yourself (or for your spouse, child, grandchild, parent or grandparent). Although you won't get hit with the usual 10% early-withdrawal penalty, the money will be fully taxed in your top tax bracket (except to the extent the withdrawal represents nondeductible contributions—that is, money on which you paid federal income tax before stashing it in the IRA). Is this a good deal or not? Well, if you withdrew the full $10,000, you would avoid a $1,000 penalty, but you would probably lose a third or more of the money right off the top to federal and state income taxes. On the other hand, if you didn't touch the money, it would probably earn you more in your IRA than the appreciation on your property would ever add to your equity. You might be more prudent to pursue the low- or no-down-payment opportunities described in the accompanying text.

About Coborrowers

"Well, we don't quite qualify for this loan," goes a typical conversation. "But if we added Grandpa's pension and social security payments, we'd qualify easily! And he said he'd be happy to cosign the mortgage."

Is that legal? Yes, and allowed by both Fannie Mae and Freddie Mac.

Usually it is not required that the coborrower (cosigner) take title to the property—that is, his or her name need not appear on the deed. In order for the extra income to be counted for qualifying purposes, the coborrower need only sign the promissory note.

However, if there is a coborrower and the down payment is less than 10% (an LTV ratio greater than 90%), the buyers must show evidence that the coborrower intends to occupy the house that is being purchased.

What Will It Cost You?

As soon as the purchase contract is signed and the sighs of relief have been heaved, every home buyer starts talking about interest rates. Most people forget, however, that the interest rate is only one aspect of what a mortgage will cost.

Points

Points are an up-front fee charged by the lender that makes the loan more profitable. One point is 1% of the amount to be borrowed. In financial circles, this fee is sometimes called the *discount.* But in this marketplace "discount" is the reverse of what you generally expect when shopping at a bargain table.

When you pay points, the value of your loan is "discounted." For example, let's take a $100,000 loan with two points. Before you get the loan or at the closing, you must pay the lender $2,000. The check the lender writes to the seller may indeed be in the amount of $100,000, but $2,000 of that is your money. So the value of your loan has been discounted by two points to $98,000.

Term

The term of a loan is the length of time scheduled for repayment. Thirty years is the most common term now being written for mortgage loans. But 15- and 20-year mortgages are gradually gaining in popularity among borrowers who are trying to grow equity quickly as a means of saving for the future.

Though few people have the discipline to take advantage of it, another option is to get a 30-year mortgage you can afford now and prepay as you can, providing that your mortgage agreement imposes no penalties for doing so.

The longer it takes to pay back a mortgage loan the more expensive the loan becomes. In fact a 30-year loan costs the borrower more than twice as much as a 15-year loan. For example, financing $100,000 at 7% for 15 years would cost the homeowner $61,789 in interest. (That's in addition to the price paid for the property.) Financing for 30 years would cost $139,508. But that interest is tax-deductible, so the numbers don't reflect an additional $21,761 in tax savings over the second 15 years, assuming you're in the 28% tax bracket ($139,508 − $61,789 = $77,719 in interest savings × 0.28 = $21,761).

On the plus side for longer-term mortgages is the amount of monthly payment. A $100,000 loan at 7% with a 15-year term requires a monthly principal-and-interest payment of $899. The same loan with a 30-year term requires a monthly P&I payment of $665. The $234-a-month difference could enable a buyer to qualify for the mortgage rather than being turned down.

And finally, remember that not all homeowners stay in their homes long enough to pay off a mortgage. The lower monthly payments of longer-term loans are usually well suited to movable people, who will sell the home and move on in a few years. The lower monthly payments facilitate making ends meet, and the difference in the amount of equity accumulated in the first few years of the mortgage is not usually enough to persuade homeowners to go without their weekly pizza-and-movie outing. The interest savings and fast equity growth of the shorter-term loans usually appeal more to rooted people, who choose to remain in the homes of their choice.

Don't Assume

• •

Don't assume that every buyer pays points, even if you're told so. Points are usually tacked on to loans with lower interest rates—the lower the rate, the more points. (Three points is considered a moderately high number.) Points can be paid by the buyer, the seller or both. Sometimes, especially when interest rates are high and real estate sales are slow, points can become an issue in negotiating a home purchase. It's not unusual for a seller to agree to pay some or all of the points for a mortgage that would get the property sold. When money is readily available and competition between lenders is high, points tend to disappear.

The Fees of Loan Processing

Like most businesses, the home-mortgage industry doesn't give its customers very much for free. The fees required for loan processing may not make or break the mortgage deal, but they are still significant expenditures and must be planned for and factored in when comparing one loan offering with another. Some of these fees (points, the appraisal fee and the credit report fee, for example) must be paid in cash either upon application, upon acceptance or at the closing.

Here's a list of the most common fees, but there may be others. Be absolutely certain that your lender gives you an accounting of all the anticipated costs when you apply for the loan. The law requires it.

It's the Law

• •

APR stands for **Annual Percentage Rate,** the effective rate of interest when all costs to be paid by the borrower are factored in. The APR in mortgage advertisements is the number in small print, almost always different from the big black number that catches your eye. Regulation Z of the federal Truth in Lending Law requires that all mortgage lenders inform a prospective borrower of the applicable APR within three days of the loan application date. By that time, however, the nonrefundable application fee has already been paid. It's far better to ask for the APR *before* you apply and compare it with other loans.

Application fee

At this writing, lenders typically require a fee of $300 to $400 to accompany your loan application. Sometimes that fee includes the cost of the credit report and the bank appraisal of the property, and sometimes it doesn't. Find out before you apply.

When lenders are aggressively competing to attract borrowers, they sometimes waive application fees. Once paid, however, the fee is usually not refundable if you decide to go elsewhere for a mortgage or even if you are turned down.

Credit-report fee

This fee is paid for a review of your credit history. Usually around $50, it's sometimes included in the application fee. If it is a separate fee, you still usually pay it at the time of application.

Appraisal fee

The lender sends an appraiser to the property to determine its fair market value. The appraised valuation then determines the LTV ratio of the mortgage. Although all of this information is gathered for the benefit of the lender, it is almost always the prospective borrower who must pay the bill.

Sometimes the appraisal fee is paid separately up front, sometimes it's included in the application fee, and sometimes it's paid at the closing.

Don't Assume
•••••••••••••••••••••••

If you are asked to pay an origination fee at the time of your mortgage application, don't assume that it will be refunded if your application is turned down. Get a statement to that effect, in writing.

Legal-review fee

Some lenders charge a fee of $100 to $300 for their attorneys to review the purchase contract and the closing materials. This fee is usually paid at closing.

Origination fee, also called a placement fee

Most lenders make this charge to cover the costs of establishing a new loan. Since there are no regulations restricting origination fees, they can be any amount. Some are as high as 1% of the loan amount. Competition among lenders, however, usually keeps these fees under control. You'll often see them drastically reduced or even eliminated when there is more money to lend than there are borrowers. Lenders may collect the origination fee upon application but more commonly do so after they've approved the loan and made the loan commitment, sometimes at the closing.

Buydowns

A buydown is a cash payment to the lender by the seller, the buyer or another party to persuade the lender to reduce interest rates—and therefore the monthly payment—during the early years of the loan. Usually the reduced interest rate applies for the first three years of the

Penny for Your Thoughts

There are few ways in which a man can be more innocently employed than in getting money.

Samuel Johnson
(1709–1784), English writer
and lexicographer

mortgage term. After that, the interest rate and monthly payments return to the original loan schedule.

A buydown can help a buyer qualify for a loan during the early years of homeownership. Loans with buydowns usually accommodate young people whose incomes keep them from qualifying for the mortgage at the outset, but who will probably earn more by the time the interest rate (and therefore the monthly payments) increases. There is always some risk that financial setback (loss of a job, divorce, illness, and so on) will derail the anticipated increase in income, making the new higher payments at the end of the buydown term difficult to meet. This situation could force the homeowner to sell.

Buydowns are accepted by both Fannie Mae and Freddie Mac for fixed-rate mortgages only.

Where to Get the Money

If you know what kind of loan you want and you are reasonably sure you are qualified, where to get the money is not a problem. The mortgage industry is huge and growing. Even small towns have a dozen or so sources in the phone book, and large cities often have well over a hundred. The problem is really where to get the best *deal* on the money.

Comparing the offerings is still the best shopping technique, no matter what you're buying. So think of yourself as "buying" a mortgage deal and start making comparisons. The box on page 239 offers some places where you can find leads, while the remaining discussion highlights some bigger-picture issues.

Should You Use a Mortgage Broker?

Like real estate brokers, who provide a service rather than sell a product, mortgage brokers provide a matchmaking service for lenders and borrowers but do not lend money themselves. A good mortgage broker will have contact with numerous lenders and will advise the borrowers on sources of the best loans for their particular needs.

More, More, More

Sources of referrals to mortgage lenders include the following:

The real estate agent who sold you the property

Representatives from mortgage companies, banks and mortgage brokers make regular stops at real estate offices to drop off information on their best and newest mortgage products. Some agencies have computerized rate and fee data. The options presented in the real estate office, however, are probably not the only ones available.

The Yellow Pages

Look under "Mortgages." Call the advertisers and ask about rates, types of mortgages and points. You can get this information by phone. Don't allow anyone to make an appointment to come to your home unless you are ready to go with that company. The rep will come with an application in hand, and you'll probably get a hard sell.

Local newspapers

Many newspapers publish the mortgage rates of major area lenders (those that buy advertising space) in their real estate sections. You can also evaluate the primary players in your area by following the lenders' advertisements for several weeks while you're still house-hunting.

Mortgage-reporting services

Several national and regional mortgage-reporting publications are available to the general public. Fees range from a few dollars per issue to $20 or so per report. These two major services can provide rate and program information from across the nation.

- **HSH Associates** (1200 Route 23, Butler, NJ 07405; 800–873–2837)

- **National Mortgage Weekly** (Box 360991, Cleveland, OH 44136; 800–669–0133)

The Internet

The Internet is ever expanding. If you have access, try exploring these Web sites, which include rate-quoting services and on-line mortgage brokers.

- **Bank Rate Monitor** (http://www.bankrate.com). Provides average national and state consumer bank rates, and samples of lenders' rates in each state's metropolitan areas.

- **HomePath** (http://www.homepath.com). Produced by Fannie Mae, this Web site offers comprehensive, step-by-step guidance to help you determine whether you're ready to buy a home, shop for a mortgage, or refinance a current mortgage. It includes financial calculators.

- **HomeOwners Finance Center** (http://www.homeowners.com). Another online mortgage broker.

- **Homeshark** (http://www.homeshark.com). This online mortgage broker allows you to shop lenders' offerings in your area, prequalify and preapprove yourself, and apply online.

- **HSH Associates** (http://www.hsh.com). HSH collects current data from up to 3,000 mortgage lenders in selected markets nationwide. You can purchase individual weekly reports of lenders' offerings in your area ($10 per report, plus shipping and handling).

- **Kiplinger Online** (http://kiplinger.com). Here you'll find an extensive array of home-buying and mortgage-shopping "what if" financial calculators.

- **Quicken** (http://mortgage.quicken.com). This online service of Intuit, makers of *Quicken* money-management software, provides an online mortgage brokerage that features six large national lenders, including online applications.

Comparing Loan Offerings

Lender	Name of rep.	Phone	Loan type

Rate	Points	Fees	Lock-in (# of days)	Notes
——	——	——	——	——————————
——	——	——	——	——————————
——	——	——	——	——————————
——	——	——	——	——————————
——	——	——	——	——————————
——	——	——	——	——————————
——	——	——	——	——————————
——	——	——	——	——————————
——	——	——	——	——————————
——	——	——	——	——————————
——	——	——	——	——————————
——	——	——	——	——————————
——	——	——	——	——————————
——	——	——	——	——————————
——	——	——	——	——————————
——	——	——	——	——————————
——	——	——	——	——————————

So why should anyone bother to hunt for the best mortgage on their own? Why not let George do it?

Fine, if George is a good broker. But when you take the easy way and let someone else do the work, you give up control and replace it with trust—or perhaps "hope" is the better word. Sometimes blind faith works. Almost always, it costs you.

Some lenders simply do not accept applications from mortgage brokers, so you'd miss out on their offerings. Some lenders accept the loans originated by the brokers, but they increase the fees they charge the borrower to cover the cost of paying the broker. Some brokers even charge the borrowers an additional fee on top of the fee they're paying indirectly through the lender who accepts the mortgage.

But you may be wondering if there is ever a situation when even the wisest and most frugal home buyer *should* seek out a mortgage broker. The answer? Whenever the prospective borrower is trying to put a square peg in a round hole. Consider using a mortgage broker if:

- **you don't quite meet** secondary mortgage–market qualification guidelines

- **you're self-employed** and have an uneven earnings pattern

- **you're buying an unusual property** that is difficult to appraise

- **you're asking for a particularly large loan**

- **you want a financing arrangement that's unusual** or "creative," perhaps a balloon mortgage or an interest-only loan (both discussed in the sidebar on page 243).

There are investors in the financial marketplace who will consider almost anything. A good mortgage broker will seek them out and the service is usually well worth the extra money it might cost.

Seller Financing

Whenever times are tough and mortgage money is scarce, seller financing becomes more common. Most sellers do not want to carry a mortgage; they would rather take their money and run—well, walk, anyway—to whatever new venture they have in mind. But when there is a need to sell and buyers are having a hard time getting financing, sellers may have to bite the bullet.

Don't assume that seller financing is the answer to your home-financing troubles, whatever they may be. Buyers who choose this kind of mortgage loan usually get short-term financing, at a price. Part of that price is increased risk, which is hidden in the need to refinance when that short-term loan comes due. If the circumstances that made it difficult for the buyers to get conventional financing in the first place still exist and can't be overcome, the buyers may lose the property.

Unless you are absolutely certain that you can't get a better deal elsewhere, avoid short-term seller financing. If

Words to the Wise

When a seller "takes back" a mortgage for all or part of the sales price, the loan is called a **purchase-money mortgage.** This type of seller financing is often used when a mortgage loan is being assumed by the buyer. The purchase-money mortgage is then a second (or junior) mortgage that makes up the difference between the buyer's available funds (the down payment) and the principal balance.

Purchase-money mortgages are rarely **self-amortizing**. (Self-amortizing means your scheduled payments over the prescribed period will pay off the principal of the loan in full.) Some are structured as **balloon mortgages.** In this financing arrangement, you make payments that would amortize your loan over a certain term (say, 20 years), but the loan is due in full in a shorter period (say, five years). When the loan comes due, you still owe most of the principal, and that's the "balloon" payment.

An even simpler structure for purchase-money mortgages is the **interest-only mortgage.** In this financing arrangement, the borrower pays interest only for a prescribed number of years. At the end of the mortgage term, the entire amount borrowed must be repaid.

Although most common in "creative" seller-financing deals, both balloon mortgages and interest-only mortgages (also called **straight-term mortgages**) can be found among the offerings of commercial lenders and mortgage brokers.

this route is the only way you can manage to buy the property, be certain that the loan agreement allows prepayment at any time and without any penalty. Try to convert to more conventional financing as soon as possible.

Assumable Mortgages

When a loan carries an assumability agreement, it means that a new buyer can take over the seller's liability for the unpaid balance of the loan at the same rate and terms that the seller had agreed to. For example, if the seller had purchased the property with an assumable fixed-rate mortgage at 7% and then sold it two years later when the going fixed-rate deal was 9%, the new buyer could assume the 7% loan by paying the seller the difference between the purchase price of the home and the principal balance on the loan.

Before the advent of ARMs, an assumable mortgage was sometimes a precious thing indeed. Today it's the assumable *fixed-rate* mortgage that can be valuable. Whenever interest rates rise sharply, a fixed-rate assumable mortgage can help to sell a house because the property becomes "less expensive" (lower monthly payments) to the buyer. FHA and VA fixed-rate loans are assumable. By assuming a mortgage, the buyer avoids qualification procedures, loan-processing fees and points.

Mortgage assumptions, however, are not common in today's real estate marketplace. Just about all conventional fixed-rate mortgage loans are written to include a *due-on-sale clause* so that the full unpaid principal is due if and when the property is sold. The loan therefore is not assumable.

Most adjustable-rate mortgages being written today do allow assumability. Usually, however, the loan includes a provision that gives the lender the right to approve the new buyer assuming the loan. Unless interest rates have skyrocketed, there is usually little advantage (beyond saving loan-processing fees) in assuming an adjustable-rate loan.

About the Application

At the beginning of this section, mortgage loans were described as business transactions. Keep that in mind when you get ready to make the actual application for the loan. Trite as they may be, remember the old sayings, "You have only one chance to make a good first impression" and "Put your best foot forward." Think of yourself as a valued customer, not a petitioner, and don't go "hat in hand." Make the extra effort to understand the *why* of what you are doing and keep as much control over the process as you can.

For example, the current practice is to have the lender's mortgage rep fill out the mortgage application by asking the prospective borrowers questions and writing down or keying in the responses. (Some mortgage applications are even taken over the phone.)

It's better, if you can arrange it, to complete the form yourself, perhaps with the rep there to answer your questions. If the rep is using a computer and you can't actually do the keying in, be sure you read over the screen or, better yet, request and carefully read a printout before you write a check for the application fee. An omission or an error as easy to miss as a misplaced decimal point can cause unbelievable delays, sometimes even a turndown.

> ## *Words to the Wise*
> •
>
> **Underwriting** is the process of evaluating the prospective borrower's creditworthiness, the collateral (property to be mortgaged), and the certitude of performance (the level of risk involved in making the loan). The person responsible for approving the loan is called the **underwriter.** The mortgage rep who takes your application really has no say in the process. Decisions are based on the information provided on the application form. Be certain it is accurate.

No-Doc and Low-Doc Loans

If you have a down payment of at least 30% of the purchase price (an LTV ratio of 70% or less), you may be able to avoid some or most of the usual paperwork of applying for a mortgage.

Some lenders offer "no documentation" loans when

their risk is lowered by a substantial down payment. These loans require no verification, not even employment verification. The price of this convenience to you? Lenders charge additional fees or points, or a fraction of a point higher interest, on no-doc loans to compensate them for the extra risk involved in taking on an applicant whose qualifications to repay the loan they have not checked.

There is a less expensive alternative that's almost as convenient. For good-risk borrowers (those making relatively high down payments), most lenders also offer programs requiring less written documentation. These mortgage applications require only enough verification to

Ready, Set, Apply

Like any businessperson preparing for a meeting or presentation, your first step is to *get organized*. Start by gathering in advance the information you'll need.

"How can I know in advance what I need?" you ask.

It's easier than you may think. Just as there are now national standards for loan qualification, there are also standards for application forms and requested information.

Check off the following items and collect paperwork in a file folder.

Starters

- **Full legal name** of each applicant

- **Current address** of each applicant, and all other addresses for the past two years

- **Social security number** for each applicant

- **Copy of the fully executed purchase contract**

- **Condominium or co-op documents** (if applicable)

- **Copy of divorce decree** (if applicable) and

documentation of alimony, child-support or separation maintenance payments due

- **VA certificate of eligibility** (if applicable)

- **Copy of the property-tax bill** for the collateral property (ask the seller for this)

- **Copies of utility bills** for the past year for collateral property (for FHA and VA loans; ask the seller for this)

Employment

- **Employment history,** including names, addresses, phone numbers and contact persons of all employers for the past two years, for all applicants

- **Copies of W-2 forms or 1099s** for the past three years if you are paid by commission, work under periodic contracts, work from a union hiring hall or earn your living from royalties

- **Copies of the past three years' tax returns** and profit-and-loss statements if you are self-employed provide adequate proof of your income and assets. Examples of alternative documentation are:

- **a verbal confirmation of your position and length of employment** from your employer rather than written documentation;

- **copies of the past two years' W-2 forms** and one month's pay stubs and bonus pay stubs rather than a written verification of your annual salary from your employer;

- **copies of three months' bank statements** rather than a written verification of account activity from your banks;

Your assets

- **Account information,** including numbers, bank names and addresses, and approximate balances for all bank accounts (including checking accounts)

- **Ownership evidence for stocks and bonds** (copies of brokerage statements are sufficient)

- **Other investment information,** including account numbers, bank names and addresses, and approximate balances for all CDs, money-market fund accounts, IRAs, and 401(k) or other retirement accounts

- **Approximate value of cars or other automobiles,** including recreational vehicles and boats (some lenders require proof of ownership)

- **Approximate cash value of any whole-life insurance policies**

- **Estimated value of personal property** such as furniture, jewelry, rugs, paintings, and so on

- **Information regarding family trusts, pensions or other annuities**

- **Other real estate owned,** including appraised value, mortgage amount if any, mortgage lender's name and address, loan number, amount of monthly payment, annual taxes and insurance costs, and rental income if any

Your liabilities

- **Auto or boat loans,** including lender's name and address, loan number, approximate balance, length of time remaining until paid off, and monthly payment

- **Mortgage loans.** (See "other real estate owned" under "Your assets.")

- **Unsecured personal loans and student loans,** including the approximate loan balance, name of lender, amount of monthly payment and remaining term

- **Other installment loans,** including the same information as for unsecured personal loans

- **Charge account and credit card balances,** with a copy of the latest monthly statement for each account

- **copies of 12 months of canceled checks showing verification of rent paid** to a landlord or payments to a previous mortgage lender.

Your Credit Report

Once you gather all the data and fill out the application, you can stop worrying if you've been both honest and thorough—except for the credit report. Because of the immense pool of credit information gathered into nationwide reporting pools, there's always a chance of some error on even the simplest report. Errors commonly occur in credit reports due to:

- **mix-ups with accounts** for some person or persons with a name similar to yours

- **accounts you have closed** that are reported as active

- **multiple entries** of the same account

- **mistaken information** reported by the creditor.

That's why it's important that you obtain credit-report

More, More, More

Just because you've never made a late payment doesn't mean your credit report is A+. Errors creep into the best-kept data. If you know you'll be buying soon, check your credit at the three major reporting agencies (listed below) at least two to three months before you go house-hunting. That will give you time to get errors corrected.

Experian offers consumers one free report a year; the other two bureaus charge a small fee for each report (unless that fee exceed limits set by state law). You can write or call to request a report.

- **Equifax** (P.O. Box 740241, Atlanta, GA 30374-0241; 800–685–1111; http://www.equifax.com)

- **Experian** (National Consumer Assistance Center, P.O. Box 2104, Allen, TX 75013-2104; 800–392–1122; http://www.experian.com)

- **Trans Union** (Consumer Disclosure Center, P.O. Box 390, Springfield, PA 19064-0390; 800-916-8800; http://www.tuc.com)

If you are having problems clearing your credit report, you can get help from an attorney or you can get advice from the **U.S. Public Interest Research Group** (218 D St., S.E., Washington, DC 20003; 202–546–9707).

information *before* you apply for a mortgage loan. Federal law has established your right to know what's in your credit files. If you find errors, take the time to clear them up so they don't get reported to the lender. If there are contested balances or other problems, try to resolve them before you apply for the loan.

The Interest Rate Lock-In

If things are relatively stable in the financial marketplace, some lenders will hold your maximum interest rate for 60 days from the date either of your application or of the bank's commitment, with a provision that you will get a lower rate if prevailing rates go down before you go to closing. Other lenders are not so generous. Some even refuse to commit to any rate, requiring instead that you accept the going rate at the time of your closing.

Many lenders, however, allow borrowers to pay for a "lock-in," which will guarantee a certain rate. The more likely rates are to go up and the longer the time between your mortgage commitment and your closing, the higher the fee is likely to be. Fees of one-half point to one point are not uncommon.

When considering a lock-in, you should weigh its cost against your probable savings. Let's say, for example, that "everyone" thinks rates will go from 8% to 8.5% on 30-year fixed-rate mortgages during the interval between your mortgage commitment and your closing. So you pay one point for a lock-in at 8%. (That's a $1,000 fee on your $100,000 loan.) It would then take 31 months of payments—more than two-and-a-half years—at the lower interest rate before you would recoup the cost of the lock-in. And the effective cost is even higher because you would not have had the use of that money during those two-and-a-half years!

> # More, More, More
> •
>
> A brochure titled *A Consumer's Guide to Mortgage Lock-Ins* is available free from the Federal Reserve Board. Send a postcard requesting the brochure to: **Board of Governors of the Federal Reserve System** (Publication Services, MS-127, Washington, DC 20551; 202-452-3244; http://www.bog.frb.fed.us).

If you are a rooted person who plans to stay in the property for 15 years or more, the lock-in described above would certainly be worthwhile. But if you are a movable person who thinks a transfer is possible within three to five years, the lock-in can be a painful out-of-pocket fee with little, if any, reward.

Sometimes lock-in fees are collected with the loan application. If this is your case, be certain you get a written statement of your lock-in rate and dates, and a written statement that the lock-in fee will be returned to you if your loan is turned down. More commonly, the lock-in fee is collected within a limited number of days after the loan commitment is made.

Commitment

The news that your mortgage application has been approved usually comes by phone. That happy call is then followed by a commitment letter. If, on the other hand, you are turned down, the lender must tell you why in writing.

Lenders have 30 days to respond to your loan application. Often the response is much sooner, sometimes in as little as 24 hours. But in times of maximum activity in the real estate marketplace, you may have to wait out the month. Be sure you allow enough time in the mortgage contingency clause of your purchase contract. (You can read about contract contingencies in Chapter 15.)

If three weeks go by and you still haven't heard, start making calls to the lender and get an extension for the mortgage contingency, in writing, from the seller. The seller will undoubtedly worry a little when you ask for the extension, but if the lenders are backlogged in applications, the real estate agent will inform the seller and there should be no problem. The request for an extension is excellent evidence that you have applied for the mortgage.

If you chose to lock in the interest rate, the commitment letter will state the interest rate, points and the amount and type of mortgage loan. If you chose not to lock in, the letter will state that you agree to pay the going rate at the time of closing.

All mortgage commitments expire by a certain date by which you need to have closed on your purchase and exercised the loan commitment. Thirty to 60 days from the date of commitment is common for existing properties, as is 60 days if you are buying a house that is to be built or is being built. If you have a long wait to closing, ask the lender for an extended commitment. If your closing is postponed beyond your commitment date, get an extension of the mortgage commitment in writing.

Once the commitment letter is sent, especially in times when money is tight, some lenders require the payment of a commitment fee, often as much as one point. This commits you to the loan and prevents you from hunting for a better deal.

So you make that commitment payment (if necessary), you inform all concerned parties that your mortgage has been approved, and you start looking forward to moving into your new home. You might even be tempted to brag a bit at a cocktail party or backyard barbecue, both about the great deal you got on a house and the great deal you got on the financing. If you do, you're likely to hear the response, "Boy! Are you lucky!"

It's politically correct to smile and nod your head. But hold in your heart this little verse by Emily Dickinson:

> *Luck is not chance —*
> *It's toil —*
> *Fortune's expensive smile*
> *Is earned.*

The Comforts
of Home

Two house hunters come into a Realtor's office and say, "We're looking for a three-bedroom ranch with two baths, no higher than $175,000."

After 14 showings during three weekends, with all properties meeting the criteria, the couple still haven't found anything they want to buy. What's going wrong here? If these house hunters could only be flies on the office wall (or have a strategically placed bug), they might hear their agent say, "They don't know *what* they want!" And truer words were never spoken.

One of the most common errors in home buying is defining housing needs by number of bedrooms and architectural style, without identifying or evaluating individual considerations of comfort. Comfort is the factor that separates *home buying* from ordinary real estate investment.

Should you take it seriously? Time tells. In the vast majority of cases, "how much we like this place" (how comfortable we are) is usually at least as important as "how much we paid" when home buyers talk about whether they got a good deal two or three years down the road.

Regardless of what gateway you've chosen in Part I, identifying your specific needs for comfort is the first step in getting the right house every time you buy. Comfort is kind of a chicken-or-egg problem: The type of home buyer you are will influence your specific needs for comfort, and your needs and resources will determine what type of home buyer you are. So, you'll probably find that this chapter complements your home-buying self-assessment from Chapter 2.

What Exactly *Is* Comfort?

Are we talking about bathrooms with 12-spigot Jacuzzi tubs? Bedrooms with skylights and three-inch-deep, wool-pile carpeting? Wraparound decks? Computerized kitchens? Fireplaces you could sleep in? A wet bar for the family room?

Not exactly. Those are luxuries, although they may indeed be part of your comfort profile. But comfort need not be expensive. It can, and should, be a factor in housing decisions within almost any price range, at any point in life and within any of the housing gateways described in Part I. What's comfortable, after all, is determined individually from a seemingly infinite number of choices.

Comfort is a feeling of ease and contentment derived from a person's response to his or her physical surroundings. You can feel comfortable because of tangible elements in a home, such as large rooms or extra-thick padding under the carpets. Or you can feel comfortable because of intangible elements, like excellent lighting and ventilation or a traffic pattern that keeps people and pets out of each other's way.

One of the most important factors in choosing a house you will love and consider valuable throughout your ownership is the awareness of what makes you—and every person who will share the house with you—comfortable. Just as some people like to sleep on rock-hard mattresses, while others like to sink in and snuggle, there is no right or wrong answer to the comfort-in-a-home question. Instead, the problem is one of identification. Most home buyers, indeed most people, know when they feel comfortable, but they don't always know or can't say *why*.

If you can identify what it is that makes you feel comfortable, you can evaluate any property against your particular needs and standards. Doing that evaluation will usually keep you from over-responding to charming decorating, carefully targeted marketing techniques or superheated marketplace pressure. You can focus on buying a house that suits your lifestyle. The worksheet on pages 254–255 will help you draw a comfort profile for yourself and your family.

A house is a machine for living in.

Le Corbusier (1887-1965), Swiss-born French architect

What's Your Family Comfort Profile?

Ask each of your family members to rate each statement, below, from 1, "not important," to 5, "essential." Average the results to establish your family's comfort profile.

	Importance ratings	
	Each family member	Family average

Privacy

I need a space that is mine alone, where I can leave everything just as I please (either in total disorder or in perfect order).

The parents' bathroom should be separate from the children's.

All windows should have blinds or shades.

Kids and teens should have a separate place where they can hang out with friends.

Backyards should be separated from neighboring yards by trees, shrubs or fences.

The family living area should be completely separate from the formal entertaining area.

Space and movement

I want all the bedrooms clustered together.

I want the master bedroom and a guest room separate from the children's bedrooms.

I want an office/den/study that is apart from the busy and noisy living area of the house.

I want to be able to remove outer wraps and footwear in a foyer or coat room before entering the main living area.

I want a big eating area where my family and friends can gather at the kitchen table.

I like cocktail parties where people can move from room to room through wide doorways without retracing their steps.

When I invite people for dinner, I don't want them even to see the kitchen, much less walk through it.

	Importance ratings	
	Each family member	Family average

Security

I feel better with an alarm system that covers all the lower-level doors and windows.

I want plenty of outdoor lighting.

I want to be able to see who's knocking at my door before I open it.

I want to be able to see the neighbors' lights at night.

I want to live relatively close to police and fire stations.

I want all my bedrooms on the second floor.

Glass patio doors make me nervous.

Luxury

I want thick carpet, even over hardwood floors.

I want indoor climate control for all seasons.

I want built-in storage shelves in the garage and basement and a pantry in the kitchen.

I want at least one fireplace.

I want a swimming pool.

I want a bathroom with a stall shower and a whirlpool tub, double sinks, and a skylight.

Walk-in closets are needed in all the bedrooms.

The living room should have built-in bookcases and a built-in bar.

Penny for Your Thoughts

Ah! There is nothing like staying at home for real comfort.

From *Emma,* by Jane Austen (1775-1817), English novelist

Before you take it on, however, let's go through some common comfort issues in home-buying. Once you exhaust this list, you may add more of your own.

A Primer on Privacy

Whether shopping for a one-bedroom condo or a 15-room mini estate, most home buyers say they consider privacy important. Funny thing, though, few of these buyers ever explain to their real estate agents who wants privacy from whom or what. Why? Probably because they haven't thought through this highly personal intangible.

Privacy basically comes down to freedom from interaction with, intrusion by or awareness of, or observation by other people. The following are some of the most common areas of concern for privacy in a home.

All in the Family

Sharing is one of those things we all learn in kindergarten. But no matter how much we love our housemates, how socialized we get or how gregarious our nature is, most of us want to keep some space that is ours alone. And most of us forget that when we house-hunt.

One couple, for example, chose to build a traditional, two-story colonial but modified its interior to a contemporary *open-space* design. The rooms in the front of the house (living room, dining room and entry foyer) were traditionally laid out, while the entire back of the first floor was built without walls between kitchen, eating area and family sitting area. On the first night in their new home, both husband and wife delighted in the open feeling, the "togetherness" of their new home.

Within a few weeks, sounds were clashing late every afternoon. Mr. Homeowner liked to come home from work and turn on the television for the latest news from Wall Street. Mrs. Homeowner had long been in the habit of listening to books on tape as she prepared the evening meal. Each activity diminished the enjoyment and comfort of the other person.

At the other end of the spectrum, many mothers of very young children appreciate an open floor plan because it allows them to keep their children in sight while working at other chores.

Some builders are answering the call for more privacy while keeping the benefits of an open plan by including a small and completely walled room, adjacent to the living area, to house a computer and perhaps an easy chair. The bigger the house, the more of these functionally "dedicated" rooms you can expect: TV, exercise, music, kids' playroom, library, and so on. There is no "right" answer to the question of room division. There is only the "right" question that all house-hunters should discuss before buying: How will this property provide the privacy that each member of our family needs? To answer that question, you'll need to analyze the privacy needs of your family. Consider these questions.

> ## *Words to the Wise*
>
> •
>
> **"Open-space" floor plans** have become increasingly favored by builders since the late '70s. These houses are built without full dividing walls between the kitchen, breakfast area, family room, living room and sometimes even the formal dining room. The "open space" saves the builder considerable money (rarely passed on to the consumer). Some homeowners enjoy the extra light and the unconfined feeling. Others, however, sorely miss the privacy of a cozy corner.

To start with, what sorts of separations might you need in order to preserve privacy? Those separations might include:

- Husband and wife from each other

- Mom and Dad from the kids

- Kids from each other

- Family from overnight guests

- Grandma or Grandpa, or both, from everybody else, and vice versa

- Pets from certain parts of the house

- A working-at-home family member from family life

Now ask yourself: What other elements in a home preserve your privacy, or the impression of it, besides walls and room division? For example, do you prefer doors rather than open doorways? Where? Do you require a certain position of rooms relative to each other? Soundproofing (determined by the way the walls, floors and ceilings are built)?

Let Me Entertain You

Affluent Victorians had very distinct functional zones to their houses. There were the working areas like the kitchen, laundry and servants' quarters. There were the family living areas. And there were the areas to which guests were admitted. Today, for the most part, there are few servants, everyone works, and many people who are not family members are invited to sit around the kitchen table.

But the current egalitarianism does not mean that we all socialize in the same way. Some of us don't mind if the business colleague invited for dinner sees the dog's bed, the cluttered desk, or the overflowing toy box or laundry basket. Others prefer to keep an area for entertaining guests separate from the areas typically used by family members.

When house-hunting, consider not only your entertainment space needs but also your entertainment style. Your space needs are determined by how many people you entertain, how often, at what seasons of the year and what times of day or night. Your style is determined by whether you prefer a sit-down dinner party or a barbecue, a cocktail party or a brunch, a children's birthday party or a sleepover—or perhaps all of the above.

Would you be comfortable with a house that invites people to move about it freely, or would you prefer an area that welcomes guests and another area that is obviously reserved for the family? In other words, do you prefer to have formal rooms and informal rooms, or one tone throughout the house?

If you have children, would you have them bring their friends to their rooms or to a common socializing area? Although it almost never adds to resale value, would a basement play area help keep peace in the household?

Do you want the kitchen closed off from the dining area to hide cooking and serving messes? Or does the chef in your household like to talk with guests while cooking? Do you like to invite your guests to join in meal preparation? (You'll need a kitchen with a lot of counter space and enough space to pass without bumping.) How much of a hike is it from the kitchen to the formal dining room?

Will overnight guests have (or need) a separate bathroom and perhaps sitting area? Is there a den or office that might stand in for a guest bedroom if necessary? Is at least one of the children's rooms large enough to allow two or more children to share it so as to create a temporary guest room?

Is there adequate closet space for guests' coats near the areas where you will most likely be entertaining? Is the location of the powder room both convenient and private?

What Light Through Yonder Window Breaks?

Most house hunters are very concerned with the views they see looking out of the windows of a house. Few consider what the world outside sees when looking into those windows. But the perception that privacy is lacking sometimes becomes a factor that diminishes comfort in a home once the moving vans have left and "normal" life has been taken up again in earnest.

But don't blame the windows entirely. Huge windows looking out from a penthouse above a city, or overlooking an ocean cliff or a wooded area, might have absolutely no effect on one's sense of privacy. On the other hand, a window of very modest proportions in a lavatory located at the front of the house can cause considerable discomfort. The truth is, most issues of external privacy arise from a combination of window location and house *siting*.

For example, you'd do well to think twice before buying a house that's located at a right-angle turn in a road or at the point where one road intersects another to form a "T." Imagine the intrusion from the lights of oncoming vehicles throughout the night. Or, if you're considering a house that's located far below grade level, imagine passersby looking into the second-story windows. Will they be looking into the private areas of the house, such as the bedrooms and bathrooms? Even if these situations don't make you uncomfortable, they can make resale difficult in the future.

Words to the Wise

• •

The **site** or **siting** of a house refers to the place where it stands. Issues to be considered with siting include closeness to the road (also called "setback"), direction of exposure (north, south, east or west), terrain (on a hill, in a valley), and proximity and exposure to neighboring properties. More about siting in the next chapter.

Road grade level refers to the elevation of the center line of the street. If you are below grade level, your house is lower than the road and your driveway slopes down from the road to your house. If you are above grade level, your house is above the road and your driveway slopes up from the road to your house.

The amount and the "feeling" of light in a house is also affected by the siting. A house that faces east-west will have morning and afternoon sun. But if the front of the house faces east and you prefer morning sun in your kitchen at the back, you're out of luck. But, if you have a lovely deck just off your kitchen, you may spend many hours enjoying late afternoon sun.

If you are in an area where winters are severe, a house that faces north-south may be considerably more expensive to heat because of the maximum wall exposure to the coldest winds. If you are in a southern climate, however, north-south exposure can prevent overheating from direct sun during the morning and afternoon while giving you a steady cool light on the northern side (great for artists) and a diffuse, warm light on the southern side (just what the indoor gardener ordered).

Of course you can go on to theorize about an east-southeast or a north-northwest front siting. The point is that the pattern of sunlight in the house in a particular climate will make a difference in your comfort level. As soon as a house begins to pull at your heart strings (or your purse strings), therefore, you should stop and check to see how it is sited. Notice if windows are essentially front and back only or on all sides of the house. Visit the house at different times of the day and make note of how the light is falling. Be aware that the change of seasons will change the amount and pattern of light.

If you are having a house custom-built in a development where all the houses are set back from the road at the same distance, you can choose from among the available lots to find one that will give you the particular orientation to the sun that you want. (For example, one house on Street A may be planned facing east, which will give you morning sun in your living room and afternoon sun in your kitchen, whereas the same house on Street B will provide the opposite exposure.) If you find a particularly large lot in an area where houses are not lined up equidistant from the curb, you can plan for the siting of your foundation to bring in the sun as you would like it.

Don't forget, apartments get sunlight, too. When shopping for a condo or co-op, check for siting just as you would in a single-family house, especially if you'll have only one exposure. For example, an apartment with a west-facing exposure in a southern climate is going to "feel" hot in the afternoon even if you have the air conditioning on. On the other hand, a northern exposure won't be kind to your plants.

While windows allow natural light into a house, they also have the potential for transmitting both heat and cold. Many a horror story has been written about drafty old houses with rattling windowpanes. Some of that fiction could become uncomfortable reality if you were to buy a "charming" old house in the summertime, only to find that it lets the cold air in and the heated air out all winter.

Most listing sheets specify whether a house has storm windows or double-glazed insulating windows. Consider that when estimating both value and comfort. And remember also to check the placement of the windows. Even with air conditioning, there may be times when you want to open a few windows to get a nice cross breeze.

How Big Is a Yard?

When most house hunters talk about "a little privacy," they mean they want a single-family detached house with a yard. But the size of the lot on which a house stands does not always correlate with your sense of privacy while living in that house.

Penny for Your Thoughts

Small rooms discipline the mind; large ones distract it.

Leonardo Da Vinci
(1452-1519),
Italian painter, sculptor,
architect, and engineer

You can own a flat acre of land contiguous to several other flat acres and not have enough privacy to give your dog a flea dip without the neighbors noticing. On the other hand, a corner-unit condo apartment located in the building that abuts the designated open-space land can be very private indeed.

We'll talk more about the effects of land on life in a house in the next chapter. Concerning the relationships among privacy, land and comfort, ask yourself:

- **Does this piece of property give you the opportunity to separate from other people when you choose to do so?** Is there some kind of screening, either natural—like hedges—or fabricated—like fences—that will let you cook some hot dogs without inviting the neighbors over?

- **Do you want your kids to be able to play safely outdoors without your constant supervision?** Does that mean a fence? A very large lot? Or several lots that run together without fences or marked lot lines?

- **Do you like to conduct certain, otherwise private, activities outdoors?** Do you want to indulge in all-over tanning, for example?

- **Do you want to keep your pets from bothering and being bothered by other people and animals?** Can you accomplish that by fencing a pen in the corner of the property, or by installing an invisible, electronic "fence"?

- **Do you consider the perimeter of your yard to be your first line of defense from criminal intruders?** Is a long driveway good (more distance between you and an opportunistic criminal passing by)? Or bad (your home is too isolated and, therefore, vulnerable)? Close neighbors a plus or a minus?

If you find that a house that you like in every way except the degree of outdoor privacy, stop and think a bit before discounting it. Would fast-growing evergreens on the lot lines help? Would the neighborhood association allow a fence? If you like everything about a house except the degree of outdoor privacy, you might spend the money for a consultation with a landscape architect.

Does Form Follow Function?

Visiting builders' "model homes" is an excellent way to prepare for house-hunting or home building. Most of today's designs and decorating schemes are based on extensive research about what appeals to the majority of people and what works effectively. Ask yourself:

- **Does this arrangement of rooms work?** Why or why not?

- **What's pleasing about it and what's not?** Is it comfortable?

Before you leave, be sure to pick up the ever-present fliers and floor plans for study at home. And as you read through each subhead in this section, refer back to these two questions and test your responses. As you attend open houses, for both new and not-so-new houses, you'll soon be testing what you see against your comfort criteria without even thinking about it.

It's a Matter of Size

What are the smallest acceptable dimensions for a bedroom? Most experts will say 10 feet by 10 feet or perhaps 9 feet by 12 feet. But what if you're looking at a 1920s house with a mystery room that measures 6 feet 9 inches by 8 feet 10 inches? Do you call it a walk-in closet? Make it into a bathroom? Or perhaps you need a room for your PC. If one of those ideas works for you, great. But will it work for prospective buyers at the time of resale?

Although there are conventional ranges of size for rooms of various types, there are no "correct" standards. For example, the so-called "science kitchen" that packs everything a cook could need into a neat (and small) U shape may be perfect for the home with only one person cooking, but a disaster for the family that cooks together. A 28-foot-long living room may be perfect for the homeowner with a grand piano who often holds formal parties and gatherings. But the same room would be an underused and costly extra for the homeowner who finds enjoyment and entertainment gathered with friends and family around chips, salsa and the TV in an informal living area.

It would seem logical, then, to advise you to pick a house with room sizes that fit your individual needs. But there's a little caveat here. Rooms outside the normal size range may work for you, but they may also make the house more difficult to sell in the future. The unusual dimensions will reduce the pool of potential buyers who find the rooms comfortable.

When odd-size rooms are a consideration, you'll have to decide whether comfort—that is, meeting your personal needs—or resale value is more important in your current home-buying situation. If you don't have an answer, go back to Chapter 2 and consider again whether you have a "movable" (turnover-oriented) or rooted home-buying character.

But the question remains: How does an average (much less an inexperienced) house hunter find out what's the normal size range for each type of room? It's not hard. You can quickly become quite knowledgeable by considering a number of properties before you begin to house-hunt seriously, making sure to observe, compare and compile your results. That's why it's important to go out house-hunting several times *without* your checkbook before you are ready to make an offer on anything.

Don't Assume

When you hear a sales agent say, "This is our most popular model" or "these are the features *everyone* is asking for," don't assume the floor plan and features are right for you. Keep-up-with-the-Joneses fever is a high-risk factor in house-hunting that can cost victims many thousands of dollars for features that will never be used or will actually cause *discomfort*. Think about these trendy features, for example:

- **The two-story entrance foyer** that wipes out valuable floor space and sucks up heat.

- **The two-person whirlpool tub** in which a person bathing alone can't get comfortable because it's both too long and too wide.

- **Ceramic floor tiles in the kitchen** that are hard to stand on, very cold in the winter, create noisy echoes, and are guaranteed to break everything that is dropped on them.

- **Palladian (arched) windows** that double in cost when you try to find shades that will give you some privacy at night.

- **Outdoor motion-detector lights** that go on at 2:00 A.M. because a deer or stray dog was crossing your driveway.

Moving About

Here's a factor that house-hunters often miss because they look at a house from the standpoint of touring or looking about rather than living in. They forget to consider even the most common questions of everyday living, such as:

- **What door will be used for bringing in the groceries?**

- **Where will the children come in and take off their boots** and jackets after playing in the snow?

- **How many stairs will you climb to do a load of laundry?** How many stairways will you have to babyproof when a child becomes mobile?

- **How will you deliver food** from the kitchen to the patio on a summer's evening or to the dining room for a formal dinner party?

- **Where will you serve the drinks** and place the hors d'oeuvres for a cocktail party?

- **Where will you housebreak the puppy?** Can a room be gated or closed off? Can you go from it directly to the outdoors—quickly?

- **What if someone is sick** or recuperating from surgery? Is there a place to rest comfortably on the main level, and is there a convenient bathroom?

More, More, More

A timesaving means of becoming more familiar with typical room sizes and traffic patterns is available at just about any magazine stand and even at your supermarket. Those *101 House Plans for the New Millennium* type magazines rarely get used for building new houses, but they're good study tools. Compare the sizes and locations of bedrooms, baths, kitchens, and formal and informal living areas. You'll quickly get to know the conventional size ranges for each type of room. And you'll also soon be able to identify unusual traffic patterns in the houses you inspect on your particular house-hunts.

Here again, you must consider your particular needs, lifestyle and buying situation when deciding whether a property with an unusual *traffic pattern* will be comfortable for you. Try drawing a floor plan of a house you think you like. Then take a colored pencil and draw traffic pattern lines on the floor plan as you imagine yourself moving through a typical day—from brushing your teeth in the morning through coming home from work, changing clothes, having dinner and spending the evening. Take another color of pencil and draw the traffic pattern for another member of the family. And another color for each additional member. When and where do they run in parallel? How much do they cross or collide? If you feel really ambitious, you can draw the floor plan again and try mapping the movements of people for a holiday gathering or a child's birthday party.

Houses with inconvenient traffic patterns that force their inhabitants to walk around things or through one room to get to another are notoriously difficult to sell. They usually bring lower prices than comparable houses with more conventional floor plans because prospective buyers feel inconvenienced or awkward. Even when the sellers assure everyone, "Oh, it's nothing at all. Once you get used to it, you don't even notice," most buyers don't believe them.

Words to the Wise

The relationship and arrangement of rooms and the access to those rooms determines the way the occupants of the house will move within the space enclosed by outside walls. The typical pathways of movement are usually referred to as the **traffic pattern** of a house.

Safe at Home

It's almost impossible to feel comfortable in a home if you don't feel safe. In fact, many home buyers choose a property because its location helps to allay their concerns for personal security. But the structure and layout of a house can also contribute to your sense of safety.

Exterior Doors

One woman refused to buy a property that met her requirements in every way and was the favorite of her husband and her children. Why? There were four access doors to the outside on the main level and two more in the basement. With three children, a dog and two cats, she had the feeling that she would never be completely sure that all the doors were closed, much less locked.

Perhaps this young mother was burdened with more cares than most, but her objection was a sound one. When choosing a house, it's important to ask yourself the following about the exterior doors.

- **Do they coincide with your lifestyle** by providing easy access to the outdoor areas you will use most often?

- **Do they meet your need for privacy** by closing off visual access to the indoors when closed? Do you need special floor-to-ceiling shades to cover 6-foot-wide sliders? Or are the sliders always open to the outdoors?

- **Can they be secured?** In theory, every door can be locked, but some locks are definitely better than others.

- **Can you see who is on the other side** without opening the door? Apartments often have spyholes. Many newer houses have glass panels on either side of the front door. Often you can see who's at the door by taking a peek from a window in the living room or another front room. But what about the recessed front door with no windows? What about solid back doors? Will you open a door without seeing who is there?

Windows and Alarm Systems

Windows are more than a source of light and a means of providing fresh air: They are also an entry point for burglars. When considering the security aspect of comfort, notice the number and position of the windows on the first floor and in the basement. Are any particularly well hidden by a corner of the building or by trees and shrubs? Do any provide easy access because of decking, closeness to the ground or position on a fire escape? And most important, can you live with that? Your answer may depend on the crime rate in the area or on other security measures in the house, such as alarm systems.

Alarm systems are usually considered a plus when evaluating a house. There are many kinds, from simple motion detectors that set off sirens to sophisticated systems that send a silent message to a monitoring center and ultimately to police. Some systems even include smoke detectors that alert a monitoring center to call the fire department whether you are at home or away. Companies that install monitoring systems usually charge a monthly fee, so factor that into your housing expenses if necessary.

Parking and Entrances

In suburban locations, you're most vulnerable to robbery at the moment you get out of your car to open the garage door. That's why automatic garage-door openers have become so popular.

In urban condominium complexes and older houses where detached garages are more common, many home buyers take note of the distance and path to be traveled from the parking spot to the door. Outdoor lighting becomes a factor here, as well as clear and level pathways.

In apartment buildings and multifamily houses with shared stairwells, there is yet another concern beyond getting to the entranceway. How is the common doorway locked—by traditional key or electronic keypad? How many keys are available to people other than yourself and your family? How often is the combination changed?

Woods and Roads

Despite popular fear, having woods or open fields behind a house does not usually increase the risk of burglary. More commonly, break-ins increase wherever road access is good. Driveways that bend around to the back of the house are an invitation to steal. Corner lots sometimes make emptying the house of its contents easier and more inviting.

In some parts of the country, greater numbers of break-ins are reported in residential communities near interchanges of interstate highways. Perhaps thieves see the nearby highway as a quick escape route. Or perhaps they get off at an interchange and cruise until they find a likely candidate for a burglary.

Just a Little Extra

A feature regarded as an extra, an enhancement or a luxury by some can be regarded as an absolute necessity or at least an essential element of comfort by others.

- **Is garaging your car essential?** How about the cars of your teenage children?

- **Do you need basement space** for a woodworking shop or some other hobby that helps to keep you sane and happy?

- **Are clothes important** enough to your job or your self-image that closet space ranks right up there with the size of the kitchen and bathrooms?

- **Is soaking in a warm tub** a form of relaxation for you, or do you save the tub for bathing the dog and prefer a tiled shower for two with nine showerheads at various levels in the walls?

- **Would your life be bleak** without a patio and barbecue?

If some items in that list seem silly and superfluous to you, be advised that they are essential concerns to other home buyers. And comforts essential to you may seem silly to them. Yes, people certainly are different! And those differences score many a point for regarding home buying as an art as much as a business transaction.

Your Piece
of the Earth

The word unique means "being the only one." If you take the word "only" seriously, that's a tall order and there really aren't many things in life that are truly unique. But each and every piece of real estate you will ever own is unique.

Did you do a double take? Are you thinking, "My split-level house looks pretty much like the split-level next door. And my brother's condo is exactly like the condo upstairs from it and the one downstairs, too. What's unique about that?" Each and every piece of real estate is a particular part of the earth. There is no other like it because nothing else can stand in the same spot. That even goes for condo apartments where the space you own, enclosed by certain walls, is different from all other space.

The unique piece of the earth that your property occupies is its *location*. There is nothing more important in the real estate marketplace.

The location you choose will affect your comfort level in your home and influence your chances for growing equity through profitable resale. Many home buyers get so caught up in the exterior appearance and interior feeling of a house that they forget to consider:

- **where the house stands in relation to** jobs, schools, recreational facilities, shopping and municipal services;

- **where it stands in a neighborhood** and what kind of neighborhood that is;

- **where it stands on the lot** and what kind of lot that is; and

- **where it is located in the building** (if you are buying a condo or co-op apartment).

If you want to buy the right home, you must consider location and comfort together. When house-hunting, location means *town, neighborhood* and *lot.* (For condo and co-op buyers, it can also mean *floor* and *number.*) Let's go over each factor as it will affect your real estate purchase. Remember: Careful attention to location is the first line of equity-growth protection. It will also save you house-hunting time as you eliminate those locations you do not want and concentrate your hunting in those areas that really interest you.

At the end of the chapter, spend some time with "On Location: A Twenty Question Quiz." This multiple-choice exercise is not a test of how much you know, but rather a kind of sounding board that will help you evaluate how closely the location of each house you consider harmonizes with your own needs and preferences.

Words to the Wise

Real estate is defined in law offices and in dictionaries as *land, including all things natural or man-made that are permanently attached to it.* The issue of what is *permanent* attachment sometimes causes problems. So does the word *land.* You see, *land* in real estate law is not only the earth's surface but also its extension downward to the center of the earth and upward to infinity. That's how owning *real estate* can mean owning the oil beneath 661 Paleozoic Boulevard or owning the space enclosed by the walls of apartment 704 on the 7th floor of Cozy Corners Condominium.

About Towns

The word town may evoke scenes from Norman Rockwell, but it's used here to describe all variety of municipality, including cities, counties (which frequently govern suburbs), townships and villages. The most common comparisons made between towns are of taxes, schools, services, recreation and accessibility to the workplace (the length of the commute, in miles and time).

Should you ask local residents about these factors? Of course. But be prepared to evaluate the answers in light of the slant that people typically put on them. Practically everyone will know the tax rate for his or her own town and maybe even some of the neighboring towns. That's a pretty objective thing to ask about and something that you can easily confirm through other sources. When you ask about the schools, however, almost everyone will tell you how good they are. They'll usually rate recreation pretty high, too. Services will draw some snide remarks. And the commute? Everyone complains. Pay careful attention when someone's response differs from these patterns. He or she may have a real insight to report.

This is not to say that you shouldn't gather both facts and opinions, but rather that you should weigh the facts and opinions according to your own standards and needs. Schools are probably the best example. The parent who wants a good high school business program for his or her son won't be impressed with the fact that Shakespeare is taught in all four years of English. The parent who thinks global communication is the key to success in the future and wants foreign languages introduced into the elementary school curriculum won't be impressed by the fact that the sixth-grade soccer program is the best in the state.

In another sphere, if you're a tennis player, it's the number of tennis courts that counts, not the number of bus trips the recreation department offers each year to area museums and attractions.

In short, the town that's "just right" for one home buyer may be all wrong for another.

What You Can Learn at City Hall

Very, very few home buyers ever set foot in the municipal buildings of the towns where they are house-hunting. And they miss so much. Let's take a look at some of the not-at-all-secret secrets you can uncover there. All are matters of public record.

Tax maps

Most towns are divided into workable subdivision maps called *blocks*. The perimeter of each piece of property on each street within a block is drawn on the map, and the lot is given a number—thus the "block and lot number" on listing forms, contracts and other legal documents related to home-buying. Owners' names and sometimes the amount of the assessed valuation (the amount on which property taxes are based) are usually printed within the space of the lot.

Looking at tax maps is an excellent way to get an overview of how land is divided and valued in a town. You can compare the overall layout of one town with that of another and get an idea of the strength of the tax base. A well-developed and maintained tax base will make sudden jumps in property taxes less likely.

As you consider and compare tax maps between towns or between parts of the same town, ask yourself the following questions:

- **How big are lots in the various neighborhoods?** Are similarly sized lots clustered in planned developments? Looking at residential lot size will give you a quick glimpse of the town's character. Is it urban and high density, where "neighborhood" will mean living close to your neighbors? Or is it country-suburban, where "neighborhood" will mean maintaining your land (a lot of work) and your privacy (not much trouble)?

- **Is assessed valuation always higher on the larger lots?** Or do you find some areas where small lots have houses with high *assessed valuation*? High valuation on small lots can mean upscale townhouse development, where there is little maintenance responsibility. Or it can mean an urban location where land is extremely expensive. Low valuation on large lots can mean an older neighborhood where small houses were built when land was cheap. (These are sometimes candidates for subdivision.) It can also indicate an area where land is still inexpensive and housing not in great demand.

Words to the Wise

• •

Assessment has two meanings in real estate language. It refers to the act of estimating the value of a property for tax purposes. One might say, "The town will be doing an assessment next year." And it refers to a tax levied on a property in addition to general taxes, usually for a special service or improvement. One might say, "Our sewer assessment was $2,000." **Assessed value** or **assessed valuation** is the actual numerical value assigned to a property by the assessor for tax purposes. One might say, "The agent says the fair market value of that house is $190,000 but its assessed value is only $127,000."

Check Points for a Long Distance Move

Your goal is to get both an image and an understanding of what it's like to live where you're going or where you think you'd like to go. Ideally, your research into an area will be done through several personal visits, but a good deal of the work of gathering local information can also be done from a distance—any distance.

Consider the following topics.

Climate and terrain

You'll need to know temperature ranges and weather conditions to judge the appropriateness and value of such home systems and features as:

- heating and cooling systems
- necessary insulation
- a fireplace or a swimming pool
- insulated windows

The topography and the soil affect:

- lot size and shape
- basements
- architectural styles
- construction materials
- wastewater disposal systems

Common weather hazards

Landslides, earthquakes, tornadoes, hurricanes, floods, blizzards, smog, drought and forest fires: Each region of the nation has its own particular weather-related problems. It's important to know what they are in the region you'll be going to so that you will be prepared, and "prepared" includes adequate insurance coverage.

Pests and other problems

Gigantic Palmetto bugs, hovering horseflies, killer mosquitoes, warring ants, rabid raccoons, howling coyotes, shrub-eating deer, disease-carrying ticks: The list can go on and on. How about mold, mice, roaches, bats, locusts, termites, No-See-Ums, spiders, snakes, geckos, and even wolves and mountain lions? Had enough? There's always something!

By knowing what pest infestations or problems to look for in a region, you'll know what features (like fine-mesh screens on a porch) might add value and comfort to a home. You can also better evaluate the home inspection report.

The socioeconomic character of the region

How do most people make their living? Business? Industry? Farming? What is the median income and what is the jobless rate? Is the region economically healthy?

Checking out the local economy is more than a matter of how much house you can get for the money (see Chapter 12). It's also a question of personal comfort and lifestyle. Most people like to live near others who have interests, values and lifestyles similar to their own.

HOW TO GET THE INFORMATION

You can and should do the detective work long before you make the move. Check out these sources.

In your local library

- **Telephone books:** Most libraries have the phone books of major U. S. cities., including the Yellow Pages. Choose the city closest to your prospective location and look under "Pest Control Services." There you'll find ads signaling which pests are common. Poke around awhile to see what else you can learn about lifestyles in the area.

- **Money-management magazines:** Libraries keep back issues of most national magazines. Publications like *Kiplinger's Personal Finance Magazine* and *Money* carry articles from time to time that compare and rank the desirability of places to live. Your reference librarian will help you find and retrieve the articles.

- **Books, video tapes and CD-ROMs:** Libraries shelve or can order a huge range of materials, from statistical studies to travel videos to street maps on CD-ROM.

By phone and mail

- **State tourism and development offices:** You can get brochures, booklets and maps, most free for the asking. If you have specific questions, you can also ask for referral to other information sources.

- **The local chamber of commerce:** Member businesses will send you information and often answer your questions.

- **The local Board of Realtors:** You can get statistics regarding home sale prices and selling times in the areas that interest you.

- **Real estate or land and urban studies departments of large universities:** Many offer free information on housing patterns, construction methods, socioeconomic growth, and more. Be prepared to be put on hold and transferred from one extension to another, however. If you're persistent, you'll usually find someone who can help you.

Online

There is so much information available! It just takes patience and persistence and some research skill to sift through it all. Many chambers of commerce now have web sites as do personal finance magazines and large real estate firms. Start by going to your favorite search engine and entering the name of the city or state you're interested in.

Local newspapers and magazines

There's nothing like a subscription to the Sunday edition of the local newspaper or a regional or city monthly magazine to get you into what's really going on in the area you are considering. For larger cities, look for Sunday editions on newsstands or at public libraries. You can even check the want ads for jobs and houses for sale.

The people who live there

There's more to life than what gets into print. Talk with people who live in the area or have lived there. This might require networking (like asking your cousin Maud for the phone number of her brother-in-law).

- **Do all the pieces of property in one part of town, on large and small lots, have relatively higher assessed valuations than in another?** That means that the tax assessor found one area of town more desirable to the buying public and therefore more "valuable" than another.

- **What areas of town support commercial properties?** How large are the commercial assessments? A healthy balance between commercial and residential property will help to keep the residential property-tax burden down.

- **Are there large tracts of undeveloped land in the town?** How are they being used? (You can check with the people in the zoning office. See the next section.) If it is designated as "open space" land, it won't bring in tax revenue, but neither will it generate expenses that could cause taxes to rise. If the land is available for development, how it is developed may change your future property-tax burden. High-density housing will probably create the need to finance and build new schools, for example, and your taxes may rise. Commercial or industrial development may shift some of the tax burden away from you, homeowners, to business owners.

Once you are seriously considering purchasing a piece of property, tax maps will help you evaluate property layout, ownership and land usage in a particular area. Property near commercial areas will not appreciate as well as that in the midst of a residential area.

You can also gather information from the assessment that may help you with your negotiating. Records from the previous tax assessment include the size of the lot; the square footage of the house; a description of the interior, including the number of bedrooms, baths, and so on; and often the date of the last sale and the price of the property.

Zoning maps and the master plan

When a municipality establishes zoning, it divides the land within its borders into zones that specify the uses allowed to owners of the real estate within each zone. For example, an R-1 zone might allow only single-family detached houses, while a commercial zone might allow both housing and businesses. When a town enacts a master plan, it establishes zoning that will presumably allow growth in an orderly, ecologically sensitive and economically sound manner.

Zoning maps can provide insight into what is likely to happen to that vacant land behind "your" house. More important, however, they will allow you to visualize how densely populated the town is, how much open space there is, and how much of that space will be used for growth, whether residential, commercial or industrial. If you take the time to read the master plan, you can even learn what kind of signs are allowed in town and whether the town sees itself as set in its ways or very much open to change.

Some history and statistics

Most towns publish materials that describe the growth and development of the community, its primary industries, population, points of interest, recreation sites, and so on. Although these pamphlets are generally available in real estate offices, few home buyers read them. And so they miss information that can be essential to understanding what a town is all about.

The type and structure of the town government is usually outlined, with the names of the people who are responsible for everything from running town hall to making sure your street is cleared in winter. You may not recognize the name of a single person in the pamphlet, but put it away in a safe place (one you won't forget about) because those names could become valuable indeed if you run into challenges in the months after you close on your house.

What the town considers important almost always

Don't Assume

Don't assume that zoning is a guarantee. Just because you saw R-1 on the zoning map doesn't mean that townhouses won't be built on the five-acre tract across the street. Although zoning is a means of planning and controlling development, it is not carved in stone. The owner of a lot can apply to the town's planning board for a **variance** that would allow noncompliance with the zoning law. And the owner(s) of a tract of land can apply to have the zoning changed. A public hearing is always required, but the vote of the planning board does not always reflect the opinions expressed by neighboring property owners. Ask the planning-board secretary how many zoning variances have been applied for in the past three years and how many have been granted.

Penny for Your Thoughts

It has long been an axiom of mine that the little things are infinitely the most important.

Arthur Conan Doyle,
(1859–1930), from
A Case of Identity

comes through in its printed publications. Ask yourself: How do these concerns compare with what I consider important? The questions might range from whether tin cans are picked up with aluminum cans for recycling to whether mentally disabled children attend regular classes or special classes in a separate school building.

Systems that keep the pulse beating

Town hall is also a good place to get information on what's in town and where it's located. Maps are usually available showing the location of schools; hospitals; transportation centers; police, fire and ambulance stations; recreation facilities; and other community services and facilities.

They'll even show the location of the town landfill—what used to be called "the dump"—and the sewage treatment plant. Such facilities, although known to local residents, may well be hidden from normal road view. Proximity to these community services does *not* facilitate growing equity.

While you are in town hall, stop in at the town clerk's office and ask about:

- **Water supply.** Is there a municipal system, community systems, private wells, or a combination of all three?

- **Wastewater disposal.** Does the town have sewers? Its own treatment plant? Do the streets have storm sewers? Do some or most houses use private septic systems?

- **Refuse removal.** Is collection included in property taxes or must a homeowner hire a private service?

- **Recycling.** Is it mandatory? What materials are accepted? Are there regular collection days or a drop-off center?

- **Leaf and snow removal.** How are they handled?

- **Special pickup.** How are large trash items like sofas and refrigerators removed?

- **Sidewalks and streets.** Is the town pedestrian-friendly, with plenty of sidewalks, crossings and "walk" lights? How are streets and sidewalks kept clean and repaired?

- **The fire department.** Is it volunteer or full-time professional? (The type of fire protection in town will affect your insurance rates.) Is it well equipped? Are there fire hydrants throughout the town? What sources of water are used for firefighting, and are they reliable regardless of the season or other demands for water?

- **The ambulance squad.** Is there one? How is it staffed and equipped? Is it a community service supported by tax dollars and private contributions or is it a private service you pay for if you need it?

- **Services for the physically disabled, elderly and mentally handicapped people.** Do they meet your needs? Are the buildings and other facilities adequate?

- **The local library.** How large is it? Does it have neighborhood branches? How about a bookmobile? Can you get interlibrary loans?

- **The police department.** How large is it? How responsive is it? Consider the ratio of officers to population, the average response time for calls, and the frequency and types of crime in the community. What additional services and programs does it offer, such as self-defense or bicycle-safety training?

- **Local celebrations, festivals and events.** Do they appeal to you? How might they affect you? Consider noise, litter, increased foot and car traffic, and parking.

What You Can Learn at School

If you have school-age children or expect to, then you'll probably want to be assured that local schools are of high quality and will meet your family's needs. But it's also important to remember that the reputation of the schools affects the desirability of a town and thus the value of the houses within it.

Because schools are generally paid for by local property taxes, even home buyers without children should be confident that their tax dollars will be used well. It's important to be aware not only of the quality of education being offered, but also of the physical plant. Outdated or inadequate buildings and facilities can make learning more difficult, and updating or replacing them almost always means a tax increase. A town whose facilities are in good shape almost always has the advantage.

It's very difficult to find answers to individual questions and concerns about education in the public information materials distributed by local school districts. When seeking information about programs and policies, you need to establish what educators call an "interactive participation with a person in a position of authority." In other words, visit the school and talk with the principal! If you haven't yet chosen a neighborhood and don't know which schools your children will attend, call the superintendent's office and make an appointment to talk with someone about the district's curriculum.

Each home buyer has his or her own concerns about schools, and you should begin to create your own list, using the worksheet provided on page 282.

Programs

- **What's the average class size** in elementary school?

- **What's the pupil-teacher ratio?** The smaller, the better. Does that include assistants to the teacher?

- **What schedules are available for kindergartners?**

- **Are there any after-school care programs?**

- **What special program**s (such as art, music, drama or a Junior Great Books discussion group) are offered at the elementary level? Are those that interest your child offered?

- **How are the needs of special-education students met?**

- **Are computers available in the classroom?** What are they used for?

- **How are physical education and exercise handled?** Is there a daily exercise period (rain or shine)? Is there professional instruction in games and sportsmanship?

- **What subjects do middle-school students study?** Is the curriculum beginning to expand to lay the foundations for citizenship and productivity in today's world? Are languages taught? An awareness of money management? Some beginnings of career exploration?

- **How do local pupils rate on standardized tests?** As compared with nearby towns? In the state? In the nation?

- **What courses are offered at the high school level and which are required for graduation?** Will students who do not choose a college preparatory program be adequately educated to find work in the adult world?

- **Is there a college-preparatory course of study in high school?** Are advanced-placement courses offered?

- **What extracurricular programs are available?** Are your child's interests represented?

- **What percentage of each high school class graduates?** Generally, the higher the percentage, the better the school district.

- **What do graduates do after graduation?** Where do graduates go to college? How many enter the military? Does the school help in job placement for students who choose to work in the community?

Physical plant

- **Are there enough buildings to house the current school population?** If not, what alternatives is the district using?

- **When were these schools built?** Are they in good repair? Will they need to be replaced? When? How will construction or renovation be paid for?

- **What are the projections for future need,** and how does the district intend to meet the challenge of increasing or decreasing numbers?

Other community services

If your primary concern with community services is not schools but perhaps recreation, public transportation, elder care or security, use the same research technique as the concerned parent: go to a knowledgeable source. Stop

Continued on page 283

Comparing Schools

Use this worksheet to compare how well different locations will meet your educational needs and concerns now and in the future. Say that the quality of grade school is on your list of concerns. It might be a low priority now because your youngest child isn't of school age, but it will be a high priority in a few years. If you expect to be in your home then, which of the neighborhoods you're considering has the best grade schools?

Our educational needs/concerns		Priority	Location _____	Location _____
1. _____	Now	_____	_____	_____
	5 years	_____	_____	_____
	10 years	_____	_____	_____
2. _____	Now	_____	_____	_____
	5 years	_____	_____	_____
	10 years	_____	_____	_____
3. _____	Now	_____	_____	_____
	5 years	_____	_____	_____
	10 years	_____	_____	_____
4. _____	Now	_____	_____	_____
	5 years	_____	_____	_____
	10 years	_____	_____	_____
5. _____	Now	_____	_____	_____
	5 years	_____	_____	_____
	10 years	_____	_____	_____
6. _____	Now	_____	_____	_____
	5 years	_____	_____	_____
	10 years	_____	_____	_____

in at the senior citizens' center, the police station or the parks department and ask to make an appointment with someone who can discuss programs and policies. Bring a list of questions.

If you are researching a long-distance move, actual visits may be above and beyond the call of duty (and available time). So, as Ma Bell used to say, "Let your fingers do the walking." The blue pages in the local phone book will give you the numbers you need.

All in the Neighborhood

What makes a neighborhood? Nearness. Whether your area of choice is a city, a suburban development, a condominium complex, a private and gated golf community or a rural road, the dwellings around your home are your neighborhood. And like it or not, your neighborhood will affect the value of your home and the comfort you feel there. Most people prefer to live among people pretty much like themselves, and homes in clusters that are more or less homogeneous in size, age and quality tend to hold their value better than homes in areas where home styles and prices are mixed and where some commercial buildings may be included.

The Good and the Not-so-good

You've already read about many considerations for choosing a neighborhood specific to the home-buying gateways of your choice, so let's focus on more universal concerns. Besides the appearance and maintenance of the houses surrounding a property that interests you, there are intangible and invisible factors in a neighborhood that can greatly affect your wealth and happiness. They are three S words—*sounds, smells and security*—and the big C word, *convenience!*

Noise
Houses near major transportation facilities such as highways, railroad tracks and airports will be subject to a

more or less constant sound buzz. Many homeowners say that you won't even "hear" the noise once you get accustomed to it. That may or may not be true for you. But the fact remains that houses in noisy areas are very difficult to sell and usually bring a lower price than comparable properties without the noise pollution. Houses near occasional noise sources such as a fire station, civil-alert and ambulance-squad siren pole, police station, kennel, and some recreation centers and gathering places also suffer from buyers' aversion to noise. Note that many real estate agents promote "quiet street" in their ads.

Don't Assume

• •

Don't assume that traffic is light on a given through street just because that's what you see from the house you're inspecting at 11 A.M. That street could rival the Daytona raceway between 7 and 9 in the morning and 4 and 6 in the afternoon. Before you sign a contract to purchase, visit the house during commuter hours.

Odors

Odors are another "you'll get used to it" item. Some people might object to the smell of a salt marsh but have no problem with the scent of sulfur from standing groundwater. Your own tolerance is a judgment you'll have to make. Just remember that it's also a factor that you'll have to deal with when you finally decide to sell your home.

Smell can be as strong as a concrete wall in preventing a sale. People do not want to live near sewage-treatment plants, garbage dumps, factories, swamps or any other place with a "characteristic" odor. On the other hand, a breeze with the scent of pine needles near a forest or the hint of salt in the air near the ocean can act as a subconscious sale-promotion device!

A safe place

When the word "security" is mentioned, most people think of the crime rate—which is, of course, a factor in choosing any location. But security can also mean a safe place for children to play, or for jogging or riding a bike. The amount of traffic on the streets around a house can affect its value and salability. It's a truism in real estate offices around the nation that houses on major through streets are slow to sell.

Convenience

Besides "quiet," another word that shows up frequently in real estate ads is "convenient"—that is, "convenient to town, convenient to the railroad station, convenient to highways, convenient to shopping." It seems everyone wants easy-to-get-to and just-a-few-minutes-away even when right-next-door-to would be a major detriment.

Of course, by easy-to-get-to some folks mean within an easy walk and others mean an easy drive. Consider what convenience means to you, then weigh each neighborhood against your own needs.

Appearances count

Because a homeowner can't force a neighbor to cut the curbside weeds that are beginning to look like road ruffles or to repaint the front of a house that is beginning to look as patchy as a harlequin Great Dane, most savvy prospective buyers check out the appearance and maintenance of nearby houses before committing to a purchase. One "rotten apple" may not spoil a whole barrel, but it will affect the apples close to it.

The Power of an Association

Some neighborhoods are actually organized communities that function almost like mini municipalities. Most people would expect that multi-unit condominium buildings grouped together in a development would fit this profile. But there are many kinds of homeowners associations beyond the condo community. The presence of one in your neighborhood and the degree of its influence and effectiveness could affect both your lifestyle and your wallet.

A well-run condo community and homeowners association can enhance the pleasure of ownership. A poorly run organization can cost you money in higher and higher fees for less and less benefit, not to mention more and more irritation. If a neighborhood you are considering has a homeowners association, even if it's not a condominium community, be sure to read Chapter 6, "Of People, Planning and Profit: The Shared-Space Gateway."

In the traditional condo community, the homeowners association governs the maintenance of the buildings (other than the inside of the individual units), the land and the improvements. In many newer, "gated" communities, however, the dwelling units look like single-family detached homes and are, in fact, owned individually. But the land on which they stand, the surrounding land and the recreational facilities are owned in condominium ownership. The homeowners association levies "taxes" (called condo fees or association dues) to maintain the property held in condominium ownership. The homeowner must pay these dues or the association can begin legal proceedings against the property.

It's the Law

• •

Requirements and restrictions on the land: Membership in a neighborhood association can be required with the purchase of a home. A legal agreement (called a **covenant**) establishing the association and requiring the membership of every owner of every home built on the named parcel of land can be written into the deed. This covenant is said to "run with the land," which means its requirements and restrictions are passed on to each new owner.

Other deed restrictions and covenants can also run with the land. They are generally noted by the seller in the listing information. Sometimes they are found in the title search conducted by a closing agent. It's never wrong to ask the agent, "Are there any deed restrictions on this property?"

In other associations, homeowners own both their houses and their lots individually but share in the maintenance of roads and recreational facilities. And in still other arrangements, the roads are owned and maintained by the municipality, but homeownership in the community carries with it use of (and responsibility for) recreation facilities such as a golf course, marina or swim club.

Required membership in a homeowners association is noted on a real estate listing and should be made known to all prospective buyers. All houses in the neighborhood belong, and the membership should be considered when evaluating the entire neighborhood.

Homing In on a Homesite

The location of a property within a neighborhood also affects your investment. Salability and value are usually most protected with a site located in the middle of, or at least well within, the neighborhood. Houses on the edge of a neighborhood of similar homes usually sell at lower prices, especially those on lots that abut a commercial zone or a residential zone of higher-density housing, such as multifamily houses, apartment buildings and condos. In either case, you can expect that you might feel more crowded, experience more traffic and enjoy less privacy.

The exception is a fringe location where the change of housing character is toward *more* expensive homes or toward a park or designated open space. In those cases, a fringe location will actually increase comfort and value with better views, more green space and enhanced privacy.

The Cheapest House Myth

The old real estate adage "buy the cheapest house in the neighborhood" is based on the theory that the value of the other houses will increase the value of yours. This sometimes works, especially in upscale resort communities, but not always. Some potential buyers are intimidated as they anticipate "keeping up" with the owners of the more expensive properties. Others simply don't want to live in the "oddball" house.

Better advice—or at least advice that brings a positive result more consistently—is to buy in the middle range of a neighborhood. While the smallest houses are brought up in value somewhat by their surroundings, the largest are brought down substantially. For example, a 3,000-square-foot, colonial-style house in a neighborhood of 1,800-to-2,100-square-foot split-levels would most likely sell at only slightly above the top split-level price. This holds true even if the same house, located in a neighborhood of similar colonials in the same town, would sell for 1½ times the top split-level price.

Generally, no matter how different the size and design, no matter how much it is "improved," a house will seldom sell for more than 20% above the mean average price in the neighborhood. Also, the time on the market required to make the sale of the "biggest and best" house is likely to be considerably longer than average. So, if you are concerned only about getting maximum living space and luxury for the money, you can sometimes do so by choosing a house bigger and better than its neighboring properties and negotiating hard.

But if you seek to protect the appreciation potential of your housing investment, you will usually do better by choosing a property in the middle price range of the neighborhood. Your financial investment in such a property is protected by strength in numbers and by the resale appeal of a homogeneous neighborhood.

Don't Assume

• •

Don't assume that a house is a fabulous bargain that will grow your equity exponentially just because it is listed at tens of thousands less than a house of almost identical size, style and floor plan. That identical house may be located in a neighborhood that supports its higher price. The bargain house, while a lot of house for the money, may be located in a neighborhood that holds the price down, making the asking price actually a little on the high side of fair market value. Location affects value more than any other single factor.

This Land Is My Land

The size of a lot does not affect its value nearly as much as its location. A tiny lot in the Georgetown section of Washington, D.C., is worth many times as much as a two-acre lot on Castlebrook Drive in Raleigh, N.C. A half acre in the middle of a block in the middle of Happy Acres will be worth more than a full acre on the corner where Happy Acres is bordered by Helzapoppin Highway.

Once a ballpark value is established by location, however, several other factors affect both the value of the property and the comfort level in living there. Use the following list as a guide in weighing your own needs and preferences.

Shape

Generally, lots with an ordinary shape—that is, rectangular or square—are preferred. They are easier to visualize as "this is what I own" and, in a funny way, easier to "defend." You can fence them, hedge them, or just mow exactly on the line. Blame it on territorial instincts.

Pie shapes and multi-angle lots work in some terrains, especially where rock outcroppings, streams or other natural barriers help define the lot. Usually, however, these lots require explanation and definition from the owner because children, guests and prospective buyers don't always understand why the property ends where it does. Many buyers object to the challenge of landscaping and maintaining a "strange" lot.

Good depth of property (an intangible measured by good feeling, not feet) behind the house is usually preferred

More, More, More ●●●●●●●

The United States Geological Survey is responsible for providing accurate maps that show the topography of the land throughout the nation. The USGS Earth Science Information Centers (ESIC) answer questions, sell maps and distribute consumer-oriented materials. For the address of the nearest ESIC, write to: U.S. Geological Survey, 507 National Center, Reston, VA 20192, or call 800–872–6277.

to a wide side yard or large front yard. Property behind a house usually affords more privacy for recreation.

Contour and terrain

Most buyers prefer level land because it is easier to maintain and easier to use for customary backyard recreation. Houses on steep slopes or with steep driveways can be hard to live with and hard to sell because maintaining the driveway and ensuring the safety of young children will be more difficult. (Imagine a child on a tricycle barreling down the driveway into the street.) Less obvious are questions of drainage during storms and after melting snow, water that collects in low points, and mudslides.

Drainage

Lots located in the lowest part of a neighborhood can collect water. And that means flooding problems in the basement, especially if the soil tends to hold water or if the water table in the area is high.

Poor drainage can also cause serious health problems when septic tanks are used for waste disposal. Standing surface water from inadequately draining leach lines can become a breeding area for mosquitoes and other insects. In wet weather conditions, poor drainage can cause toilets to back up into the home and virtually shut down its wastewater removal system.

If you are suspicious about drainage, ask your home inspector or real estate agent about getting a soil analysis or a "perk" (percolation) test done (see page 200).

Lots located in a "flood hazard area" will require federal flood insurance. Area lenders and real estate agents usually can tell you which properties are in areas designated as flood hazard areas by the Army Corps of Engineers. Be aware that "flood plain," a more common reference, doesn't necessarily mean an area as obvious as the Mississippi River valley. Coastal property and the property surrounding small natural streams and even drainage canals can flood under some conditions. That makes a check with the USGS worthwhile whenever you see nearby water.

The view

Some views (such as waterfront or mountaintop) can greatly boost both the pleasure and the value of real estate. But what you see from most homes is rarely that dramatic. Pleasant views (which usually include trees and other greenery, some open space, or a somewhat distant neighbor's house) are generally calming and unthreatening and help maintain value. Unpleasant views (power lines, commercial buildings, parking lots, cemeteries, used-car lots, and so on) may not "bother" you once you "get used to it" but they can decrease value and slow down resale time.

Privacy and landscaping

Whether pine trees or cacti are valued depends on the character of the region. Generally, the best landscaping uses plants that occur naturally in the region and are appropriate to the climate. Inappropriate choices will cost you extra effort for maintenance and extra money to replace failed plants or water nonnative plants.

Appropriately located trees can enhance privacy and serve as a heat-preserving windbreak or a source of cooling shade. Provided they're healthy and well-formed, mature trees almost always add value to a property. However, you may have to pay an arborist (or at least a leaf-spraying service) to help keep them that way. You must also be prepared to clean up your yard, roof and gutters after them (or pay someone else to do it). The plants, shrubs and trees that are planted in beds contiguous to the house are called "foundation plantings." They should create a visual transition—call it a blending or softening—from the building to the natural landscape. They should not block the light from entering the windows, and they should not grow out over walkways. When appropriately maintained, foundation plantings, too, add value.

Fences in good taste are also usually a plus. What constitutes good taste, however, is often a personal evaluation, and it may even be dictated by a neighborhood association. The usual guideline, again, is harmony with the surrounding area.

Added lot size when it increases privacy will often facilitate a sale. Sometimes, however, the extra maintenance required for a very large lawn will actually decrease the comfort level in the home and the ease of resale. Remember, too, that a gorgeous lawn didn't get that way by itself. Are you prepared to maintain it yourself or hire a lawn-treatment company to do so?

Easements

The effect that an *easement* has on the use and value of a piece of property must be judged individually. There are no general rules that apply to all easements. The following are some typical examples:

- **When a shared driveway is bisected by the property line of two neighboring lots,** each owner holds an easement over the other's land. This means shared maintenance because neither owner's car can get in or out without going over the land of the other owner. Will you shovel half a driveway in winter or share the cost of plowing?

- **A waterfront lot** might have an easement along one property line that will allow other community residents to get to the beach. Will you mind the parade of beach umbrellas every day during the summer months?

- **A drainage easement** might run along a lot line where a storm-drain pipe is buried to collect water and carry it to a retention basin. This kind of easement actually helps to keep the owner's property usable and rarely requires servicing. Its only negative factor might be the metal grates over the access points for water. They are not exactly aesthetically appealing, and some people with young children see them as a hazard.

- **An easement for a natural-gas line** might run along the edge of a property or right across it. If it is near an in-ground swimming pool, it will often hold up a sale because buyers fear damage should the gas line need unearthing for servicing.

- **A flag lot,** one that is usually set back behind another lot, can require the use of an easement in order to get to a road. It will usually be more difficult to sell than a lot with road frontage. (For more on flag lots, see page 91.)

Words to the Wise

• •

An **easement** is the right that one party has to use the land of another. Many public utility companies have the right to cross and use private land. A real estate agent might say to a prospective buyer: "There is a gas line easement across the northwest corner of this lot." A private party that owned neighboring and otherwise inaccessible land might also hold the right to cross another person's land. This type of easement is often called a **right of way.**

This Space Is My Space

If you are buying a condo or co-op apartment, you will need to be concerned with town, neighborhood and lot (the land the apartment complex stands upon), just as any other home buyer would be. But you will have an added concern: the location of your particular space within the building. In effect, you're choosing a "lot" indoors. You must consider views, noise and traffic (albeit foot traffic).

To help make this choice, consider the following factors. They may prompt you to think of others.

- **The orientation to the sun.** Will you have morning light? Northern light? Sunsets? All of the above?

- **The view.** Will you look toward the street? Garden? Ocean? Pool? If your apartment faces the alley, will you hear garbage trucks at dawn or smell curry all evening?

- **The floor.** Usually the higher in the building, the more expensive the apartment. But if there is no elevator, that may not be true. Some people prefer a top-floor apartment to avoid neighbors "clunking" around overhead.

- **Nearness to the elevator or the parking lot.** Many people don't like the extra noise and traffic.

- **Nearness to common areas** such as a recreation space or lobby. Some people enjoy having others nearby for socializing, others do not.

The Survey

A survey is the measurement of the boundaries of a lot or parcel of land. It is done by licensed surveyors and then a drawing (also called the survey) is rendered. In residential real estate, a survey includes a drawing that locates the perimeter or outline (also known as the footprint) of each building on the property. Driveways, walls and fences are indicated. Sometimes a survey includes the topography. Slope is indicated on the survey drawing by lines that show the distance above sea level.

Both lenders and title insurance companies (more about them in Chapter 15) require a survey, and you, as buyer, will probably have to pay for a new one. Long before you sign a contract to buy, however, ask the real estate agent or the seller whether a current survey is available. That survey is your best available description of the land you're considering. Walk the property lines with it in hand. Check whether the buildings you see match the buildings drawn on the survey. (If they don't, read page 334 carefully.)

Now take a long look at what may be your future piece of the earth. You've gotten to this spot by narrowing your focus from town, to neighborhood, to lot. Run through it all again in your head. Does it feel right? Practically everything about a piece of real estate can be changed *except* its location.

On Location: A 20-Question Quiz

This quiz is designed to help you consider location as an essential factor in your search for a better home. To use it most effectively:

- **Underline the description in each category that most nearly fits your idea of "best" possible location.** If you have a buying partner or family members, you may have to negotiate your top choice.

- **Give the quiz to each house you're seriously considering.** For each of the 20 questions, choose the one answer that most nearly describes the location of that piece of property (sometimes more than one answer will be equally descriptive). If it matches your preference, check it off.

- **Add up your checkmarks for each location.** The closer its total score is to at least 20, the more likely the location is right for you.

	House Address	House Address
	_____	_____
	_____	_____

1. The personality of the town is:
Progressive	____	____
Stable, not changing	____	____
Safe	____	____
Exciting	____	____
Old fashioned and homey	____	____

2. The commute to work or school from this town will be:
Short and easy	____	____
Short but hectic	____	____
Long but easy	____	____
Long and hard	____	____
Not bad	____	____

3. The schools in this town are:
Efficiently run	____	____
Warm and supportive	____	____
Academically excellent	____	____
Flexible and adaptive to individual needs	____	____
Great for sports and character-building activities	____	____

4. Recreational opportunities in this town are:
Abundant in all seasons	____	____
Mostly for kids	____	____
Primarily indoor activities	____	____
Primarily outdoor activities	____	____
Dependent on an individual's own resources	____	____

5. Police, fire, rescue and ambulance services are:

Available 24 hours   ____   ____
Staffed by part-time and volunteer people   ____   ____
Responsive and reliable   ____   ____
Somewhat outdated   ____   ____
Not there when you need them   ____   ____

6. Town government is:

Open to contributions by new people   ____   ____
Run by a few old-line families   ____   ____
Efficient and businesslike   ____   ____
Wrapped in red tape   ____   ____
Corrupt   ____   ____

7. For the tax dollars paid, property owners get back:

Probably the best return in the area   ____   ____
Good schools but few services   ____   ____
Good services but mediocre schools   ____   ____
About the same as surrounding towns   ____   ____
Less than surrounding towns   ____   ____

8. The personality of the neighborhood is:

Married with children only   ____   ____
A delightful potpourri   ____   ____
In transition   ____   ____
A bedroom community for singles and professionals   ____   ____
Personality? What personality?   ____   ____

9. Surrounding houses are:

Similar in age, size and price   ____   ____
Generally larger and more expensive   ____   ____
Generally smaller and less expensive   ____   ____
Each different from the others in size, style and age   ____   ____
Still being built, or being changed or remodeled   ____   ____

10. Neighborhood lawn care and landscaping is:

Casual: edged in weeds   ____   ____
Diligent: mowed every Saturday   ____   ____
Professionally planned, planted and tended   ____   ____
Country natural   ____   ____
Mostly blacktop and concrete   ____   ____

On Location: A 20-Question Quiz, Cont'd.

11. Socializing in the neighborhood is:
Planned by the homeowners association
Just about nonexistent
Centered around children
Frequent, casual and inclusive: seems like each house
   has a party or cookout once every year or two
Limited to small cliques

12. Traffic on the street and nearby areas is:
Always heavy but slow-moving
Always heavy and fast-moving
Heavy during commuting hours only
Light but pretty steady
Pretty much limited to neighborhood cars

13. Considering convenience, the neighborhood is:
Walking distance to town and transportation
A short drive (three to five minutes) from town
   and shopping
More than a five-minute drive from the nearest
   convenience store
A pretty long drive to everything
Close to shopping but far from recreational facilities for
   children, meeting places, schools and restaurants

14. Within the neighborhood, the lot is located:
At the edge and near a more expensive neighborhood
At the edge and near a less expensive neighborhood
In or near the center, or well within the neighborhood
At the edge and backing up to woodlands, open-space
   land or parks
At the edge and near commercial property or a
   municipal building, or near a school or church

15. Considering topography, the lot is:
On the high ground of the neighborhood
On the low ground of the neighborhood
Above the grade level of the road
Below the grade level of the road
On level ground similar to other houses

16. *The appearance of the lot is:*

Wooded and natural   ___ ___
Recently professionally landscaped   ___ ___
Full of mature trees and shrubs   ___ ___
Easy to landscape or maintain   ___ ___
Unusual and maybe demanding   ___

17. *Views from the lot feature:*

Mostly other houses   ___ ___
Houses and commercial buildings   ___ ___
Vistas: distant mountains, ocean, meadows, a lake   ___ ___
Nearby trees, greenery, or forest   ___ ___
Buildings and blacktop   ___ ___

18. *Considering privacy, the lot is:*

Fenced or separated by shrubbery from all exposure   ___ ___
So large that neighbors don't matter   ___ ___
Exposed to view by neighbors on both sides and back   ___
Exposed to view by neighbors on one or both sides but
  backing up to woods, open space, or other separating
  factor such as a hill or lake   ___ ___
Exposed to view from roads on two sides or more   ___ ___

19. *Drainage on the land is:*

Excellent: porous soil and high ground   ___
Not great: boggy, on or near water, or on clay-like soil   ___ ___
Occasionally poor: pooled with water on the land, possibly
  indicating a rock ledge under the topsoil   ___ ___
Risky: Drainage is good but lot is located within a flood plain ___ ___
Precarious: on a hillside and subject to running water
  or mudslides   ___ ___

20. *Owning this piece of earth would:*

Feel right   ___ ___
Be convenient for present needs   ___ ___
Not be ideal—but the house is just perfect   ___ ___
Be a challenge that would probably help in growing equity ___ ___
Be affordable and would be acceptable for a short term   ___ ___

Total checkmarks   ___ ___

The Price and Value Question

In the real estate marketplace, it's not, "To be or not to be?" but, "How much?" *That* is the question that dominates every real estate deal from the Trump Towers to the little Cape Cod around the corner.

"How much?" is the essential price and value question. But actually it is two questions: "How much will I *have* to pay?" and "How much is it *worth*?" From the moment you get that first twinge of desire for a particular house until the bank has finished its appraisal and calls to say your mortgage has been approved, these twin demons inevitably bounce off each other in your head. Needless to say, that creates a good deal of worry and sometimes colossal headaches.

You may be surprised to learn, however, that these two questions merge again into one after all the negotiating is done and the contract to purchase is signed. At that point, when the property is "sold," *the agreed-on price decides the worth of that property.* The fair market value has been determined.

How Price Tags Get Their Numbers

Haggling over price is not an inborn part of the American character. Really, the only things we seriously negotiate over are houses and cars, and automakers are trying to eliminate their half of that pair. So most Americans must *learn* good negotiating tactics. You should begin by understanding how asking price is determined.

A seller can choose any number for the asking price. It might be a dream number that adds in a few thousand dollars for prize rose bushes or many more thousands for the view of a distant mountaintop—factors few prospective buyers would pay for. Much more rarely, it might be a number that reflects the owners' unhappiness in a home and a resulting undervaluation. (These houses sell fast!)

When the Asking Price Is Set by the Pros

Computers have become an integral part of the Realtors' trade, and they have the potential to take a lot of the guesswork and emotional judgment out of the business of selling a home. But they won't ever overcome the human factor, and that's why, as a buyer, you needn't accept a computer-generated asking price as gospel. Consider all the elements the computer presents and then add in what's right for you and your family. But let's look at what a computer can do.

By accessing stored information, agents can pull up lists of recently sold houses of similar style, age and size within the same neighborhood as the property about to be sold. Data on these "comparable" properties includes original asking price, actual selling price, reductions in price and length of time on the market. Using this information, the real estate agent suggests a range for the asking price and predicts a range for the probable selling price.

Since real estate is neither consistently scientific nor mathematical, this process, usually called a *CMA* (for comparative market analysis), can come up with numbers that are sometimes right and sometimes wrong (although usually more nearly right than wrong.) The problem in establishing asking price, however, is that the seller is *not* required to accept the *fair market value* estimate and suggested asking

> # *Words to the Wise*
> •
>
> The age-old definition of **fair market value** is the highest price a ready, willing and able buyer will pay and the lowest price a ready, willing and able seller will accept—in other words, the point at which there is a meeting of the minds. No owner, appraiser or real estate agent can ever *set* fair market value before a contract is signed. It can only be estimated.
>
> **CMA** stands for comparative market analysis. This is a service provided free by most real estate agencies to prospective sellers to help them estimate the market value of their properties and set an asking price. As a buyer, you can ask for it, too.

price generated by the CMA. At the seller's request, Realtors often list and advertise houses at tens of thousands of dollars above the asking price recommended in the CMA.

So, when you're in the market to buy, don't consider asking price as anything more than asking price. Despite the tremendous amount of buyer-protection legislation enacted during the past two decades, you are still on your own when it comes to paying a fair price for a house. The old adage "Buyer beware" still prevails.

The Effects of Time and Pressure

You may have noticed by watching the newspapers ads or from previous house-hunting experiences that asking prices are subject to change—usually reduction. These price changes can be indicators of your negotiating power so when you ask "how much?" it's important that you ask the real estate agent or the seller several other questions:

- **How long has the property been on the market?**

- **What was the original price?**

- **Have there been any price reductions?** If so, how much, and when?

There is rarely much downward negotiating opportunity when a house is new to the marketplace. After two to three months, however, most of the unrealistic dreams of "making a killing" have withered away and sellers are not only willing to listen to an offer but also ready to reduce their expectations in order to put a sale together.

Price reductions may also indicate that the sellers are under pressure (perhaps they have already bought another house, or perhaps foreclosure looms). If you detect such pressure from something the Realtor or seller says, you might be on the trail of a genuine bargain. If you are working with a buyer's agent, he or she can inform you of any known factors that might affect the final selling price (for information about buyers' agents, see Chapter 13).

On the other hand, price reductions may just mean that the owners are feeling the discouraging effects of over-pricing (for example, very few people are coming to look at the property). But, in this case, the new "reduced price" may *still* be far above other comparable houses (sort of like shopping in a Ralph Lauren outlet store).

What's Happening—or Not—Locally

The very same factors that determine the price of carrots and coffee ultimately determine the price of real estate—supply and demand. As has been true since prehistory, when supply increases beyond demand, prices decrease; when demand increases beyond supply, prices increase.

But like everything else in real estate, this basic premise of economics takes on some complications. In the first place, every property is unique and anchored to the land. The supply of real estate, therefore, cannot be relocated to relieve a superabundance in one area or satisfy a greater demand in another. In addition, home buyers (who create the demand) are often restricted to a geographic area because of their jobs. This immobility of people and houses creates the local character of real estate markets across the nation.

Don't Assume

Don't assume that the price you see advertised in the newspaper should be your guide to negotiating. Many inexperienced home buyers think that getting 15% off the asking price means they got a good deal, but the property could have been priced 20% above its competition. Many "For Sale By Owner" and "Just Listed!" houses are overpriced. Comparison shopping is a safeguard against paying too much. Real estate agents can help, too. Be sure to read Chapter 13, "Efficient and Effective House-hunting."

The figures for the national economy may be upbeat and positive while the real estate market in your local area may be sagging. Within a state, home prices can be increasing in one town and decreasing in a neighboring town. Even within a single city, home prices can be increasing in one neighborhood and decreasing in another.

And all that theory boils down to one of the most important axioms of real estate: *Know your local marketplace*. If you want to buy near where you already live, you probably have been keeping tabs on the marketplace, perhaps subconsciously, just by reading the local newspaper and listening to the gossip on the golf course or among the parents at after-school activities. If you will be relocating, you will need to rely on facts and statistics. Fortunately, the information is readily available.

Here are a few sample questions to ask your real estate agent. As you get into researching communities, neighborhoods and housing styles, you'll certainly come up with more queries of your own. Once you've got some pricing benchmarks for the area and you know whether the market is heating up or cooling off, you can better judge the value of any house you consider in that market: Is it a bargain, is it fairly well-priced or is it overpriced?

More, More, More

• •

Current computer technology allows boards of Realtors and real estate offices to keep track of what types of property are selling best, what types are selling slowly, where prices are going up and where they are not. Information on national trends and local trends in other states and towns is available through the National Association of Realtors, through computer access to state and local boards in other areas, and through the relocation services to which many real estate companies subscribe. This information may not be offered to you when you shake the hand of your agent, but ask and (usually) you shall receive.

• **What is the range of prices** of a three-bedroom, two-bath (or whatever size you're interested in) house in the town(s) or neighborhood(s) you're considering? What's the median price? (When working with a median price, remember that half of all similar houses are priced above it and half below; you could call it the midpoint of the market.) Is what you can afford close to the median, or out at one of the ends of the range? Will you feel comfortable with that?

• **How has this median price changed since last year?** You want to know if the trend is up or down, a good indicator of whether demand is increasing or decreasing.

• **How does the median price compare** in a given town or neighborhood for a ranch house, a colonial, a raised ranch or a contemporary of approximately the same size? You are looking to see which styles are in demand and which are not.

- **What is the median time for all homes on the market?** The length of time it takes to sell a property is an indicator of demand in an area (more about that in just a bit).

- **Can you give me some demographic profiles of area communities?** You want to know where the population is growing—creating increased demand—and anything else that will help you decide whether a town is desirable to home buyers.

- **Where is the school population growing or falling?** This is an indicator of the makeup of the community. Communities with young populations have a growing school census; communities with older populations usually have a falling school census.

- **What is the proportion of homeowners to renters?** Owners tend to be less mobile and therefore more committed to their communities. They tend to volunteer more, allowing the community to offer more to its members and making it more desirable.

The Slow Swings of Fortune

Because the real estate marketplace is inextricably tied to the economics of supply and demand, it responds with periods of growth, periods of stagnation and periods of recession. That's true of most investments. The major difference, however, is *time*.

The real estate marketplace responds very slowly to economic changes because of the immobility of both the supply (houses) and the demand (people). The highs and lows therefore occur over longer periods of time. For example, the baby-boomers needed starter housing as they came into home-buying age in the late 1970s and early 1980s. So condominium communities sprang up like dandelions in springtime and prices were appreciating so fast that that you could sign a contract to buy a to-be-built apartment and sell it for a profit before completion!

But the baby-bust followed the baby-boom, and by the late '80s certain condos were among the most difficult housing to sell because there was too much supply and too

Penny for Your Thoughts

It is a capital mistake to theorize before one has data.

Arthur Conan Doyle (1859-1930), British physician and novelist, creator of Sherlock Holmes

little demand. As the new millennium approaches, the condo market is again showing signs of revival as boomers scale down from their suburban four-bedroom, 2½ bath mansions and seek a longed-for city pad or a maintenance-free gated community.

The generally slow swings of the real estate marketplace can be bad news if you are a homeowner in an area where real estate values are about to come out of a depression because the rebound may take more time than you are willing to spend. You may have to settle for a smaller gain, or even take a loss, in order to move on.

On the other hand, the slow response of real estate to economic pressure can also work to your advantage. The savvy buyer can choose to buy in an area where demand is just beginning to increase and thereby improve the odds of appreciation. Later, you can sell when you notice that a downward trend has begun and therefore avoid economic loss.

Penny for Your Thoughts

• •

"Power is held in check by competition and only by competition."

John Kenneth Galbraith (1908–), Canadian-born American economist

When he wrote these words in his autobiography, *A Life in Our Times,* Galbraith was referring to power among business firms. The idea, however, is an appropriate insight into the real estate marketplace, especially if you think of "power" in terms of price. So remember: To increase the odds of successful home buying, you must know the local marketplace. In every transaction you will ever enter, ask yourself: *What is the local competition?*

What's Hot and What's Not

Although not as immense and difficult to alter as the forces of economic supply and demand, certain features of property also affect value. Two decades ago, buyers wanted formal dining rooms. In the late '80s, bathrooms the size of a small bedroom were in demand. Today the trend is toward informal living space, and most buyers would rather have an extra room to house the computer than space for a mini greenhouse in the bathroom.

Specific features that add or detract from value have been discussed in each housing style and decision in the earlier gateway chapters. But for the purposes of evaluating value and resale value in a house under consideration, let's take a brief look at some general features. Those marked + tend to increase value, those marked = either have no effect or can have a positive *or* negative effect, and those marked – usually decrease value.

+ Privacy

One of the most often requested features. It could mean a large lot, a mature stand of trees or, in a condo community, a corner unit near the woods.

+ Safety

Few home buyers are eager to live on a busy through street. You might get a good deal at purchase, but the house could be difficult to resell.

Gated communities and towns with low crime rates add to the value of a house, at purchase and later.

+ Bathrooms

Two seems to be the minimum for a "desirable" rating among most house hunters. If you're looking at an older home with just one bathroom, this may work to your advantage pricewise. And, you can easily alter the floor plan later and add bathrooms.

+ Kitchen

Large, sunny and shiny-new will almost always command more money.

+ Garages

The more garage space, the more you'll pay. Home buyers appreciate space for their cars and storage—within limits! Beyond the three-car garage, you're either aiming for a mansion or about to open a home auto-repair shop for teens and their friends.

= Swimming pool

Its value depends on where you are in the nation. In warmer climates, it adds value. In colder climates, it often hinders a sale. Questions about safety and liability also deter some buyers.

= Basement and attic conversions

Rec rooms are still used everywhere, but they rarely add value to a property.

– Mixed use or commercial zoning

Few home buyers want to live next door to Betty's Billiards, Burger King or even the local high school. If you can put up with such neighbors, you're sure to get a lot of house for your money. But you'll probably have some trouble selling and are unlikely to make a killing—unless, of course, McDonald's wants to move in right on the spot where you sit and will pay you for the privilege.

– Corner lots

They're valuable in commercial real estate, less desirable in residential. Home buyers don't like the added exposure to the street, which means reduced privacy and often exposure to more traffic.

– Inappropriate additions or overimprovement

The need to walk through one bedroom to get to another can make a house extremely difficult to sell. So can getting too big and too grand for the neighborhood.

Negotiating for the Best Price

Effective negotiating does not begin with an offer. It begins with knowledge. Its success does not depend on being tough but on having both a goal and a plan before you begin. You should be able to place a check mark for "accomplished" at each of the following items before you ever mention to anyone what you might be willing to pay.

Know how much you can afford to pay.

Then ask yourself how much you *want* to pay for housing. You may not want to stretch to your financial limits and be forced to live on pasta and video rentals for a few years until your income goes up. You'll find guidelines in the home financing section, beginning on page 209.

Estimate the fair market value of the property you want to buy.

If you are working with a Realtor, you can get this information by using the comparables file as discussed. If you are buying directly from a seller, you'll need to go to the town hall. Ask the people who work there where the records of recent real estate transactions are kept. Try to find some properties comparable to "yours" and compare their selling prices with their tax assessments. How much above assessed valuation seems to be fair market value? Then compare the tax assessment of your property with its asking price. Is it in the ballpark?

Consider the tempo of your local marketplace.

We've already discussed the median length of time on the market as an indicator of local housing demand. Now use the tempo of the marketplace to help set the tone for your negotiating on a specific property. Start with these two questions. Answers to both are available through local boards of Realtors:

- **What is the median time on the market for your type of property?** Be specific. Don't ask about four-bedroom houses. Ask about four bedroom, 2½ bath, two-story houses with two-car garages. You want to eliminate, for example, four-bedroom raised ranches (which, if included, would make the figures inaccurate since raised ranches are a less desirable style of housing than the traditional two-story style). Under three months is considered a fast market. Over six months is considered a slow market by sellers and real estate professionals alike.

It's the Law

• •

Negotiating protocol: Don't let a real estate agent—yours or the seller's—intimidate you by saying something like, "That's a ridiculous offer. I can't possibly present that." In every state, the law requires that an agent present every written offer, whether in person or by phone or fax. If the seller lives in the local area, insist that your agent present the signed offer form in person with the earnest-money check in hand. In-person presentation maximizes your negotiating power because it emphasizes that yours is a serious, signed offer, not just a probe to see if the seller will come down in price.

- **At what percentage of asking price are most houses selling?** If the pace is fast and houses are selling near or even above asking price, you will probably have to act quickly and make your first offer close to your estimate of fair market value. (Remember, this is not the same as "close to the asking price," which could be a trap.) If the market is slow, you may have the opportunity to "test the waters" by making a low offer.

Words to the Wise

• •

The check you give the agent with your written offer is called **earnest money** or **hand money.** It is meant to show that your intention is to buy the property. Usually $500 or $1,000 will suffice. By custom, the check is shown to the seller but is not cashed until all issues are settled and the contract is fully executed (signed). If agreement cannot be reached, just say, "Please return my earnest-money check."

Set a top dollar figure.

In some cases—an especially well-located and appealing house, for example—you might be willing to pay a little more than your estimate of fair market value for the property. Do not under any circumstances tell anyone what your top price is!!! If you let this cat out of the bag, you can almost be certain that that's the price you'll pay.

Set a goal for closing title and taking possession.

Make note of your flexibility. Would you wait longer if the price were lower? Would you close sooner if the price were lower? Would you pay a little *more* to close sooner—or later?

List the extras you'd like to stay with the house.

Those might include draperies, lawn furniture and appliances. Differentiate between those you really, really want and those you are willing to give up if the price is just right.

How to Do It

Make your first offer in writing. If you are working with an agent, you will need to accompany the offer form with a check. If you are working directly with a seller, do not offer a deposit of any kind. If you hand over a check before you have a written agreement, you may never see the money again. That money should go into an escrow fund held by a fiduciary, not into the owner's bank account.

When buying without the help of a real estate agent, negotiate price and terms with the seller at the kitchen table, then have a contract drawn by a lawyer. The lawyer can hold the deposit money in escrow *after* a contract has been signed. (Read more about these safeguards in Chapter 15, "Protection Under the Law.")

Even if your first offer is a very low "probe" nowhere near fair market value, make it in writing. Offers presented by phone are too easy to say no to and you rarely gain the benefit of a counteroffer or a discussion of the sellers' position.

When you make a low first offer, it's usually a good idea to make it as simple as possible. Do not include a long list of extras or a complex formula for determining the date to close title. The first issue of concern should be price and only price. Requests for extras can be added as you raise your offer; often they're hardly noticed that way. And the closing date may become a factor in price negotiations if the sellers have a specific time in mind. For example, if they ask for a quick closing, say you can do it if the price is lower.

Remember throughout your negotiating that you must never lose your temper—tantrums invariably cost money. Proceed step by step, increasing your offer or changing the terms until everyone reaches a meeting of the minds. Don't take words like "this is my final price" too seriously. Wait a bit and try again; people do change their minds. And don't accept any contract, especially a scratched-out, initialed and addendum-laden one, without safeguarding yourself with an attorney-review clause.

It's the Law

• •

Your safety net: Even if lawyers do not usually close title in your area of the country, you can give yourself a few days' thinking and checking time by including an attorney-review clause (required in some states) in your contract or offer form. Most agreements give three working days, though you can specify a longer period of, say, five days. The clause should read: *This agreement is subject to review and approval as to form and content by an attorney of the buyer's choice. The attorney may rescind the contract for any reason before midnight of [insert date].*

Do You *Really* Know What You're Doing?

Most people sign contracts without reading and understanding all the fine print. This can be extremely dangerous in the real estate marketplace because there is so much money at stake, not to mention the many legal entanglements. In Chapter 15, we'll go over what goes into a contract and how to protect yourself. But remember, if you ever feel that something's not quite clear or quite right, get the help of a real estate lawyer—one you pay to work for you. The expenditure for contract review is small (as little as $100 and hardly ever more than $300) compared with what it could cost to fix an error or get you out of a situation you don't want to be in.

Efficient
and Effective
House-Hunting

Home buying! It's like no other shopping experience in American life. There are no showrooms where you can see the products, handle them, or try them on for size. Exchanges are not allowed. Warranties, if they exist, are minimal. Catalogs are ineffective. Comparison of competing products is difficult. Duplicates cannot be ordered. Price tags are unreliable. And efficient home buying usually means getting involved with professional salespeople. No wonder some people choose, if they can, to make it a once-in-a-lifetime experience!

On the other hand, some people enjoy the challenge. They enter the real estate marketplace with interest rather than apprehension. They effectively use the services offered by professional salespeople. They develop methods of keeping records and making comparisons. And they use the opportunity to negotiate a price to their decided financial advantage (more on this in Chapter 12).

Well, maybe you can't quite see yourself actually enjoying the hunt, but you can gather information and learn techniques that will make the process more efficient and less bothersome. Careful house-hunting is a major factor in getting the best possible house for the best possible price. So take a little time in this chapter to go over some marketplace business facts and some tips that experienced buyers know well.

About Real Estate Agents

Does any child dream of growing up to be a real estate agent? Hardly! But the industry employs more than a million people, and brokers assist in the sale of more than 85% of the houses sold in this country each year. Still, not many adults know what real estate agents really do.

"They sell houses, don't they?" you ask. Yes, and they:

- **advise** sellers on pricing and marketing techniques

- **advertise** properties

- **select and suggest** suitable properties to buyers

- **collect** tax, survey, title and other information necessary to the sale

- **assist** in negotiating

- **advise and assist** in finding mortgage loans (for more on this, see the special section that begins on page 209)

- **make** preparations for the closing

- **most important of all**, they keep up with the local marketplace, knowing its pace and its inventory (the properties that are for sale).

It's the Law

Who is your licensed agent? Only a licensed real estate *broker* can act as an agent for the seller or the buyer in a real estate transaction. (An agent is a person authorized to act for or represent another person—called the principal.) Each state sets its own requirements for licensing a real estate broker. Only a licensed broker can hang out a sign and open an office.

A real estate *salesperson,* however, will probably show you houses. In addition to driving you from house to house, the salesperson will act as the go-between in your negotiating and probably sign as a witness on your purchase contract.

How can this be if only brokers can act as agents? Well, a real estate salesperson is also licensed. He or she works as a kind of sub-agent who can partake in a real estate transaction only under the supervision of a broker. If you sign a contract to work with a particular salesperson, you are actually hiring the broker.

If questions of competence, ethics or legality ever come up regarding a salesperson or the broker that you are working with, you can seek help from the real estate commission in your state. You'll find the number in your phone book's blue pages.

Realtor With a Big 'R' or Small?

There was a time when the *New York Times* didn't allow its real estate writers to use the word *Realtor* unless it started a sentence. Editors at the *Times,* being correct and proper, knew that the word was a registered trademark of the National Association of Realtors. If it appeared in the middle of a sentence it needed a capital *R,* and that would give the trade group a free punch. Competing newspapers, however, were not so discriminating; they used "realtor" for real estate agent just as the rest of us use "kleenex" for tissue.

The enduring popularity of this story in journalism and real estate circles illustrates how significant that capital *R* has become—at least to Realtors. But it has meaning for you, too.

The National Association of Realtors (NAR) is the largest and one of the oldest trade associations in the nation. But that does not mean that every licensed real estate broker is a member. To be a member in good standing, a broker and all affiliated sales agents must subscribe to the NAR's code of ethics. Since Realtor status is an important aspect of doing business in most areas of the country, most brokers and salespeople not only subscribe to the code, they also adhere to it.

Besides that commitment to ethical practice, the major advantage of dealing with a Realtor is his or her access to the multiple listing service. The MLS, supported by the local board of Realtors, is an easy access tool by which all local Realtors make their listings known and available to all other Realtors. The listing broker and the selling broker split the sales commissions, typically 6% of the selling price (though they range from 4% to 7%).

Words to the Wise

● ●

Listing in the real estate world has nothing to do with names or words arranged in columns, such as membership lists or grocery lists. It is the word used to indicate the agreement by which a seller employs a broker to sell a piece of property and earn a fee or a commission. You'll hear sellers say, "We signed a listing at 6% for three months" or "We listed at 6% for three months."

Listing is also used in the marketplace to refer to a piece of property that is or has been listed. You'll hear Realtors say, "There's a listing on Maple Road" or "That listing has been reduced."

Whose Side Are They On?

Loyalty is a big question right now in real estate. For decades all agents were committed by contract to work only for the seller, either as listing agents or as subagents of the listing agent when listings were shared. But many buyers didn't know this, and, thinking the agent was dedicated to helping them find a house, were simply too trusting. They revealed financial and negotiating information—like "we can go a little higher, but we don't really want to"— that inevitably helped the seller.

The buyer's broker

Then the idea of the buyer's broker emerged. These agents pledged themselves to work in the best interest of the buyers (who signed a contract similar to a listing contract). The only problem was: *how would the brokers get paid?* Since real estate commissions had traditionally come out of the sellers' proceeds from the sale of their property, buyers understandably hesitated to shell out thousands of dollars just to have devotion and loyalty added to the service they had always gotten without cost.

The creative solution? Pay the buyer's brokers out of the proceeds of the sale as usual (in other words, the seller pays), just let them *represent* the buyers. And surprisingly, few sellers objected.

But then another problem arose, especially among large and multi-office brokers. Let's say a salesperson in Bonanza Realty *listed* 21 Oak Street. Then another salesperson in the same Bonanza office *sold* 21 Oak Street to a buyer who had signed a buyer's broker contract. Since only *brokers* can actually represent anyone in a real estate deal, we now have Bonanza as the seller's agent *and* the buyer's agent. Does a bell go off? Something about no one being able to serve two masters? In real estate, serving two masters is called *dual agency.*

The future of the buyer's broker movement is still questionable. Some brokers have decided to represent buyers only and take no listings. A trade association has been created and several companies are franchising buyer's broker offices.

Some traditional brokers, however, are sending their agents to buyer's-broker training courses and allowing them to assume both roles, acting as listing agents with sellers and buyer's agents with buyers. In some cases, this has resulted in locking office files so that no agent acting on behalf of an opposing party can snoop in the records of listing and showing data. In some offices, word from the top has come down forbidding discussion of listings or customers among office personnel—a virtually impossible rule to enforce because agents sell properties by talking about them. Some brokers ask their sales agents to choose one role

It's the Law

Dual agency occurs when one broker represents opposing parties (the buyer and the seller) in the same transaction. It is illegal *unless* both parties agree to the dual agency. No matter what the customary practice for disclosure in your area—whether the agent reveals dual agency at the first showing of the property or waits until you're about to make an offer—don't make a written offer on the property without *written* agreement on dual agency by all parties concerned.

or the other. The brokers then put up partitions between agents representing sellers and agents representing buyers. Some brokers are even housing their seller's agents and their buyer's agents in different buildings. And some brokers are going about their business as though there were no buyer's-broker movement. In fact, some agents will look at you a bit strangely if you mention it. They're just doing what they've always done. It's a little like hoping that threatening news will go away if you ignore it.

On the other hand, some state real estate commissions are looking with disfavor on the problems and questions being caused by dual agency. There are movements within some states to redefine whose side the salesperson is on. One solution, for example, is to determine loyalty on a first-come basis—that is, all agents will owe primary loyalty to the sellers of all properties listed with their brokers. When they show buyers properties listed with other brokers, however, they can work in the best interests of the buyers. But that approach raises the question for buyers of *when* to confide anything to the agent since you won't know whose side he or she is on until you choose a house.

In an attempt to deal with dual-agency conflicts, some states have decided to create nonagency relationships wherein transactional brokers agree to represent neither party in a transaction. (In some areas, these brokers are calling themselves "facilitators.") Similar to mediators, they can't take sides. Of course, you should ask yourself whether you're willing to pay someone for *not* representing you.

So what do these quandaries of loyalty mean to you, the educated home buyer, in the marketplace? (Why have we used all this paper?) Well, at least now you know that there are choices and risks when you choose a real estate agent to work with. Perhaps awareness of the controversy will reinforce the most important message of the home-buying process: *Rely on yourself.*

In the 19th century, utopian author Edward Bellamy wrote: *Buying and selling is essentially antisocial.* These are good words to remember when dealing both with real estate agents and with sellers. They may be friendly, but they are not your friends. (And even if your agent or your seller is a friend or relative, he or she is not necessarily acting in that role during the selling process.)

Do not share any confidences. Do not volunteer any more information than is necessary. Think of television police reciting the Miranda warning: "Anything you say can and will be used against you." You may be shopping for a *home,* but the shopping process is *business.*

More, More, More

If you want to know more about dedicated buyer's brokers or would like a referral to one, you can contact your local board of Realtors or one of the following organizations:

- **The National Association of Exclusive Buyer Agents** (NAEBA; 7652 Gartner Road, Suite 500, Evergreen, CO 80439–5204; 800–986–2322; www.NAEBA.org)

- **The Buyer's Agent Inc.** (1255 Lynnfield, Suite 273, Memphis, TN 38119; 800–766–8728; www.forbuyers.com) This is the first national franchiser of buyer's-broker offices. If you call the agency, you will get both information and referrals. Be aware, however, that the call would be similar to calling any traditional real estate franchiser, such as Century 21 or Remax. The agency will want to get you working with one of its agents.

Good Help Is Hard to Find

The worst way to find a real estate agent is to get "picked up." You call for more information on a property advertised in the newspaper, and the salesperson who answers the phone persuades you to come in to the office to look at pictures. The next thing you know, you've signed a buyer's-broker agreement, and the house you originally called about no longer interests you.

If you continue on this path, you run the risk of inspecting homes priced beyond the range you indicated, asking questions that don't get answered, and watching with bewilderment as the agent gets lost between houses because he didn't do the essential homework.

Of course, not every agent acquired by chance is a bad agent. Sometimes you might just be lucky and have your phone call answered by the firm's best. But if you're not so lucky, an unpolished or unprincipled agent may pressure you to make an offer when you express the slightest interest in a house.

Incompetence in real estate, as in practically every other profession, can be masked with snappy dressing, sensational smiles and sweet talk. In the marketplace, it can cost you long days, tedious repetition and corrections, and big bucks. One buyer told her agent (let's call him Rip Van Winkle) that she wanted to make an offer. Rip couldn't find time to write up the contract for two days and then allowed another two days to elapse before presenting the offer to the seller. What happened? Another offer came in during that time and was accepted because, as the seller said, "We had no idea that Mr. Van Winkle had a contract in hand."

But you have a choice. Once you've spent a little time in the marketplace, you'll become quite adept at judging which agents are working efficiently and which are not. And you'll feel no qualms about switching agents if you're dissatisfied. Of course, if you've signed a buyer's-broker contract, you will have to get a signed termination of that contract. If you don't, that agent can claim commission due if you later buy through another broker. If you have

Penny for Your Thoughts

If I am not for myself, who is for me?

Hillel *the elder,*
(30 BC – 10 AD),
from *Talmud,*
The Wisdom of the Fathers

Judgment comes from experience, and great judgment comes from bad experience.

Bob Packwood, former
U.S. senator from Oregon

not signed a buyer's broker agreement, you owe no particular loyalty to any agent and can switch. You can even use two or more agents simultaneously (perhaps one for each town or area).

Use the checklist on the following page to help in your evaluation of each agent you go out with.

Finding an agent

Even with the best evaluation standards, however, you still have to *find* that good agent. There are several methods and you may have to try more than one:

- **Ask friends or colleagues** who have recently bought a home in the area where you want to live. Copy the "Checking Out Real Estate Agents" quiz at right and ask them to rate their agent by its standards.

- **Tour open houses.** There is an agent on duty at every open house. Start a conversation. Ask questions that will allow you to fill out the quiz.

- **Watch for notices in the real estate sections of local newspapers.** Real estate people who win awards and the acclaim of their peers are not usually sitting on their hands.

- **Call a brokerage firm with a good reputation** and tell the office manager you want to work with an experienced agent who has continuing-education designations. The NAR awards the GRI (Graduate Realtor Institute) and the CRS (Certified Residential Specialist) designations for experienced Realtors who complete prescribed courses of study.

A-Hunting We Will Go!

Sometimes it strikes suddenly and sometimes it creeps up, but there is always a moment when the brain recognizes the thought: It's time to start looking for a house. So how do you begin?

It depends on how far you are from the area in which you intend to buy. If you're close, you've probably been driving around for months and already know the reputable

Continued on page 320

Checking Out Real Estate Agents

	Plus points	Minus points
Professional experience	❏ licensed for 3 years or more ❏ primary interest in residential	❏ licensed for less than 3 years ❏ primary involvement in commercial property listing and sales or rental property, or primarily a manager
Community knowledge	❏ local resident for 2 years or more ❏ community involvement ❏ children in the schools	❏ lives outside the area in which he or she works ❏ new resident in the area
Commitment	❏ full-time agent ❏ earns his or her living through real estate ❏ in real estate to further own investing	❏ part-time agent with another career ❏ part-time agent with another income
Competence	❏ shows properties in the price range indicated by buyers ❏ plans most-direct showing routes ❏ has pre-inspected all properties to be shown ❏ can answer questions when asked or gets the answers promptly	❏ shows properties above buyer's stated range ❏ shows properties of a different style or size than requested ❏ plans routes to avoid "undesirable" areas or those she thinks you would be "uncomfortable" living in ❏ is not familiar with the properties being shown ❏ doesn't know how much comparable properties sold for during the past year
Ethics	❏ alerts buyers to problems in location or condition of property ❏ does not pry for personal information that might affect negotiations ❏ allows buyers "thinking time"; no pressure to make an offer	❏ neglects to mention known or suspected problems ❏ "bad-mouths" other areas or other agencies ❏ pressures for an offer

names in real estate and the desirable locations. Then it's just a matter of actually stepping out into the marketplace. If you're far away and have done all the long-distance research you could, you may still feel uncomfortable about finding an agent there, choosing neighborhoods and touring houses (as outlined in Chapter 11). Enter the relocation specialist.

Professional Help With No Sales Pressure

Corporations began using relocation specialists (often called relocation counselors) in the late '60s to encourage their employees to accept a transfer. The profession grew rapidly in the early '80s and is now well established.

Although it's rare in today's marketplace, some corporations employ their own full-time relocation specialists. More often, relocation specialists are subcontractors hired when and where needed. Some relocation specialists are salaried employees of the larger real estate firms; others are independent owners or employees of small relocation specialty companies. In all cases, they do not sell real estate.

A relocation specialist introduces prospective home buyers to the communities in which they might choose to live. This introduction includes counseling on prices and values; information on the character of each community and the neighborhoods within it; information on schools, services and recreation; and usually several driving tours. Question-and-answer sheets, pamphlets, maps and videotapes are among the tools of the trade.

Corporate rates for the counseling of transferees vary by location, but an hourly rate of $80 isn't unusual. For buyers without corporate support, some real estate firms offer free relocation counseling. After the counseling sessions, the specialist helps to choose the firm's sales agent who is most likely to be compatible with the prospective buyers.

If the hint of conflict of interest in that arrangement makes you a wee bit uncomfortable, you may want to hire an independent relocation counselor. Noncorporate rates vary by area of the country and degree of service provided.

You can usually negotiate a fee somewhat lower than the published corporate rate. Look in the Yellow Pages under "Employee Relocation" or "Relocation."

Working on Your Own

Besides working with a Realtor, there are several ways to start your hunt and augment the work of sales agents. You may not use all of these, but you will certainly use some.

The Internet
Most larger real estate firms now have Web sites where you can browse through listings without being disturbed. Call any of their offices for their online addresses or check for publication in their weekly display ads. Be aware, however, that the information on a listing (even with a photo) doesn't always give a true picture of the property. Some owners selling without a broker are also listing on the Net. Use "real estate" for a key-word search on whatever Web search engine you use.

Local newspapers
Newspaper advertising is by far the major source of market information for the general public. Sunday papers usually carry the most ads. But a great many properties that are for sale are not advertised in any given week, and this week's new ads may advertise last week's houses with different copy. This, of course, makes house-hunting by newspaper unreliable at best. Local papers are, however, the best source for For Sale By Owner (FSBO) information.

Open houses
Open houses are a good way to get a feel for market value without committing to any particular real estate agent. Attending them is a good beginning tactic but generally a waste of time once you are hunting in earnest.

On the golf course or at the Little League game
You'll hear or overhear some of the most valuable information at recreational or community functions. Who's

A good beginning makes a good ending.

English proverb

planning to move? Who's getting divorced? You'll have to track these leads down tactfully.

Cruising

Driving about the streets where you might like to live is a good house-hunting technique. You may even see a FSBO sign go up. If you find an area you really like, you can try "prospecting." Get the names of the owners on the entire street from the town tax maps and write a pleasant note to each saying you'd like to buy in the area. Sometimes you'll catch someone who has been thinking of selling.

Working With a Realtor

Once you have chosen a Realtor, it's important to do some homework. You should bring to the first meeting a sheet of paper with:

- **the price range** you want to hunt in (allow some space for negotiating)

- **the towns or neighborhoods** that interest you

- **the style or styles of house** you will consider

- **the number of bedrooms** you need

- **the probable time to a purchase** (are you looking to move in six weeks or six months?)

Beyond this point, you should divide the paper into two columns, one for needs and one for wants. List those features you must have under *needs* and those features you would like under *wants*. Give each *want* feature a rating from 1 (lowest) to 5 (highest) to indicate how important it is to you. Your profile for the Realtor is essentially a condensed and edited version of your "comfort" and "location" worksheets (pages 254 and 294, respectively). Don't bring the worksheets themselves, however, because they might contain information that would influence your negotiating strength.

Be certain you absolutely must have your *needs* because they will set the limits on the computer search of the

MLS. "Must have a fireplace," for example, could eliminate dozens of otherwise acceptable houses, including one that you might have chosen. If a *must* is really a *really want,* put it into the *want* column with a 5 and circle it.

Do not tell the real estate agent whether this is a "movable" (turnover-oriented) or rooted house-hunt. Your motivation will affect the likelihood that you will bid higher, and that is information no agent should have.

In most offices you can sit down and look through the listing book. Searches, however, are now usually conducted by computer because listings are most current there. But beware the limitations of computer searching. If you tell your Realtor that your only limiting factor is four bedrooms, for example, you will get all the four-bedroom houses in Happyville, including many that are too expensive or otherwise inappropriate. On the other hand, if you state your exact price range as your limiting factor, you may miss a house that would be perfect for you but has an asking price only $900 higher than your top dollar. So you and your Realtor will want to start with wide searches that will produce lists, then narrow down your selections and call up individual listings with pictures.

Tips for the Trail

Keeping track of what you saw in which house is one of the challenges of house-hunting. In fact, it's even hard to remember which house was where. But a little planning and some sorting strategies can go a long way toward eliminating what you don't want and keeping for consideration what you do. Here are some tips to start you off; after a time you'll probably add many of your own.

- **Ask your Realtor to copy a local street map** and mark the locations of the properties you will visit. Get a separate copy of the map for each day's house-hunting trip and date it at the top. Number the properties in the order you will see them.

- **Have the Realtor print or copy the listing information sheet** with a photo of each property you will visit. Number them to coincide with the numbers on the street map.

- **On the reverse side of the listing sheets take notes** on what you like and don't like about the property. Some home buyers like to sketch the floor plan.

- **Carry a flash camera with you and take color photos,** indoors and out, of houses that particularly interest you. You might find it handy to use a disposable flash camera or a Polaroid so you can label them instantly.

- **Buy an inexpensive three-ring photo album with self-adhesive pages** (about $10) and keep the listing sheets, photos, sales brochures and any other information given away in each house (a copy of the survey of the lot, for example) on all houses that interest you in *any* way. Even though you are sure you won't buy a particular house, if you think it's fairly priced and find it at all appealing, you may be able to use it to make price and value comparisons once you do find a property that you might buy.

- **Return in your own car after the showing and drive about the neighborhood.** Observing traffic between 4 P.M. and 6 P.M. on a weekday will give you an idea of the worst you can expect. Look at neighboring properties to estimate their relative value. If you return on a weekend and see people working in their yards, stop and chat a bit. Ask questions about the schools, children in the neighborhood, pet policies (do dogs roam free?), the nearest pizza parlor, the best way into town, and so on.

- **Before you make an offer, try to draw the floor plan from memory.** Often we remember what we hope to see, so this is a good reality check. Be sure to indicate stairs, doorways and windows in your drawings. If you're buying with someone else, go into separate rooms, do the drawings and then compare them. They'll surely be different. Then return and evaluate the house with your drawings in hand, noting especially where you got it wrong and the items on which you differed with your partner.

Dealing With Discrimination

No one should have to deal with discrimination but, unfortunately, it does still happen. The federal Fair Housing Act (Title VIII of the Civil Rights Act of 1968, with amendments in 1974 and 1989) prohibits discrimination in housing because of race, color, religion, sex, national origin, disability or children in the family. Some states add other factors as well.

The law strictly prohibits "steering"—a practice in which agents don't show minorities some neighborhoods on the assumption that they would (or should) feel out of place there. Realtors' listing contracts also advise sellers that it is illegal to discriminate. Under some circumstances, however, a seller can refuse to sell his or her own house. For example, the owner of a duplex in which he makes his home may be able to refuse to sell the other half to a family with small children.

Don't accept discrimination. Change agents and go on with your house-hunting. At the same time get help from an attorney, your state real estate commission, or one of the national or local fair-housing enforcement or advocacy groups. See the starter list above.

More, More, More ......

For more information about and help with discrimination problems, contact:

The Fair Housing Information Clearinghouse (Box 9146, McLean, VA 22102; 800–343–3442; www.CIRCSOL.com/Fairhousing)

The National Fair Housing Alliance (1212 New York Ave., N.W., #525, Washington, DC 20005; 800–910–7315)

The HUD Housing Discrimination Hotline (800–669–9777)

Good Working Order

Throughout this book, heart, soul, individuality and even eccentricity have been suggested as acceptable contributors to judging how a home will meet your personal needs. Sometimes these elements of personality also get a voice in judging the structure and condition of that home. When they do, the results can be unfortunate.

In the home-inspection arena, the voice in our heads that is prompted by feelings does not usually identify a need or hold to a preference. Instead it often raises a din of denial that can drown out all the rational voices working to judge quality and condition.

People who have "fallen in love" with a house don't ever say, "I want that sagging roof" or "I like a wet basement." Either they somehow don't see the uneven roof line or smell the dampness of wet stone, or they say, "It really doesn't matter." That denial can lead to financial disaster. So look carefully, see clearly, and keep your rational senses in control, even if (or especially if) you *love* the house. And listen to your home inspector.

Fear of faulty working systems and unsound structure is one of the most common reasons prospective home buyers hire professional home inspectors. The inspector brings experienced judgment, the knowledge of acceptable standards for product performance, and—if you choose carefully—an impartial eye to the evaluation process. A good inspection will make you aware of exactly what is in good working order and what is not (more about professional inspections later in this chapter).

This short chapter couldn't possibly substitute for the professional inspection of the working systems and structure of any property that you might offer to purchase. But it may keep you from the time-consuming and stressful process of entering into negotiations on a property that has obvious structural or serious working-systems problems that you're not prepared to deal with. And when such problems are not so obvious, it will help you to use and understand the professional home-inspection report to protect your financial and personal interests.

All of which is another way of saying that this chapter is intended to help you avoid trouble. Making a fully informed purchase decision will help you avoid any risks you haven't bargained for. You certainly don't want "surprises" to increase by many thousands your actual cost for a home. And you certainly don't want to put up with the discomforts and anxiety such surprises cause. So let's take a tour of what most people *don't* see when they look at a house.

The Risks You Run

"**G**ood working order" is a phrase used in most residential real estate purchase contracts to describe the condition of the working systems of a house (plumbing and heating, for example) and the appliances that are included in the sale. But don't let the positive tone ease you into an unjustified sense of security. "Good working order" doesn't mean "like new" or even "without fault." It only promises that at the time of title transfer, a system will do the job for which it was designed.

Any system could break down the morning after closing and cost you thousands in *out-of-pocket dollars*. This is a nightmare for most home buyers because:

- **Few buyers have much ready cash available** immediately after closing on a house.

- **Getting the cash is usually expensive. A second mortgage, equity line or other credit source** usually comes at higher rates than a first mortgage.

- **Unlike improvements, repairs rarely add value** to the house for resale. A new septic system adds no value even though (or perhaps because) it is essential to habitability. On the other hand, a new paint job does add to value, probably because it improves the appearance.

The trouble with most people is that they think with their hopes or fears or wishes rather than with their minds.

Will Durant
(1885–1981), American
historian and writer

• **A breakdown can cause considerable discomfort** if you can't afford to repair it immediately.

Just as the good working order of the systems and appliances is an essential element in getting a good buy, so is what might be called the good working order of the structure. Of course, that particular phrase isn't used in purchase contracts since most people would stumble over the idea that foundation blocks are working.

But think about it: If the foundation, frame, siding, windows and roof, and their components and support systems, are not working as they should be, the house cannot provide safe shelter. When dealing with a nonworking or poorly working structure, your home-buying risk is increased to include danger to the inhabitants and, taken to the extreme, the possibility that you could be left both *without* a place to live and *with* the burden of owning an unsalable property.

In purchase contracts, the common phrase used to describe the acceptable condition of a building is *structurally sound*. That soundness is the primary concern of every professional home-inspection service. It should also be among the essential criteria of your purchase. Even when buying property for rehabilitation (see Chapter 3), the essential structural elements must be sound or you're probably better off demolishing the structure and starting over.

Words the Wise Know Well

In the process of buying real estate, the phrase **out-of-pocket-dollars** usually refers to necessary cash which cannot be financed with a mortgage loan. Closing costs, for example, are out of pocket. So are the dollars that must be spent immediately after occupancy for repair, landscaping and decorating.

Structurally Sound

To consider structural soundness, you have to understand what holds a house up and holds it together. Now, you're probably not an architect, a builder or even a home inspector, so how can you possibly understand so complex a subject? You can't, at least not entirely. But you can be aware of enough information to look for signs of trouble and to ask relevant questions of the real estate agent, the seller and, of course, the home inspector.

The Foundation

When talking about a house, the word *foundation* refers to any construction that is below or partly below ground level and upon which the house is built. Everything, literally, rests upon it. A foundation might be poured concrete, concrete block, cinder block, cut stone, brick, or in older properties, fieldstone. Poured concrete is most commonly used.

Foundation height ranges from a *slab* that separates floor joists from the ground, to a *crawl space* that puts anywhere from a foot and a half to four feet between ground and floor joists, to a *full basement*, which is usually seven to ten feet high.

Each type of foundation has specific characteristics and danger signals.

> # More, More, More
> •
>
> If you want to get into home inspection, up close and personal, these two books will help:
>
> *The Home Buyer's Inspection Guide,* by Warren Boroson and Ken Austin (John Wiley & Sons, $17.95).
>
> *The Complete Home Inspection Kit,* by William L. Ventolo (Dearborn Financial, $15.95).

Slab

The concrete should lift the wooden floor joists at least six inches above ground level to guard against termite infestation and rot. To prevent frost heaves and moisture penetration, the slab should be poured over a layer of crushed rock and a permanent vapor barrier. Wide cracks and/or crumbling corners are danger signals.

Crawl space

Some crawl spaces are built above a poured concrete slab; others are built right over the ground. When a dirt floor is used, it's essential to have adequate ventilation throughout the foundation. To prevent moisture from penetrating up into the house, the ventilation devices (usually iron grates) must be kept open throughout the year. In areas that are frequently damp, it's advisable to have a polyethylene plastic vapor barrier laid on the ground. Watch out for standing water in corners and low spots.

Basement

A wet basement is more than a nuisance. Besides dampness and mold, water in the basement can undermine the soundness of the foundation. It can threaten the functioning of the furnace and water heater. And a water-logged basement is virtually unusable for storage, hobbies, or a children's rainy-day play area.

So be aware that foundation materials are not waterproof. Whether a basement is prone to collect water depends on the water table in the area, the existence of hidden springs or underground creeks, and the grading outside the house.

Don't Assume

• •

Don't assume that floors and countertops are level. Carry a small ball or a marble when you inspect a house. Place it on the surface in question and see if it will roll and in which direction. A rolling ball may indicate uneven settling, which could undermine structural soundness. Talk with your home inspector!

If you see a yellowish-brown or white line at an even level about the basement walls, it is probably the high-water mark either of a flood or of the risen water table during a period of heavy rain. Moisture collecting outside the walls might be indicated by a white fuzz called efflorescence that seems to be "growing" here and there on the inside of the walls.

Random hairline cracks in a foundation do not usually indicate a problem, but cracks that are wide or that start as a hairline and get wider, cracks that extend from top to bottom, and all horizontal cracks should be investigated by a professional. They can indicate an unstable or deteriorating foundation.

The Framing

The horizontal and vertical boards that define and create the space that is the house (some would say its skele-

Continued on page 332

Parts of a House (Everyone) Knows

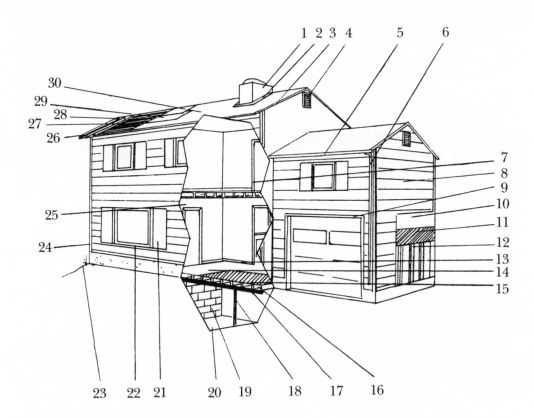

Key

1. chimney
2. flashing
3. cornice
4. louvers (for attic ventilation)
5. gutter
6. downspout
7. interior door trim
8. siding
9. exterior trim
10. building paper
11. sheathing
12. studs
13. base molding (baseboards)
14. finish floor
15. sub-floor
16. joists
17. girder
18. girder post (lally column)
19. foundation wall
20. cement floor
21. shutter
22. window frame
23. grade
24. corner board
25. sheetrock (sometimes called drywall or plaster board; in older houses may be plaster)
26. rafters
27. roof boards
28. ridge board
29. roofing felt
30. shingles (roof)

ton) are called framing. Uneven settling of the foundation or the use of improperly seasoned lumber for framing will create cracks on the interior walls at the door jambs and window corners. Floors that slope and separations between the floors and baseboard moldings can also indicate uneven settling or improper construction, and may or may not be a serious problem. In earthquake- or hurricane-prone parts of the country, you'll want to know whether appropriate framing techniques have been used—originally

Some Words You Thought You'd Never Need to Know

As you follow the home inspector around a property, you're likely to hear many of these terms. He'll explain them, of course, but here's a preview.

- **Anchor bolts.** Bolts set in the foundation to which the sill plate (the horizontal base of the framing) is anchored.

- **Beams.** Supporting members of a structure, typically made of steel or wood (see also girders and joists).

- **Bleedout.** What you see when the effluent from a septic system is rising to the surface rather than draining into the earth.

- **Bridging.** In home construction, crisscrossed pieces of wood secured between the floor joists. The bridging reinforces the joists and distributes the loads.

- **Building code.** A municipality's laws and regulations that control the construction of new buildings. Codes cover design, materials, construction techniques, working systems, use, repair, remodeling and other factors.

- **Downspouts.** Vertical pipes leading from the gutters of a roof to the ground.

- **Ductwork.** A system of tubes to convey air from a heating or cooling unit to the individual rooms of a house.

- **Eaves.** The extension of the roof beyond the walls of a house.

- **Efflorescence.** White, fuzz-like powder that forms on basement walls when moisture is present behind the walls.

- **Effluent.** Treated sewage from a septic tank, usually 99% water.

- **Fascia.** A flat horizontal board enclosing the area under the eaves. The gutters are hung from the fascia.

- **Flashing.** Angled barriers at intersections of the roof planes or at places where a chimney or vent pipe protrudes. Designed to keep water from seeping into the attic, they should be inspected and sealed every year, but that is rarely done.

- **Flue.** The passageway in the chimney through which smoke rises to the outside.

- **Girder.** A main supporting beam.

- **Gutter.** A channel (usually aluminum but sometimes wood) run along the eaves of the roof to carry rainwater to the downspouts.

- **Guy wire.** A cable for holding, guiding or steadying something, most frequently seen on utility poles and sometimes on fence posts. Note that it can be a hazard for tripping both children and adults.

or remedially—to help prevent damage where possible.

The framing underlying the roof in today's houses is usually prefabricated and structurally sound. Older houses, however, have been assembled in many different ways. When considering a house, look at the roof line. It should be straight. If you even think there is a sag, call for a professional evaluation to make sure you're not getting a weak or leaky roof.

- **Jamb.** The side of the door frame that faces the opening.

- **Joists.** Beams (or wood members) that rest on the foundation, sill plate, or outer walls to support the boards of a floor or ceiling.

- **Lally column.** A column, often filled with concrete, that supports a girder or sometimes other floor beams.

- **Leader.** A downspout or a channel that conducts water from the gutter down and away from the house.

- **Pilaster.** A reinforced projection of the foundation wall that gives additional support to a floor girder or strengthens a length of wall.

- **Riser.** The vertical part of a step.

- **Sash.** A window frame.

- **Sheetrock.** A trademarked name for plasterboard or drywall.

- **Siding.** The covering on the outside walls of a house. Wood is the most common material. Vinyl, aluminum and stucco are also common.

- **Sill plate.** Horizontal framing set on the top of a foundation wall.

- **Soffit.** The visible horizontal underside of an eave.

- **Splashblock.** A stone or concrete block placed under the downspouts to take water away from the foundation.

- **Stud.** An upright member of the framing, usually wood.

- **Subfloor.** Material (usually plywood) nailed to the floor joists. Most building codes require that finished wood floors, ceramic tile, wall-to-wall carpeting or other flooring materials cover it.

- **Sump.** A pit in the basement floor or crawl space that collects water to be pumped out.

- **Tongue and groove.** A type of interlocking-boards construction.

- **Tread.** The horizontal part of a stair.

- **Vent pipes.** Pipes that allow gas to be vented outdoors from the plumbing system.

- **Window well.** An excavation around a cellar window.

The Roof

Life insurance agents will tell you that the job of roofing contractor is one of the most dangerous and accident-prone. So don't plan to inspect a roof yourself! Leave it to a professional home inspector, and ask him about the roofing materials, the flashings, and the gutters and downspouts (see the definitions on pages 332–333).

Asphalt shingles are among the most common roofing materials in older homes, and their life span is approximately 16 to 25 years. If the house you are considering is more than 15 years old and has its original roof, ask whether there are barren places on the shingles where the granular mineral coating is worn away. If there are many, you will need a new roof in a few years. Negotiate for a lower purchase price.

Fiberglass shingles are a relative newcomer to roofing materials. They can be found on some new houses and on some that have been reroofed. A high-quality fiberglass shingle should last longer than the typical asphalt shingle.

If the house you are buying has several changes in roof planes where wings have been added or the orientation of the house changes, be sure that the inspector checks the flashings. Ask if the gutters and downspouts are

Don't Assume

If you suspect unrecorded additions or alterations, ask the sellers or the real estate agent if any changes have been made to the structure since it was first built. (Trust your intuition; if the deck strikes you as strange-looking, there may be a reason you should know about.) Ask whether a survey was done when the sellers purchased the house; the survey will show the exterior footprint of what they bought. Compare this with the present situation. Note any changes and ask whether they were made with the necessary building permits. A smart homeowner might even have copies of the permits to show you.

If you have even the slightest doubt that all necessary permits were obtained, go right down to the town hall and do some detective work. In the tax records office, ask for the assessor's inspection report from the last general tax assessment. Is the suspicious addition mentioned? In the buildings department, ask to see any records of building permits for the house in question. It's all public information.

in good condition and clear of debris. If they are clogged with dead leaves from last autumn, you may find yourself on a ladder one rainy day trying to clear them out! If water is overflowing clogged gutters or if the downspouts are not directing the water away from the house, you could find your basement flooded.

You can sometimes detect a leaking roof from inside the house. The water will leave irregular brown stains on the ceilings or walls. If you can get into the attic, shine a flashlight beam at the rafters. That's where the water usually runs. Look for water stains where the wood is darker with an irregular edge to the shading. Another common place to look for water stains is near the chimney or vent pipes.

Don't Assume

If you are house-hunting for a condo or co-op apartment, don't assume that the building's structure and working systems are A-OK just because such things are the responsibility of the homeowners association or the board of directors. Since each unit owner owns an undivided interest in every brick in the walls and every shingle on the roof, poor construction or maintenance can cost you money. You can hire a home inspector to inspect the common elements of a community as well as the individual unit you wish to buy (see Chapter 6).

Windows

Windows seem to come in an endless variety of sizes and shapes. They may open upward, outward, or side to side, but it's most important that they open with ease. Windows that stick or get stuck may indicate improper framing or uneven settling, though they could also be due to humidity, a broken rope or a bent pulley. You should open and close every window in the house before you buy. In older houses, look also for gaps between the sashes of double-hung windows—a real draft-producer and heat-sucker.

Decks, Porches and Additions

Although an added deck or porch may not greatly affect the purchase price of a house, it could affect your wallet in a surprisingly painful way. Sometimes a homeowner will add a deck to the back of the house or perhaps convert a garage to extra living space without obtaining the necessary building permits, thereby avoiding the required inspections and approval process.

These additions may not meet current building codes, and they may not be safe. If the change is discovered by the town (during a tax re-assessment, for example), local government agencies can force you to return the structure to its former (approved) state, take it down or rebuild it in accordance with local building code. It makes no difference that you, the new owner, did not make the illegal changes. *You* can be required to make them right.

Chimney Construction

If a house has a fireplace or a heating system fueled by gas, oil, coal or wood, it has at least one chimney to supply air to the fire and carry off smoke. Current building codes have strict requirements for chimney construction, but—nothing on Earth being perfect, much less the local building inspection process—problems still exist. Check to be sure that the fireplace is not pulling away from the building. Also check, or have an inspector check, the flashings between the chimney and the roof and the quality of the masonry.

It's the Law

• •

Required disclosures: In addition to the old and still-prevailing "Buyer Beware," there's now a new marketplace motto: "Seller Be Truthful!" In more than half the states, sellers and their agents must warn buyers of "material" defects in a property that would not be apparent during a routine inspection. Each state puts a different twist on the definition of "material," but generally it means defects in the house or its systems that might affect the buyer's assessment of the property's value.

Gallant idea, but don't believe every word you read or check mark you see. There's another saying in the marketplace that goes: "All sellers are storytellers." Also keep in mind that few sellers really have the technical knowledge and impartial perspective necessary to correctly evaluate the structure and working systems of their homes.

All Systems Go

While the structure of a house creates shelter, its working systems make that shelter livable. Can you imagine day-to-day life without good drinking water, toilets that flush, warm showers, lights at night, heat in the winter, a stove, oven, dishwasher, even a fire alert system?

You can't? Well, join most other American home buyers! Value diminishes in a property whose working systems are aging or suspect. It's best to rely on professional inspections for both system and product life-expectancy predictions and for efficiency reports, but there's no harm in knowing what to watch for. Read on.

Water

There are two ways to get running water in the modern home: public and private. Public water is supplied through

> # Words to the Wise
>
> **Potable water** is water suitable for drinking. Lab-test results will show what substances are present and in what quantity. Both states and municipalities set standards for safety that must be met.

the public works department of your municipality (commonly called *city water* on Realtors' listing forms). Private water supply usually comes from under the earth (better known as a *well*). Some condo communities, resort communities and large developments, however, have independent water supplies from wells or reservoirs. That water is sometimes stored in huge "holding tanks" that break the skyline like flying saucers. Such water sources are usually referred to as *community water*.

If the house that interests you is supplied by a well, make your purchase contingent upon acceptable *potability* test results. If you are applying for a mortgage, your lender will probably also require the test because a house without safe drinking water is virtually unsalable.

You should also discuss with your home inspector:

- **The depth of the well.** Water from a source close to the surface is more easily polluted.

- **The age and type of construction.** Is it appropriate to home use and likely to last throughout your homeownership tenure?

- **The type and age of the pump.** Pumps break down and are expensive to repair. Ask about warranties.

- **The size of the storage or "pressure" tank.** This determines how much water you have in reserve.

- **The current gallons per minute of pumping capacity.**
  This affects your water pressure.

Needs and standards for the rate of flow and storage capacity vary by area of the country and family-use patterns. Your home inspector will be able to give you guidelines for what is acceptable in your area and for various sizes of house and family-use patterns. If the well water is unacceptable or has a high mineral content, you can have a water purification system installed. These systems can be purchased or leased. Check your phone book under "water purification."

Public water supplies in the U.S. are subject to rather strict standards and inspections and are generally safe. If you are buying a house with city water, you may still elect to have the water lab-tested, however, to determine its biological and mineral content, hardness, and acidity. If the results are unacceptable to you, you might decide to look for a house in a neighborhood or suburb with a different source of public water. Or you can have a water purification system similar to those used with well water installed. (Or, you can purchase bottled water for cooking and personal consumption.)

Also have your inspector check water pressure by opening several faucets at the same time. If the water from an upstairs spigot is reduced to a trickle, you may have insufficient pressure or corroded lead pipes. Have a plumber come in to estimate the cost of fixing the problem.

And finally, consider *hot* water. There are many ways to heat and hold hot water. What do they all have in common? None of them lasts forever. Ten to 15 years is a ballpark figure for the life expectancy of most water-heater tanks. Ask the sellers how old theirs is. You should also discuss with the inspector the tank's capacity and reheat rate in light of your use and demand patterns. Consider everyday use, and then consider the demands that would be made on the system if you had guests, a party, or your kids all come home from college for the holidays with five weeks' wash in tow.

Plumbing

Indoor plumbing has been around for most of this century, which means it's often quite old in older houses. It's also difficult to inspect in houses of all ages because most of it is hidden behind walls or under floors (which means it's expensive to repair or replace). You're going to have to rely heavily on your inspector in this field, but here's a list of pipe types and some of their pros and cons. The best place to get a glimpse of what you're dealing with is usually the basement.

- **Galvanized iron:** 25+ years old by now and probably pretty near the end of their useful lives. Detected by the attraction of a magnet, rusty-looking water and restricted water flow.

- **Brass:** less common than galvanized iron but almost as old and almost as worn out. These pipes cannot be replaced in sections, only by whole lines.

Don't Assume

• •

Don't assume that a hookup to municipal sewers is a free ticket to wastewater disposal. When sewers are originally installed in the streets, the local government has the right to levy a special sewer assessment. Homeowners can usually choose to pay this over the course of several years, and it may not be fully paid yet in a house you are buying. You can negotiate to have the balance paid by the sellers at the closing or you can assume the payment schedule. Even after all sewer assessments have been paid off, many municipalities and some private communities charge annual sewer-use fees, which will be listed with all other tax assessments on the listing form and on the closing statement. If you are buying without a real estate agent, ask the owner directly.

- **Copper:** the most common pipe material and many say the best, though it's also the most expensive. Pipes can easily last 50 to 75 years and are still being installed in many new homes.

- **Plastic:** the new kid on the block and still to be tested over the long haul. They are inexpensive, but breakable and, some people say, noisy.

- **Mixed:** different types of pipe in the same house indicate replacement and repair, which usually indicates that there may be more repair to come. Remember that lead pipes are thought to be health hazards by some authorities.

Wastewater Disposal

Like water supply, wastewater disposal is either publicly or privately managed. Public management means a sewer system. Bear in mind, however, that the presence of a sewer line in the street does not necessarily mean that an individual house is connected to it. Some homeowners with working septic systems elect not to connect to public sewers. The listing sheet will indicate the wastewater disposal system that is being used.

The manufacture, installation and maintenance of private wastewater disposal systems is a growing industry encompassing many methods beyond the old-fashioned hole-in-the-ground system commonly known as a cesspool. Building codes dictate an array of septic tanks, holding tanks and leaching field possibilities, and the environmental protection agencies of federal and local governments further police wastewater disposal.

Since about the middle of this century, most towns have kept records of the location and type of septic tanks and leaching fields that were installed when houses were first built. If the seller doesn't have this information, get it from the town. (The town clerk's office will tell you which department houses the records.) You need this information so you can check for spongy soil over the tank, which could mean poor drainage and possible backup. Also, septic tanks need cleaning from time to time. If yours were to need an emergency pump-out and you didn't know where it was, you could experience considerable delay, not to mention stress and inconvenience.

Talk with your home inspector about the age, type and adequacy of the wastewater disposal system. You can get the age and type from the seller or the town; your inspector should know if that particular system is performing well in the area. If you are tempted to skip this bothersome

---

Words the Wise Know Well

• •

Leaching fields, leach lines and **leach trenches** all refer to methods of removing liquid waste material from sewage by filtration through sand, gravel, tiles, stones or other means. You can often see where they are buried in a lawn because the grass will be noticeably greener above them.

detail, try to imagine how much it might cost you to repair a system that begins to leak contaminants into the neighbor's water supply (among other nasty possibilities)!

Heating and Cooling

Appropriate heating and air-conditioning for a particular house is very dependent on where that house is located. Heat pumps, for example, are popular in the South, but they are usually inadequate in cooler northern areas. On the other hand, people in New Hampshire often can't understand why anyone would spend an extra penny for central air-conditioning. To find out what is appropriate in a new area, check local listings while you are still house-hunting. Note the most common kinds of systems in use and the most common heating fuels. You can also go to some open houses for new construction and note what systems builders have installed. Their choices are usually appropriate to the area and the availability of the fuel source.

The most common heating systems are circulating warm air (which can share ductwork with a central air-conditioning system), circulating hot water and, in older houses, steam. Electric heat with its individual room thermostats has lost favor in some parts of the country because of high electric rates. Oil and gas are the most commonly used fuels, with coal and wood still burned in many areas.

Most professional home inspectors adequately check out heating and cooling systems. If you are particularly concerned about a system (if it seems unusual for the area, for example, or, in an older home, if it's leaving soot on the windowsill) you can make inspection by a heating/cooling engineer a contingency in the purchase contract. (You can read about such contingencies in the next chapter.)

Electrical Systems

Electrical codes are quite stringent in the U.S., and you'll find that just about all houses built during the past 40 years are wired safely and adequately. Electrical service to older houses may be inadequate, however, and some

---

Penny for Your Thoughts

To be worn out is to be renewed.

Lao-tsu (604–531 BC), Chinese philosopher regarded as the father of Taoism. Well, maybe he didn't really mean to replace what's not working, but the phrase is worth remembering.

rewiring may be necessary to meet current needs for electric stoves, self-cleaning ovens, clothes dryers, and even computer terminals.

Aluminum wiring, introduced more than a decade ago as a cost-saving measure, has proven to be something of a hazard. In some cases expansion and contraction of the wiring at the connections have caused poor service and the possibility of fire.

When inspecting a house, you should turn on every light switch. Your inspector should check the power to every outlet. Discuss with him the adequacy of the service and the safety features, such as fuse box, circuit breakers, underground wiring, smoke detectors, and fire-alarm and security systems.

It's the Law

• •

Before there was a law: Properties that were built and in use before certain building codes or zoning ordinances were enacted are said to be **grandfathered.** Grandfathered properties are allowed to continue in use even though they do not meet current standards. But beware: If you decide to renovate, build an addition, or even just change some aspect of electrical wiring or other noncode feature, you can be required to bring the entire building up to current code.

Appliances

Whether appliances convey with a house or move with the seller depends primarily on local custom. In most states, cooking facilities (a stove and oven) are included in the sale of a house. In some areas a refrigerator is also provided, and washing machines and clothes dryers often remain with the property.

Dishwashers are another story. Real estate law generally recognizes anything permanently attached to the building as "real property," which means it is part of the house, and its ownership is automatically transferred with the house. With that in mind, most people would say that an installed, working, under-the-counter dishwasher goes with the house. But many a dishwasher has been known to disappear before closing day. If you want it, write it into the contract.

On the other hand, room air-conditioners are generally considered personal property, even though the supports that hold them are securely nailed into the siding. There is also frequent controversy over curtain and drapery hardware, shades and other window treatments. Lighting fixtures are usually considered "attached to the house," but sometimes a seller will replace the chandelier you see in your inspections with a less valuable fixture. Installed wall-to-wall carpeting generally goes with the house, while area rugs do not.

The only way you can be certain of getting everything you see when you inspect the property is to list it specifically, item by item, in the contract. Then you must keep that list and recheck it during the walk-through you do on the day of closing. The home inspector will have run and tested all appliances during the inspection. You have the right to get these in "good working order." Run them all again on the day of the closing walk-through.

> # *Words the Wise Know Well*
> •
>
> The real estate legalese for personal property is **chattel.** Generally, it's chattel if it isn't nailed down, screwed in or well rooted. Technically, chattel is *not* included in the purchase price (see Chapter 15, "Protection Under the Law").

Pests and Problems

Less than a quarter of a century ago, termites were usually the only threat to homeownership important enough to merit a separate inspection and a contract contingency. Today we are wiser—or at least more worried. We have radon, lead paint, asbestos, buried waste, leaking buried oil tanks and formaldehyde in the foam insulation (Urea-Formaldehyde Foam Insulation, abbreviated on listing sheets as UFFI), to name only some of the most common concerns.

Will we stop buying houses? Hardly. But like it or not, home buyers must address these concerns, even if only to eliminate them from concern. Some home-inspection companies include these specialized inspections in their contracts; others do not but will advise you on where to hire the necessary professionals.

About Lead Paint

HUD and the Environmental Protection Agency (EPA) estimate that nearly three-quarters of all houses built in the U.S. before 1978 contain some lead-based paint. (In 1978, lead-based paint was banned for use in all homes and most other buildings.)

Why the fuss? Lead is a highly toxic metal that, when present in the human body, attacks the central nervous system. Children under age 6, fetuses and women of childbearing age are particularly susceptible to lead poisoning. Ingested lead—typically from lead chips and dust—can result in anemia, hyperactivity, kidney dysfunction, lowered intelligence, stunted growth, mental retardation, and even death.

A federal law enacted in 1996 requires that homeowners and landlords disclose their knowledge of the presence of lead-based paint before renting or selling any property built before 1978. An EPA booklet titled "Protect Your Family From Lead in Your Home" is being distributed by real estate agents to every prospective buyer of affected property. It outlines lead hazards and ways to reduce the risk of lead poisoning.

"So, what's the problem?" you ask. "Get the inspection done, and if there's lead paint, get the seller to remove it."

More easily said than done. First, the inspection can be expensive, depending on the type you choose, whether the less expensive dust-wipe samples or the most expensive x-ray fluorescence (XRF), which peers through layers of paint to detect the lead. If you're planning to remodel by tearing down any walls, an especially dusty process, the latter method is preferred.

Then, the removal process is very expensive. In some instances, getting the lead paint out would cost more than

---

More, More, More
● ●

Call your local public health department or department of environmental regulation for references to government-certified labs, or to contractors who do lead testing, hazard assessment or abatement work.

The National Lead Information Center (800–424–5323; http://www.nsc.org/ehc/lead.html) can also provide more information.

the building is worth. But that could be overkill anyway. The EPA brochure notes that, in most cases, lead-based paint that is in good condition is not a hazard. Otherwise, there are alternatives to tearing out painted wood, such as paneling or painting with a thick paint called an encapsulant, a kind of plastic "skin" that bonds with the lead and is supposed to last 20 years. Worst case, you could hire a lead-abatement contractor to remove the lead hazard—say, by replacing all the windows and frames, a common source of lead dust, and then cleaning up any hazardous dust raised during construction.

If you're in the market for an older house and your family fits the profile for risk, you may want to make your purchase contract contingent on appropriate testing. If the seller has already had it done, he or she must disclose that to you. You might also specify what constitutes an acceptable level of lead and stipulate that the deal is off if the lead level is too high. You could negotiate a change in price to cover whatever lead-abatement solution is advisable.

To avoid a conflict of interest, get your hazard assessment done by a contractor who doesn't also do the remedial work. Get a written report along with the actual test results. Don't let anyone start ripping out old windows and woodwork unless you've received a well-thought-out lead-abatement plan from a certified assessment contractor whose references check out.

More, More, More

Professional associations are always happy to provide prospective clients with the names of local members.

- **The American Society of Home Inspectors** (ASHI, 85 W. Algonquin Rd., Arlington Heights, IL 60005; 800–743–2744; http://www.ASHI.com) is the largest professional home-inspection association.

- **The National Institute of Building Inspectors** (NIBI, 424 Vosseller Ave., Bound Brook, NJ 08805; 800–424–4202; 908–469–2138, fax; http://www.NIBI.com) trains and certifies home inspectors.

- **The Association of Construction Inspectors** (8383 E. Evans Rd., Scottsdale, AZ 85260; 602–998–8021; http://iami.org/aci) is one to try if you are building a home, buying a new home or doing a rehab.

The Inspector as Guardian Angel, If You Please

So how do you choose the professional home inspector who will do a thorough and competent job of examining the structure and working systems of the home you want to buy? The easiest way is to take the advice of the real estate agent who showed you the house, right? After all, agents work with these inspectors all the time. They must know who's best.

That's true. But "working with these inspectors all the time" can also be the source of a problem for you. When home inspectors know they have gotten a referral from a real estate agent, some of them hesitate to "rock the boat" by bringing up seemingly minor issues or by projecting the probability of a serious and costly problem. They want to do repeat business with the agent, and they know that a happy agent—one who has made the sale—will call again.

What to do? If possible, get your referral from relatives, friends or business associates who have recently bought a house and been satisfied with their home inspection. Or call one of the national trade groups with high certification standards and ask them for the names of member firms in your area (see the box on page 345). If you do ask your real estate agent for recommendations, get more than one name, make a choice, and don't mention that the referral came from the agent until after the inspection report is signed, sealed and delivered.

Besides providing a professional opinion of the quality and maintenance of structure and working systems, an inspector can also buy you time to reconsider your purchase and a second chance to negotiate the price. To get these bonuses and make the inspection worth the inspector's weight in gold, you *must* include a professional-inspection contingency clause in the purchase contract. It's already written into many printed contract forms. When you see it, don't hesitate to add the strongest wording possible to make the purchase entirely contingent on a satisfactory inspection.

Satisfactory to whom? Why to you, of course. The contract should be contingent on an inspection report "which in the sole judgment of the purchaser is deemed satisfactory."

If everything isn't perfectly satisfactory (and it never is), you can get out of the contract if you want to. Or you can approach the seller with a list of faults and problems and ask that the price be reduced to cover their correction. (The actual dollar number is usually negotiable.) Or you can ask that the seller correct the problems to your satisfaction before the closing.

There's more about contract protection in the next chapter. Be aware also that in some parts of the country, home-inspection contingencies, and indeed home inspections themselves, are not the norm and may be discouraged by real estate agents and sellers. Don't let the raised eyebrows and sour faces get you down. If you want a home inspection (and you should), get one.

Protection
Under the Law

It happens every day. A Realtor presents an offer with an earnest-money check in one hand and a purchase contract signed by the buyers in the other. The sellers make a counteroffer. The buyers make another offer. The sellers counter again. The buyers accept. The earnest money is deposited in an escrow account and the deal moves forward toward closing. *Meanwhile, no member of either the buying party or the selling party has read through the entire contract!*

That's right, most people are so focused on the price during negotiations that they see the contract only as a means of presenting offers and counteroffers. Most real estate purchase contracts are long, and they are full of details, small print and unfamiliar language. "Who has the time to go through all that?" is the subconscious protest.

Both buyers and sellers usually think they'll attend to the contract after the price is settled. Few do. And once the contract is signed by both parties, it's too late; the deal is made. Changing a fully executed contract will usually require the agreement of both buying and selling parties, the help of a lawyer, or the threat of using an escape clause—or all of the above.

It's dangerous to view a contract merely as a price-negotiating tool because the printed form was never meant to *determine* anything. Yet for those home buyers who sign it without reading it, the printed form determines almost everything.

In theory, the contract should merely *record* the agreement reached between two parties. Realtors see many contracts where the price is crossed out, rewritten and initialed by all parties again and again. Those scratched-out entries demonstrate the buyer's and seller's efforts to reach an agreement.

Once there is a meeting of the minds on price, however, many buyers and sellers assume that the rest of the details will be covered by the printed *blah, blah, blah.* There are often no initialed cross-outs anywhere else on the long legal form. Those buyers and sellers who don't really know or understand what they have signed are allowing the "usual and customary" clauses to create, define and safeguard the orderly transfer of title. In addition, the buyers are accepting *whatever is printed* as being good enough to stand as their primary protection against financial disaster.

You should not only read your contract carefully, you should also *rewrite* it whenever and wherever necessary to protect your interests. This chapter will help you to focus on those points that can cause trouble and to make additions or changes for your protection.

The "Standard" Contract

There *is* no standard contract. The term is tossed about in the real estate marketplace whenever a printed form is brought out and offered to someone to sign. Any signed agreement between two parties that is based on offer and acceptance can be considered a contract. A dozen lines scribbled on the back of an envelope, dated and signed by all the parties involved can commit a home buyer to spending hundreds of thousands of dollars.

There are, however, commonly used contract forms. Many are designed and written by the larger real estate firms in the nation. Most are based on National Association of Realtors recommendations and most make good contract forms. In other words, most preprinted contracts are a good place to start.

But remember this: Each real estate contract to purchase must reflect the unique terms of an agreement between two parties for the transfer of a unique piece of property. That's why every contract form has blank spaces to be filled in, and that's why there is always space for additions and always the opportunity to delete.

Beware the Binder

Though it's rare, in some parts of the country negotiations are still conducted using a short form called a binder, or memorandum of agreement. The language and appearance of this paperwork varies from one real estate office to another. Usually a binder contains the names of the buyer and seller, the address of the property, the date, the price, the amount of the earnest-money check, and a date by which a contract must be *executed* by all parties concerned. Essentially it is an agreement to agree, that is, to sign a purchase contract.

Words to the Wise

• •

In the language of real estate contracts, to **execute** does not mean to *put to death* as in "the murderer was executed" nor to *put into effect* as in "the plan was executed." It means to *sign*. One might say, "The contract must be executed before Friday," meaning all parties must sign it by Friday.

The danger in using a binder rather than a purchase contract to present an offer lies in the lack of buyer-protection clauses. For example, Dick and Jane use a binder to negotiate a price of $110,000 for a starter home. The binder doesn't specify that the agreement to buy is contingent on their ability to get a mortgage loan of $100,000 at an acceptable interest rate. It simply states "contract to be drawn within three business days."

Two days later a formal contract has not yet been signed, but Dick and Jane are told that they do not meet the income requirements for an FHA mortgage in the amount they need (see the special insert beginning on page 209 for more about mortgages). They notify the broker that they cannot buy. The seller, however, wants to make the deal and offers seller financing. The catch is that his loan is offered at a rate two percentage points higher than the rate on the FHA loan. Dick and Jane say they can't afford that loan and don't want it. The seller says, "Okay, I'm going to keep the $1,000 earnest money deposit because you agreed to buy the house and you are refusing the loan that would make the purchase possible."

Can he do that? Technically, yes. An earnest-money

check is usually held (not deposited) until a written agreement is signed. But the binder Dick and Jane signed is a written agreement, so the earnest-money check was deposited in the broker's trust account. It's now more difficult to get it back because the seller has to agree to its release. The binder did not contain a clause stating that Dick and Jane's agreement to purchase was subject to an acceptable contract and void if no contract was drawn and executed. The seller has a good case for keeping the money. (Dick and Jane should, of course, object. But if the seller refused and further discussion failed, Dick and Jane would have to go to court to get the money released from the escrow account. That would probably cost them more than $1,000 in court costs. Because of the cost of fighting over a legal issue for so small amount of money, most sensible people avoid binders.)

Don't Assume

• •

Don't assume that a binder is easier to get out of than a contract. The reverse can be true. If you must use a binder to negotiate, be absolutely certain it contains wording to this effect: "This agreement is subject to a contract *acceptable to both parties* being drawn and executed before midnight *[date]*. If a contract is not executed by both parties, this agreement is void, and all deposit monies will be returned to the buyer."

What Makes an Agreement a Contract

Here are the bare minimum requirements necessary to create a valid purchase contract. The more precise the information, the less opportunity for legal confusion.

The date
To be a legal instrument, a contract must be dated.

Names of the parties
The full names of all the buyers and all the sellers should be written out and identified as "buyer" or "seller." It's also a good idea to include their addresses, especially when the seller lives somewhere other than in the house

being sold, when the sellers are divorced or when the buyers are currently living separately.

Don't Assume

• •

Don't assume that buyer protection is written into the printed contract form you sign when making an offer. Most real estate agents are under contract to work in the best interests of the *seller*. You, the buyer, must guard your own best interests. You can, however, get some help by using a buyer's broker. A good buyer's broker will review each clause in the contract with you before you sign it. But not all agents are buyer's brokers, nor are all agents "good" agents. (Read about buyer's brokers and how to evaluate an agent in Chapter 13.) The best bet is attorney review.

The address of the property to be sold

The street address is acceptable, but the block and lot number on the town tax map is preferred. In condo ownership, unit and building numbers and the name and address of the condominium community are essential.

The price

The full amount of the agreed-upon purchase price should be indicated no matter what financing arrangements have been made.

Earnest money

The amount of the check that accompanies the offer must be indicated. The contract is a legal receipt. The amount and required date of deposit for any agreed-upon additional earnest money should be recorded. (Earnest money is usually paid into an escrow account in two stages: The initial check for $1,000 or so that is presented with the contract, and the balance, which you shouldn't part with until all the contingencies have been fulfilled.)

The closing

Where and when the title will pass from one party to the other is often changed by mutual agreement, but at least a preliminary date and place must be given as a point of reference in the contract.

Signatures

Each person buying the property and each person who currently owns the property must sign the contractual agreement. A missing signature can invalidate it.

That's the skeleton. But a contract that will enable you to own the house you want while guarding your interests during the transfer-of-ownership process needs more flesh and blood. Let's consider what makes a contract appealing, powerful and protective.

The Ultimate Buyer-Protection Plan

If a contract is so critical for buyers, why is it so many people dismiss theirs with hardly a glance? When the opportunity exists to mold a contract to meet one's needs, why are there relatively few additions and deletions in the contracts that are written every day?

Often contracts are not read, much less adapted, because the content, language and legal rhetoric intimidates people who are unaccustomed to dealing in the real estate marketplace. Many of us don't buy more than two or three houses in a lifetime, so, by definition, home buying is an amateur venture. Most home buyers usually don't know what to look for, ask for, question and dispute. Worse yet, they are also afraid to appear foolish.

It's hardly foolish to ask for an explanation of the tan-

Don't Assume

Don't assume that an attorney can step in to help you after a contract has been fully executed. That can only happen if your contract has an **attorney-review contingency.** Without one, an attorney presented with signed contracts will have a weak voice in negotiating changes, and any changes that can be negotiated will usually cost you considerable time and money.

The attorney-review clause was mentioned in Chapter 4, but it's so important that it deserves a second printing. Write these words at the end of your contract above your signatures: *This agreement is subject to review and approval as to form and content by an attorney of the buyer's choice. The attorney may rescind the contract for any reason before midnight [date].* The date is usually three to five business days from the signing.

Remember you can choose *not* to use attorney review even though it is written into the contract. But you can't choose to add the contingency after the contract is signed. Don't miss this. It's a no-lose insurance policy.

gled sentences often found in contracts. And it's anything but foolish to seek professional help if you yourself don't know how to "put it in writing" in a way that is clear and comprehensive.

Sometimes you can express your concerns to your real estate agent, who might have a contract form in the office with exactly your points spelled out in nice legal language. If not, however, and you are uncertain, take the time to consult an attorney before putting anything in writing. Some real estate firms have attorneys on retainer for just such help. Some local Realtor boards also have attorneys who will give advice on proper wording. If you are feeling time pressure and can't get the legal advice you want, write in your points as clearly as you can and be absolutely certain the contract contains the *attorney-review contingency* mentioned in the box on the previous page.

What follows are clauses and contingencies commonly found in or added to real estate purchase contracts. This is not a complete list because it doesn't include everything anyone ever wanted. But it should make you more aware of what others have done to protect their interests, and perhaps stimulate your thoughts regarding your own needs and goals. If you want something that's "a little different," write it in. If you don't understand something, ask for an explanation. If you object to something, speak up.

What Kind of Deed Am I?

Although it is not essential to a valid agreement, a good purchase contract will describe the kind of deed (a written, legal instrument) by which the seller will transfer *title*, or ownership, to another party. Transfer of title, of course, assumes that the seller actually holds legal title, but no one type of deed absolutely guarantees that. That's why, in some purchase contracts, there is a statement as to how the seller will prove ownership, whether by title search, certificate of title or some other means. (Of course, there's the added protection of title insurance, which will be discussed in just a bit.)

Bargain and sale

Bargain and sale deeds offer the buyer no protection regarding clear title. Most closing agents and lenders therefore insist on title insurance to protect the new owner (and, of course, the lender) against suits in the future.

Essentially, in a bargain-and-sale deed the seller is saying: *To my knowledge, I own this property legally, but I don't guarantee that all the transfers of ownership that preceded this one were done without errors, omissions or willful deceit, nor do I guarantee that nothing affected title while I owned the property.*

Bargain and sale with covenant versus grantor's acts

This is a commonly used deed. Like its namesake above, this deed does not guarantee clear title, but it does attest to the fact that the seller did nothing to damage the marketability of that title while owning it. Essentially, this means: *I guarantee that I'm passing on to you exactly what I got.*

A warranty deed

A *warranty deed* provides the buyer with the best protection. Not all sellers and their lawyers, however, are willing to use it. In a warranty deed, the seller guarantees clear title and promises to defend the title against himself and all others who have *ever* owned the property. Essentially, this means: *I'm so sure this title is clear that I guarantee to assume the responsibility to defend it against any claim no matter how long ago that claim might have originated.*

A warranty deed could require the seller to pay court costs and damages to the new buyer if, for example, the seller's longtime companion sued and won for a half interest in the property three years after the closing. It could also require payment by the seller if a direct descendent of a Georgia resident who lost a New York state property during the Civil War could prove that the property was transferred illegally.

Why Title Insurance?

Generally speaking, it's advisable to get title insurance no matter what kind of deed is used to transfer ownership. Title insurance is issued by a title insurance company to protect against loss resulting from a title problem. Title hazards might include a claim by a divorced spouse, an unrecorded lien or an error in the land survey. The policy can be written to protect the mortgage lender and the new owner in an amount that covers only the mortgage loan, or any other amount up to the full purchase price.

The fee for title insurance is calculated as a one-time charge paid at the closing. Some buyers include seller payment of title insurance as a part of their negotiations. This is a great way to save out-of-pocket dollars. In some areas, seller payment of title insurance is customary.

Buyers typically use the title insurance company recommended by their lawyer, lender or closing firm. But money's at stake, and you can choose to buy your title insurance from another company that offers a better deal. If you decide to shop on your own, compare what each company insures against and what it will pay. (See the accompanying box for more information.)

More, More, More

• •

The national trade association of the title insurance industry is the **American Land Title Association** (ALTA, 1828 L Street, N.W., Suite 705, Washington, DC 20036; 202–296–3671; 202–223–5843, fax; http://www.alta.org). It will answer your questions about title insurance and provide you with the names of member companies working in your area. It also offers printed information available free or at minimal cost. Among the currently available booklets are:

• "Why Title Insurance?"

• "Protecting Your Interest in Real Estate"

To order a copy of either booklet, send a self-addressed, stamped business envelope to ALTA at the above address.

What If? (More Protection)

There should be provisions in a purchase contract that settle what will happen in the event of a named occurrence (such as a tree falling on the roof of the house prior to closing) and determine how certain responsibilities and liabilities will be handled. These *what-if scenarios* are sometimes printed in the very fine type on what seems to be the back of the contract, but they are no less important than what you find on the front and should get equal attention. They include protection against:

Liens and other encumbrances

The seller should state that clear title can be delivered at the closing. Usually this means that all *liens* are to be paid from the proceeds of the sale and thus removed, and all other encumbrances are to be resolved. If other arrangements are made (say, if the buyer agrees to continue the payments for the sewer assessment), they should be in writing.

What if clear title cannot be delivered? The contract should state that all deposit money is to be returned to the buyer and the contract is to be declared void.

Words to the Wise

A **lien** (pronounced *lean)* is a charge or legal action against real estate for the settlement of money owed. A person who repaired a roof but was not paid could place a mechanic's lien against the property. Debts including mortgages and junior mortgages (a financial term meaning all mortgages after the first mortgage) recorded as liens create a "cloud on the title" and must be paid by the seller before title can be transferred.

An **encumbrance** is also a cloud on the title, and, in fact, a lien is a type of encumbrance. But an encumbrance can also exist without a debt owed. A legal action by someone who claims an ownership interest in the property—a divorced spouse, for example—can be an encumbrance. So can a dispute about the corner of the neighbor's garage that crosses the property line. An encumbrance does not necessarily prevent the transfer of title, but it could cause serious legal problems later and might make the property ineligible for title insurance.

Buyer or seller default

This clause describes what remedies are available in the event that either party defaults—that is, the buyer can't or won't buy, or the seller can't or won't sell. The remedies usually include forfeiture of escrow money, the right to sue and the right to force the seller to sell through a court order called specific performance.

Damage or destruction of the property

This provision explains the effect on the contract should the property be destroyed or severely damaged between signing of the contract and closing. This clause usually states that the seller is responsible for maintaining the property in the condition it was in at the time the contract was signed and for maintaining insurance coverage. Essentially, it means the property will be delivered to the buyer as the buyer saw it on the day the contract was signed. If a tree falls on the roof two weeks before closing, the roof must be repaired and paid for by the seller.

Disposition of outstanding monies

This part of the contract describes how outstanding monies or obligations will be divided if they exist at the time of closing, including:

- How real estate taxes will be prorated

- How liability and fire insurance policies will be prorated if they are assumed

- Who will pay for any fuel remaining in the oil tank

- How rental income will be allocated (if applicable)

- How condo or association fees will be prorated

- How any special assessments will be transferred or paid.

More Questions Resolved

Other provisions in the purchase contract deal with questions of personal property, responsibility and payment of fees. Check to see what stays, what will be taken out, and who's doing what in the following clauses:

A list of any personal property that will remain

This could include lawn furniture or draperies. Check the definition of chattel on page 343.

A list and description of appliances or other built-ins that will remain

This could include electrical fixtures, an air-conditioner, even wall-to-wall carpeting. Remember, what appears to be built in may not be.

The identification of any real property that will remain or be removed before closing

"Real property" usually refers to buildings attached to the land, but ask about storage sheds, children's treehouses, even young trees and shrubs that are still small enough to be taken out.

The appointment of a closing or settlement agent

Who conducts the closing differs by state. Your purchase contract should describe the local procedures.

The amount of real estate commission

This is usually a clause at the end of the contract naming the real estate agents involved and stating that the seller is to pay commission at the closing. If a buyer's broker was used, this clause should state who will pay that portion of the commission. It often comes out of the "proceeds of the sale," which means the seller pays.

Handling of the deposited escrow monies

Who will hold the money in trust? It can be the closing company, a lawyer, or even a real estate broker.

When will it be turned over to the seller? Usually at the closing, but it can be released to the seller earlier.

This clause should also describe who will get the interest on the escrow deposits. It's usually split between the buyer and the seller, but it can be divided any way or it can all go to one party.

Wondering why you shouldn't get all the interest?

After all, it's still your money until it's handed over to the seller at closing, right? The seller would say that the only reason you can't close immediately is that you have to get a mortgage. So the money is really his and he should get the interest. By law, once all contingencies are met, the buyer has "equitable title" and the seller has the right to the money. So the seller should get the interest *after* all contingencies are met and the buyer should get the interest *until* all contingencies are met—which is why it's usually split.

The provision for an inspection of the property by the buyer just before closing

This is often called a walk-through. This clause usually states that the property will be delivered in *broom clean* condition and that all systems will be in working order. (See Chapter 14 for more on what constitutes "working order.") Broom clean means that the floors will be free of debris. You can stretch it to mean that old appliances (nonworking refrigerators, for example) will also be removed, but if you think you might need that stretch, write it in specifically. You cannot, however, stretch it to mean that windows, walls, doors and woodwork will be washed to remove handprints, pawprints or what have you. Some buyers add that the lot will also be free of trash and debris just to protect themselves from having to haul away what the sellers couldn't sell and wouldn't move.

Contingencies—or How to Get Out Gracefully

Because the purchase of real estate involves really big bucks that very few buyers have on hand, a purchase contract almost always includes a *contingency* for getting the money. Essentially, the buyer wants to sign a contract that says, "I think I can get this money. Give me x weeks to try, but if I can't get it, I'm out of the contract."

In addition, the seller is offering something for sale that cannot be fully seen or understood by the prospective buyer who doesn't have professional tools and training. So the buyer wants to sign a contract that essentially says, "I like what I see, and if all things are as they appear to be, I will buy this property. If I'm not satisfied with what a professional inspector reports, however, I may choose not to buy this property."

In theory, anything can be a contingency. Your deal could be contingent on a certain stock's reaching $100 a share, on your great-aunt Tillie's dying within the fortnight and leaving you the downpayment, or even on your daughter's winning a scholarship that will relieve your tuition responsibilities and free up more of your income to put toward a mortgage payment. But both buyer *and* seller must agree to a contingency before the contract is signed, and most sellers are not at all interested in "creative" contingencies that would take their house off the market while they waited for something that has only a chance of happening. So let's focus on the most common contingencies—those clauses that will allow you to get your earnest money back and walk away from the deal gracefully if all does not materialize as expected.

Words to the Wise

• •

A contingency in a real-estate contract is a clause that creates conditions that must be satisfied before the contract is fully enforceable. From the buyer's point of view a contingency means: *"This* must happen or we will not buy this property." A buyer might say, "We want a home-inspection contingency in the contract." A seller might say, "We'll allow three weeks for the mortgage contingency to be met."

The Mortgage Contingency

Unless you have the full purchase amount readily available, you will need to take out a loan to purchase the property. A mortgage is the most common means of securing borrowed money for a home (see the insert beginning on page 209). Be sure the following items appear in writing as part of your mortgage contingency, so that all necessary numbers will be accounted for:

• **The full amount of the loan** that you will need to purchase the house.

- **The type of mortgage** you will be applying for (conventional, FHA, VA, and so on).

- **The term of the mortgage,** or how long to the final payment. Thirty years is common, and you should make that term a part of your mortgage contingency even if you plan to get a shorter-term loan. Payments on a 30-year loan are lower than those on a shorter-term loan. If there is any question of qualification, you are buying yourself some space.

- **The maximum interest rate you are willing to pay,** or a statement that you will accept the prevailing rate.

- **The number of discount points** you are willing to pay.

- **A named period of time to apply for and get a commitment on the loan.** This is written as a date, often called the cut-off date, after which the contract is canceled if you have not received a mortgage commitment from a lender. Ask for a week more than you think you will need. Then, if the date is almost upon you and you haven't yet received a commitment letter, you can ask for an extension of the mortgage contingency.

Other Financial Contingencies

A gift

If you are expecting a gift of all or part of the downpayment money, you can state the amount and make the contract contingent upon your getting that amount. Most sellers will set a cut-off date and require a "gift letter" from the giver stating the intention and the amount. Many contracts require that the gift money be deposited in a bank account in the buyer's name by a certain date.

Sale of your home

A contract contingent on the sale of a house you currently own is more complex. Few sellers will sign on the dotted line if the buyers' house is on the market or about to be put on the market unless they have unlimited time to sell, that is, they don't have a contingency clause of their own to worry about on the purchase of their next house.

If the buyers already have a signed purchase contract on the house they are selling, however, the script is quite different. Few sellers object to making their deal contingent on the sale of the buyers' house when it's already under contract and will go to closing by a known date.

An appraisal

A small number of buyers include an appraisal contingency in their purchase contract. This is usually worth doing only when you think you are getting an exceptional bargain and want reassurance of that fact, or when there is some question about the value of the property and you want a professional opinion to present to the lender.

Essentially, an appraisal contingency clause says that if, in the opinion of the professional appraiser whom the buyers choose, the property is worth less than an agreed-upon figure (which could be the purchase price or a higher amount), the buyers can walk away from the deal.

A professional appraisal will cost in the neighborhood of $300 (the price depends on the size of the house and the hours of working time required). Many buyers, especially those who can afford only a minimal down payment, rely instead on the mortgage lender's appraisal, betting that the loan will not be approved if the house is appraised below purchase price.

Professional-Inspection Contingencies

Professional-inspection contingencies are a part of most preprinted contracts. If you don't see one in the contract your agent has filled out for you, insist that it be added.

But beware of taking too much for granted. There are so many things that seem more important than the details of the inspection contingency that you think all you need to do is fill in the date by which the inspection must be completed and you can move on to more important things. But whoa! Don't skip to the next clause. What does the contract say about what happens if you don't like what the inspector reports?

Know your response options ahead of time and make sure that you respond prior to the cutoff date. In most contracts, if the inspection is not completed and the seller notified of the buyer's response before the cutoff date, the inspection contingency is waived and the buyer is committed no matter what the inspector finds.

If you're the kind of person who doesn't take dates too seriously, imagine this nightmare: Your inspector says the foundation could be buckling. You call in a specialist in foundations who is a little slow in getting his report to you. Meanwhile the cutoff date passes unnoticed. When the report comes in saying it will probably cost from $8,000 to $10,000 to repair a basement wall, you want out of the contract. If you haven't notified the seller of the potential problem and received an extension of the inspection contingency in writing, you not only can't get out, you can't even get a price concession for the anticipated cost of repairs!

Most sellers will grant the extension of the inspection contingency cutoff date if there are extenuating circumstances. Have the real estate agent get the extension in writing. If a seller refuses to extend the inspection contingency date, notify him in writing that the contract is terminated, specifying the extenuating circumstances that prevented you from having adequate inspection by the stated date. If an inspection report that was delayed then comes in with no evidence of serious problems, you can return to the seller and propose to rewrite the purchase contract. But be wary. Ask yourself, "Why did the seller refuse the extension? What was he afraid of?" A refusal of an extension doesn't happen often. When it does, be extra careful.

Don't Assume

• •

Don't assume that a professional-inspection contingency guarantees you a way out of the contract. Some preprinted contracts allow the seller to choose to take care of all the necessary repairs and thus hold the buyer to the purchase agreement. Cross out that wording and rewrite the clause. Be absolutely certain that the purchase contract is contingent on an inspection report **"which in the sole judgment of the purchaser is deemed satisfactory."** In other words, if the back stairs creak and you don't like creaky stairs, you can walk away from the contract and get your deposit money back.

In addition to the overall inspection for structural soundness and the good working order of all systems, many contracts contain contingencies for specific tests and inspections. Each should have its own cutoff date by which time the report must be completed and the buyer's acceptance or rejection reported to the seller. The following are some of the most common areas of concern, but you can always add any others that are important to you or the house in question:

- Termites and other insect infestations

- Radon

- Lead paint

- Asbestos or other hazardous insulation

- Potable water

- Adequacy and good working order of septic or other waste-disposal systems

- Availability of flood or earthquake insurance

Getting Your Money Back

If a contingency cannot be met and you must abort the purchase, don't dawdle. The longer money stays out of your pocket, the more it *seems* to belong to someone else. Notify the seller in writing that the contract is to be considered void, and request the return of your deposit money from the *fiduciary* agent. Once you have your money back, the contract to purchase is officially void and you can go on to other things.

If the seller refuses to return your money, you may have to go to court. You can usually avoid the expense of legal tangles, however, by reminding the seller that a court case could take *years* and that the property cannot be put back on the market until the matter of your purchase contract is settled. In other words, as long as you, the buyer, have not violated any of the provisions of the contract, the seller must return your deposit before the house can be sold to anyone else. Most sellers would rather get on with it than wait around for a court date. The vast majority of escrow funds are returned without a problem when a contract is declared void.

The Good News

The good news is that only a small percentage of real estate purchase contracts are declared void. Most deals go through. When problems do come up because contingencies cannot be met, extensions are usually granted and solutions or compromises are usually worked out. After all, sellers and real estate agents want to sell and buyers want to buy; when that finally happens, everybody wins.

The keys to making a contract work are simple:

- **Take** every word seriously.

- **Don't** assume.

- **Ask** for what you want.

- **Object** to what you don't want.

- **Leave** as many escape routes open as possible.

- **Work** diligently to do what needs to be done by the deadlines set in the contract.

Most important, remember to make your contract contingent on attorney review, even if you never plan to see an attorney. That little clause will give you time to "sleep on it" and change your mind if you have nightmares.